GENOCIDE BAD.

GENO CIDE BAD.

NOTES ON PALESTINE, JEWISH HISTORY,
AND COLLECTIVE LIBERATION

Sim Kern

Interlink Books

An imprint of Interlink Publishing Group, Inc.
Northampton, Massachusetts

First published in 2025 by

Interlink Books
An imprint of Interlink Publishing Group, Inc.
46 Crosby Street, Northampton, MA 01060
www.interlinkbooks.com

Library of Congress Cataloging-in-Publication data available.
ISBN-13: 978-1-62371-636-3 (paperback)
ISBN-13: 978-1-62371-635-6 (hardback)

Printed and bound in the USA

For Heba, Elena, Manal, and all the babies born in Gaza over the past year. I'm so sorry we didn't fix it before you arrived.

Contents

Foreword

Let the record show, I would not have presumed to write a book about Palestine had a member of the Moushabeck family not invited me to do so.

I am not a historian, nor an expert in the region. I have never set foot in Palestine or those occupied Palestinian lands called Israel. And I am not Palestinian!

I *am* Jewish, in a secular, patrilineal*, fun-holidays-only kind of way. But because I have a Jewish grandmother on my dad's side, the state of Israel claims I have some special connection to Palestinian lands. I could move there and claim civil and property rights that are denied to Indigenous Palestinians, even though my Jewish ancestors all immigrated to the US, not from Palestine, but from lands now called Ukraine, Poland, and Russia. Whatever mystical connection Zionists** want me to feel for "the Holy Land," I've never felt it. In the eyes of many people in the world, though, this ancestry gives me some special authority to speak about Palestine.

What I really am is a sci-fi novelist and aspiring "book influencer," who started making video essays about Palestine and anti-Zionism*** in October of 2023. I was uniquely positioned to make this content for a few reasons. I

....

*   *Patrilineal* Jews have a Jewish father and a non-Jewish mother.

**   *Zionism* is an ideology that insists on the necessity of a Jewish nation-state, where only Jewish citizens get full rights. Liberal and far-right Zionists may disagree about the methods that should be used to maintain this state, and what the borders of this state should be, but all Zionists agree that Israel, a Jewish-supremacist ethnostate, should continue to exist on stolen Palestinian land.

*** *Anti-Zionists* believe that a Jewish supremacist ethnostate should *NOT* exist on stolen Palestinian land (or anywhere). Not because we're anti-Jewish (as Zionists claim) but because we're anti-religious-supremacy, anti-apartheid, and anti-stealing-peoples'-land.

had been organizing in anti-Zionist Jewish spaces for several years. I had also just spent a year researching Jewish history for a novel set in seventeenth-century Europe.

Many Ashkenazi* Jews in the US know little about our history in Europe prior to the Holocaust. That ignorance is intentionally cultivated by Zionist historical institutions, because a deeper appreciation of our European roots would disrupt their propaganda. Because I happened to be already immersed in this research in October 2023, I could offer unique historical parallels between Jewish and Palestinian history.

Finally, I chalk up my success as an influencer to my former career as a freelance journalist and the ten years I spent teaching middle school English. From those jobs, I learned communication is most effective when you're concise, clear, and at least occasionally funny—even when the topic is bleak. If more academics took a tour in sixth-grade English classrooms, they'd be far more successful in spreading their ideas.

For these reasons, my videos on Palestine and Jewish history over the past year have frequently gone viral, and now I'm more well-known as an "influencer for Palestine" than I am as an author or book influencer. Despite the popularity of my video essays on Palestine, it never occurred to me to turn them into a book. I am uncomfortable with how my voice, as a Jewish USian,** is given precedence over actual Palestinians with lived experience under Zionism. So even if it *had* occurred to me to write a book about Palestine, I would've felt it wasn't my place to do so.

But in May of 2023, Hannah Moushabeck, a Palestinian author I admire both for her online advocacy and her brilliant, hilarious picture book *Homeland: My Father Dreams of Palestine*, approached my literary agent with an idea. "Sim has broken down Zionist talking points in a unique and accessible way," Hannah wrote. "Their video about how 'no one deserves an ethnostate' is a foundational idea that has propelled this movement for Palestinian liberation in ways we may never quantify. I hear friends of mine

....

*   *Ashkenazi Jews* are an ethnic group of Jews from central and eastern Europe.

**   I use the term "USian," rather than American, to mean "person from the US" because there are thirty-five countries in North and South America. So if you just say "American," it's like, *which one??*

who have been doing this work for decades quote them! I want to capture their content and share it in a new medium—a book!"

Hannah had just left Simon & Schuster to join her siblings in taking over the reins at Interlink Publishing. Hannah's parents, Michel and Ruth Moushabeck, had founded Interlink back in 1987, and for nearly forty years, they have operated the only Palestinian-owned publisher in the United States.

I was humbled and honored by Hannah's invitation to write for Interlink, and so, despite intense feelings of imposter syndrome, I agreed to write this book!

What is this book?

Just like how, in a more logical world, a US Jew's opinion wouldn't be centered in discussions of Palestine, so too, in that better world, this book would not need to exist. Because all the tens of thousands of words that make up this book can be boiled down to just two: Genocide bad.

GENOCIDE VERY FUCKING BAD!!! OBVIOUSLY!!!

It *should* be that simple. All you should need to do is point at a genocide, name it, and the people of the world should rise up in unison to put a stop to this most horrific of crimes.

But our society is not particularly logical or moral. Zionists have successfully obscured "Genocide bad" beneath such a dense web of propaganda that many people remain confused about what's going on. Even after a year of the most well-documented, live-streamed genocide in history, even after the UN has found Israel's warfare "consistent with genocide,"[1] and Amnesty International has concluded that "Israel is committing genocide against Palestinians in Gaza,"[2] most Western journalists still refuse to use the word "genocide" in their reporting. And in the US, where dozens of billions of our taxpayer dollars have purchased the US-made bombs that have blown tens of thousands of Palestinian children into pieces, burned them alive, and buried them beneath rubble, many of my fellow citizens asked throughout the last election, "But is genocide *so* bad? And what does it have to do with *me?*"

This book is designed to clear up any misgivings you may have about using the word "genocide" to refer to what Western media calls "the Israel-Hamas war." In fact, my secret, nefarious agenda is to convert you, throughout the course of these essays, into a fellow comrade in the fight against genocide.

And if you're already engaged in that fight, I hope this book will hone your rhetorical skills and arm you with additional useful information.

In Part I, I share the historical knowledge, life experiences, and educational philosophy that have made me an effective anti-Zionist activist. Maybe my story will give you ideas for how to get involved in the struggle for Palestinian liberation. Or, if you're a veteran of the movement, maybe it'll be therapeutic to read about someone who has been shouting "Genocide bad!" along with you.

Part II is designed to help you communicate "Genocide bad" to all those unactivated, apathetic, or even proudly Zionist people around you. I've boiled down the zillions of Zionist comments I've encountered over the past year into nine pillars of Hasbara.* Then I dissect each one and expose why it's bullshit.

In Part III, I explain what I really mean when I say, "Free Palestine," sketching my personal vision of collective liberation and suggesting how we might get there.

Finally, in the afterword, I turn my book over to voices from Gaza. In the spring of 2024, shortly after my baby was born, I began fundraising in earnest for pregnant people in Gaza who were hoping to evacuate before giving birth. Through my followers' generous donations, we were able to raise enough money for one family to evacuate, and baby Farah was born in a hospital in Cairo. But the rest of the families I supported were trapped in Gaza when Israel closed the Rafah border crossing in May 2024. Those mothers have since given birth in tents and in field hospitals under bombardment, all without anesthetic, and they have struggled to keep their children alive in the most horrific conditions imaginable. Meanwhile, I recovered from a C-section in a hospital and enjoyed life with a newborn from the comfort of my home within the imperial core. More than anything in this life, I wish I could give these families all the care and security I have been afforded. But I can't shield them from bombs and gunfire. I can't force Israel to open its borders and allow more than a starvation-amount of humanitarian aid to get through to Gaza. All I can do is fundraise and share on my platform. So the final chapter of this book will be letters written by the family members of three babies born amidst this genocide. My hope is that their powerful messages will anchor you and fuel your resistance.

....
* *Hasbara* is a Hebrew word that literally translates to "explaining," and it is the Israeli term for propaganda.

Who are you, reader?

If you're reading this on or close to its publication date, I'm guessing you already follow me on social media. Welcome, mishpocha!* While some of what's included in these pages may be familiar to you from my videos, much of the book is brand-new content. Freed of the ten-minute time constraints of TikToks and Reels, I've been able to delve deeper into topics, add more context and nuance, and connect big ideas that I never had time for in my video essays.

For those of you who are new to learning about Palestine, I imagine there will be many moments of disbelief throughout this text. Zionist crimes have been so extreme, and their hypocrisy so absurd, that learning Palestinian history can be truly mind-boggling. There's a sense of, *How the fuck am I just now hearing about this?* that makes you question your sense of reality. *Surely these villains can't be this villainous. Surely there's more both-sides nuance the author has missed!?!*

But genocide really *is* that one-sided—that's why it's so bad! So I one hundred percent welcome you to fact-check me and dig more deeply into all my sources, which you'll find listed in the endnotes. For ease of further research, I've prioritized linking to non-paywalled resources wherever possible. And you can find a digital version of these endnotes—with hyperlinks to all my online sources—at my website: simkern.com/genocide-bad-endnotes. I will also use that page to capture any corrections I may need to issue after this book goes to press. Events in Palestine are highly volatile, investigations into facts on the ground are ongoing, and new stories may come to light that better illuminate the situation after the ink on these pages has dried. So I will use that website to correct any distortions or misinformation I may have inadvertently repeated here, if the need arises.

I've also defined certain terms in the footnotes at the bottom of each page. Often these are terms that are frequently used but rarely defined in movement spaces, like "apartheid" and "neoliberalism." Or they're terms with highly debated definitions, such as "communism" or "Zionism." So I hope, reader, you won't feel like I am insulting your intelligence with these footnotes! I provide these definitions in order to 1) be precise, 2) avoid

---

* *Mishpocha* is a Yiddish word for family, a term I lovingly use to refer to my followers on social media.

misunderstandings, and 3) make this book as accessible as possible to a broad, international audience.

My dearest hope is that this book has time-traveled to a free Palestine of the future. Perhaps some history student is reading it on the beach in Gaza, where the only sounds are of wind, waves, and children laughing. No whining of drones, no distant bombardment, gunfire, or screaming can be heard.

Hello, young historian! I hope you find this book to be a mildly interesting, but totally obsolete, artifact. I hope you find it too heavy for a beach read. I hope you set it aside and go for a swim.

For the rest of us here in the bloodthirsty present: lock in. Gaza is the last stand of an Indigenous people resisting the death cult of an empire that threatens all life on earth. The weapons manufacturers and petrochemical shareholders who are profiting off the Palestinian genocide are the same group of elites dooming all life on earth to extinction through runaway climate change caused by burning fossil fuels. The struggle to free Palestine is inextricable from every other liberatory struggle on earth.

In short: if we can free Palestine, we can free the world.

And if we can't free Palestine, we're all fucked.

Part I. How I Became a Reluctant Influencer for a Free Palestine

I can't stress enough how surprised I am to find myself in the role of "Jewish Influencer for Palestine." I get recognized in public once or twice a week now—with my family at a restaurant, taking my kids back-to-school shopping at Target, in the waiting room of my ob-gyn's office, even while changing in the locker room at my gym. (Side note: if you recognize a celebrity or influencer while they are partially naked, please wait until they are fully clothed to introduce yourself!)

I feel lucky that all these interactions, so far, have been with supporters, and not with any of those people who have wished death upon me over the past year for expressing my views on Palestine. Most of the time, the person approaching me has introduced themself as Palestinian. Sometimes they cry, expressing heartfelt thanks for my videos. Sometimes they ask for a picture. Almost always, they tell me something along the lines of, "Never stop." I'm honored by these interactions, and I try to be as gracious as possible. But I'm not going to lie—getting recognized scares the hell out of me. I feel overwhelmed by the weight of my responsibility to these people. Deep down, I know that I tumbled into that responsibility, largely unintentionally, and that their admiration for me is undeserved.

Because I am no hero. I have never had a gun pointed at me, or lived under a threat of bombing, or pulled a neighbor from rubble. In the context of where I live in Houston, Texas, I experience ever-so-slight marginalization as a visibly queer Jew, but compared to the global median, I am enormously privileged. Like most regular-degular people, sometimes I do things that take courage, but more often, I operate from a place of fear and prioritizing my

1

own comfort. It scares me to be placed on a pedestal I know I can't balance on forever. And I worry that if I let other people lionize me, that might discourage other regular-degular people from taking up the cause of liberation. So let me set the record straight on just how reluctant all my activism was.

A few years ago, I made my TikTok and Instagram accounts, not to change the world, but in order to promote my own indie-published sci-fi novels. I named my channels "Sim Booktoks Badly" and "Sim Bookstagrams Badly," as a reminder to myself to not take social media too seriously, and to keep most of my energy focused on my goal of making a career as an author. Today, however, most of my 500,000 followers smashed that "follow" button because of my views on Palestine, and they have little interest in my novels or book reviews. On a daily basis, I wonder, like David Byrne of Talking Heads, "How did I get here?" and sometimes, "My god, what have I done?"

On October 7th, 2023, my social media feeds divided into two contradictory realities. Many Palestinian, communist, and otherwise anti-Zionist accounts I followed were cheering a video of Gazans knocking down a wall, alongside sentiments best summed up by Mariam Barghouti in her viral tweet: "Gaza just broke out of prison."

Pretty much everyone else I followed—extended family, former co-workers, fellow authors, and publishing people—quickly transformed into flag-waving Zionists. They posted fierce condemnation of all forms of violence alongside graphics of Israeli flags, not realizing the absurd contradiction of those mixed messages.

Logically, I understood both groups' reaction to the news of October 7th. But I shared neither excitement for the resistance fighters' success, nor shock at what Western media was reporting that Hamas had done.

I had followed news out of Palestine long enough to know I should be skeptical of any reporting we would hear over the coming days. Sure enough, much of the story of October 7th, as it was told by mainstream Western media that first week, has been called into question. Hamas did not behead babies.[3] Some accounts of mass rape initially shared have been disproven,[4] although the UN Secretary General on Sexual Violence in Conflict concluded in March 2024 that there were "reasonable grounds" that rape and gang-rape had occurred on October 7th, and the UN investigation is ongoing.[5] The number of Israeli fatalities attributed to Hamas has also been cast into doubt.

The Israeli newspaper *Haaretz* broke the story that the Israeli army had invoked its "Hannibal Directive" on October 7th, which allows the military to fire on its own people, if necessary, in order to prevent them being taken hostage.[6] We've also learned that Operation Al-Aqsa Flood did not take Israeli forces entirely by surprise. *The New York Times* has revealed that Netanyahu had some foreknowledge of the plan over a year in advance.[7] And *The Times of Israel* reported that an Egyptian Intelligence Minister called Netanyahu ten days before the attack to warn him Gazans were preparing to do "something unusual, a terrible operation," and the Minister was "shocked" by Netanyahu's indifference.[8]

While many of these details of October 7th will take years to sort out—and others will forever remain unknowable—the actions of Hamas, and other individuals who escaped Gaza during the operation and attacked nearby settlements, include war crimes. The accounts of the murder, rape, torture, and abduction of Israeli people are, of course, horrifying. Nothing justifies atrocities. As I will show throughout this book, however, Israeli forces and settlers have committed many such war crimes against Palestinians throughout the past seventy-six years. At the time of writing, dozens of hostages remain in captivity in Gaza. At the same time, nearly ten thousand Palestinians[9] are being held captive in Israeli prisons, and the Knesset recently passed a law to allow even children under fourteen to be imprisoned.[10]

So, no, I was not shocked on October 7th that Hamas had engaged in armed struggle and taken Israelis captive, in part to force a prisoner exchange for the over 5,000 Palestinian political prisoners who were being held in Israeli custody at that time. What I mainly felt on October 7th was an overwhelming despair for the genocide that was sure to follow. For the past seventy-six years, Israel had responded to any killings of Jewish Israelis with the collective punishment of Palestinian civilians, at a greater order of magnitude. For every individual Israeli killed by a Hamas fighter on October 7th, I knew the IOF* would slaughter tens or hundreds or even thousands more Palestinians in retaliation.

....

*   Israel calls its own military, in English, the IDF, or Israel Defense Forces. But I and other anti-Zionists disagree that the Israeli military is a *defensive* force. Apartheid, ethnic cleansing, and genocide are not forms of self-defense (although their perpetrators, invariably throughout history, make this claim). So, throughout this book, you'll see me refer to the Israeli military instead as the IOF or Israel *Occupation* Forces.

3

But on October 7th, I did not feel qualified to wade into the explosive discourse on social media with my own thoughts. Despite having been an anti-Zionist Jewish activist for years, a founding member of my local Jewish Voice for Peace chapter, I still felt like I was not well-informed, clever, or brave enough to share my own opinions on Palestine. While I had attended local demonstrations organized by the Palestinian Youth Movement, I never volunteered to speak on behalf our JVP chapter because others were so much more insightful on Palestine than I was. When counter-protesters or Zionist relatives would confront me about my support for Palestine, I often got tongue-tied, flustered, and could not think of responses to their arguments until hours or days later.

So, on October 8th, I decided to post something that felt comparatively "safe." I encouraged my social media followers to read some of the books that had led me to support Palestinian liberation. After all, it was reading about Palestine that had led me to deconstruct Zionism in the first place. As a secular Jewish kid who grew up in the US in the 1990s, I had been indoctrinated with a passively Zionist worldview that had normalized the existence of Israel, characterized Palestinian resistance as merely anti-Jewish hate, and required me to remain ignorant and incurious about Israel's blood-soaked origins and apartheid structure. A single book had proven powerful enough to puncture that worldview.

I still vividly remember picking up Joe Sacco's graphic novel *Palestine* off a shelf at Half Price Books and feeling like I was holding a bomb in my hands. Just the title, just the word *Palestine*, felt charged and strangely forbidden, and for the first time in my life, I determined to figure out why that was. For years, I had been meaning to get around to figuring out what I thought about Israel, and a graphic novel seemed like an easy, accessible place to start.

I read *Palestine* that afternoon in one sitting, learned the meaning of the word *Nakba*, saw the stark injustice of Israeli apartheid rendered in Sacco's reporting and black-and-white drawings, and it set me on the path to writing these words today.

So of course, on October 8th, 2023, my first move was to recommend people read Sacco's book and other books about Palestine I had read throughout my anti-Zionist journey. In doing so, I would be "sticking to my lane" as a book influencer. And in a deliberately cowardly move, I did not speak or show my face in that first video. To a clip of the song "Milliardat" by the Palestinian hip-hop group DAM, I filmed myself throwing the following books on top of the JVP protest signs I had made for that afternoon's emergency demonstration. I highly recommend y'all head to your local indie bookstore or library and pick up these absolute bangers, ASAP!

Books about Palestine to read RIGHT NOW
Posted October 8, 2023

1 *Palestine,* by Joe Sacco – Journalism in graphic novel form
2 *A Land with a People: Palestinians and Jews Confront Zionism* – An anthology of anti-Zionist writings by Jews and Palestinians
3 *Salt Houses,* by Hala Alyan – A multigenerational family epic
4 *Against the Loveless World,* by Susan Abulhawa – This novel will radicalize you
5 *Palestinian Walks,* by Raja Shehadeh – History as hiking memoir

I did not expect this video to do numbers. Back in 2021, following Israel's Operation Guardian of the Walls, a bombardment which killed over 250 Palestinians, including 66 children, I had organized a "Palestine Reading Challenge" on YouTube, which only two other book-tubers had joined. To date, only 248 viewers watched the final video of that readathon. Despite this feeble turnout, the event earned me a profile on Canary Mission, a Zionist website that vilifies and doxes Palestinian activists. Now, when you search my name, one of the top results would forever proclaim: "Sim Kern has trivialized anti-Semitism and spread hatred of Israel and America. Kern has also engaged in anti-Israel activism." All because I'd encouraged folks to read Palestinian books! The profile seemed like such a comical overreaction, that, if anything, I vowed I would keep pushing Palestinian literature on book socials out of spite!

So on October 8th of 2023, when I posted this reading list, I was expecting the video to similarly flop. All my efforts online to get people to care about Palestine in the past had never gotten traction. Honestly, part of me was hoping the video would amass no more than 248 views. Because then I could tell myself that "I tried to do something" and move on.

But the video broke 100,000 views, which was a lot for me at that time. And the responses were surprisingly positive. The algorithm had delivered the video to a largely receptive audience. But some long-time mutuals expressed a sense of betrayal in the comments. I was a Jewish author, wasn't I? Why was I encouraging people to read Palestinian books—and *only* Palestinian books—right after so many Israelis had been killed? Why not encourage people to read Israeli books, or at least books from "both sides"? How dare I? Was I a self-hating Jew?

I wanted to explain myself to those mutuals. And so, sitting in my backyard, speaking in a soft voice because my neighbor was outside painting his garage, and I didn't particularly want him to overhear me, I recorded a video. After a brief internal debate, I decided to add the caption, "Jewish Author Speaks..." at the top. I always find it a little cringe-y to preface my ideas with my identity, even though I know, from my time organizing with Jewish Voice for Peace, that it's often useful to do so. Palestinians *should* be centered in any conversation about Palestine, not Jews from the US. But Israel has weaponized charges of antisemitism against anyone critical of their state for so long that I knew that for many viewers, the only way my opinion wouldn't be instantly dismissed as anti-Jewish would be to clarify that I was Jewish before my first breath.

I had never had a video pass a million views before, but this one would be watched over 20 million times across various social media platforms. Over the next few days, I would gain over 300,000 new followers on Instagram and TikTok. The video would be "stitched" by hundreds of people, including one MAGA influencer with several million followers. In a video that was ultimately an ad for his "I Stand with Israel" T-shirts, he would clip my words out of context and send legions of his followers into my comments and DMs, to leave me thousands of more and less explicit death threats. That experience gave me months of agoraphobia so bad I could hardly leave my house, and I still brace myself and look over my shoulder whenever I'm in public.

My video would also be seen by Jewish family members and lifelong friends who would call me a Nazi and end our relationships. It would alienate me from Jewish community in ways I wasn't fully prepared for. I would struggle to celebrate Hanukkah without contributing to Zionist Judaica companies, substituting watermelon gummies for chocolate gelt. I got rid of all my decorations and Jewish paraphernalia that featured the Star of David, because after months of witnessing genocide beneath that flag, it made me sick to look at that symbol. I was pregnant at the time, and at the top of my list of potential baby names were "Shoshanah" and "Lailah," because I had wanted a traditional Jewish name. But over the ensuing weeks, dozens of Shoshanahs and Lailahs would call me a kapo and fantasize aloud about all the ways they imagined Palestinian men wanted to rape or murder me for being a Jew or a queer person, and I soured on those monikers. We ended up naming our baby after a fictional character who was decidedly not Jewish.

That video irrevocably changed my life, thrusting me into being A Main Character™ on social media for a few days' time. But in it, I didn't say anything particularly novel—nothing that Palestinian activists and long-time anti-Zionist allies hadn't been saying for decades on end. I don't think it would have gone viral at all if I hadn't slapped on the "Jewish Author Speaks" caption at the last second. But in that moment, on October 9th, I said the right thing, at the right time, as the right identity, and the algorithm gods smiled upon it. I was a *Jewish Author*, which carried some gravitas, I had a decent TikTok following of 50K, and I could effectively contradict the Zionist narrative that was sweeping social media *because I had done the reading.*

The real lasting impact of my flopped 2021 Palestine Reading Challenge was that *I* had read enough Palestinian books to cobble together my own coherent statement. By standing on the shoulders of brilliant Palestinian authors I had read, like Raja Shehadeh, Hala Alyan, Susan Abulhawa, and Mohammed el-Kurd, I was able to make a video that was essentially just "Anti-Zionism 101."

Jewish Author Speaks ...
October 9th, 2023

"So right now, if you are putting out a statement talking about how your heart goes out to the hostages in Israel, but you are not saying that your heart goes out to the people of Gaza...

If you are condemning Hamas, but you are not simultaneously condemning the Israeli Government and the US's unconditional support for the Israeli Government...

If you didn't give a fuck about what's happening in Palestine up until two days ago...

That is because you see Israelis as people, and you do not see Palestinians as people.

And if you live in the US and that's you, it's understandable if you haven't been paying attention! Because Western media is extremely white supremacist, and that is how racism works:

Israelis get to be white. Palestinians are non-white. And they are therefore: *not people*.

You see this difference in humanization when you look at the rhetoric the media uses to describe Israelis being "killed" as opposed to Palestinians "dying." You see it in the obfuscation of settler and Israeli military aggression by calling such violence "clashes."

And maintaining the dehumanization of Palestinians is so important to the project of white supremacist imperialism in Palestine that it is extremely threatening to do anything to humanize Palestinians. Which is why my suggestion yesterday— (which I always make whenever there's violence in occupied Palestine) that people read a book, any book, by a Palestinian author—is so threatening.

People take that as antisemitic. Because if you read a book by a Palestinian, it is going to humanize Palestinians for you. And it will change the way you see this conflict forever.

So before you fix your mouth to say anything about what is going on in Israel and Palestine, ask yourself: have you sought out Palestinian voices to listen to? Have you ever read a book by a Palestinian author? If you need suggestions, check out my last video."

By the next day, that video was racking up millions of views on both Instagram and TikTok. My notifications were a never-ending flood of comments. The vast majority of them, at first, were an outpouring of love from Palestinians—thanking me, blessing my family for generations, and telling me how brave I was. There was also a steady stream of hate messages from Zionists, wishing me a violent death, but these were just a trickle at first (until that MAGA T-shirt salesman stitched me!). And there was a third category of people somewhere in the middle—the slightly-informed liberal—who didn't know much about Palestine beyond what they'd absorbed from mass media and the "I Stand with Israel" posts that had been ubiquitous on social media over the past three days. These were people expressing genuine confusion as to why a Jewish author's response to October 7th would be to say, "Free Palestine." These were people who did not realize they were repeating Hasbara talking points in my comments, because they had never heard this term for Israeli propaganda. I thought these people might be reachable, so on October 10th, I decided to make a more in-depth video, addressing some of the most repetitive comments.

To be honest, I felt a great deal of dread hitting "post" on that third video. I had a feeling like I was wading into a pool of water that would prove to be bottomless. I had a feeling that Israel's violence this time around would be worse than anything we'd seen in my lifetime. And part of me knew that the more I talked about Palestine, the more I would never be able to stop talking about Palestine. And I knew how much I stood to lose: relationships with loved ones, career opportunities, my emotional well-being, my privacy, my safety just *existing* in public. I did not want to become a spokesperson for Palestine, because I knew just how dangerous that would be.

Plus, I was leaving for my book tour in two days' time! For six years, I had been working towards cobbling together a semblance of a writing career. *The Free People's Village* was my fourth book, but the first one that I would actually see on the shelves of bookstores. And this was certainly the first time a publisher was flying me anywhere to promote my book, do readings and signings, and meet my followers! I was supposed to be hyping my novel and upcoming events, not arguing with Zionists on TikTok. Especially not at a time when social media was flooded with tearful statements of unwavering support for Israel.

But all those thousands of loving, thankful messages from Palestinians had shamed me. I had not been particularly brave, because I knew just how much I had held back in those first two videos. All I'd done was tell people to read Palestinian books. I hadn't used my own words to contradict any Zionist misinformation about the settler-colonial history and apartheid present in Palestine—and there was so, so much misinformation about the history of Palestine going around.

It's one thing to know that Israel is a settler colonial* apartheid** ethnostate,*** but it's another, much harder thing to explain what that means. Explaining things is hard. That's why overwhelmed parents resort to, "Because I said so," and snarky Tweeters say, "Google is free." It's why we're set to burn up what's left of international commitments to limit global warming to 1.5 degrees Celsius, in exchange for carbon-guzzling AI text generators that will do the onerous task of stringing words together for us.

But I've come to realize that perhaps the most fundamental and vital labor, of all liberatory organizing, is the act of explaining hard truths. In your own words. To your own people. As clearly and compellingly as possible. Over and over and over and over.

By October 2023, I had spent years reading Palestinian authors and deconstructing the Zionism I'd been raised to believe. I knew that so much of what I'd been told about Israel growing up was lies and propaganda. But I still felt overwhelmed by the thought of contradicting this Hasbara! Because there is so fucking much of it! Where do you even start?

I do believe that Israel has obscured the violent colonial nature of its existence with the largest concatenation of bullshit ever accumulated in one geographic location in the history of planet Earth. Maybe even more bullshit than we tell about our origins here, in my own genocidal settler colony of the United States of America. When you start arguing with Zionists, for each lie

---

*   In a *settler colony*, Indigenous people are displaced from their ancestral lands by settlers who form a permanent colony there.

**   An *apartheid* nation makes racism the law of the land. Certain groups of people are segregated, discriminated against, and lack civil or political rights on the basis of their race.

*** In an *ethnostate*, full citizenship is restricted to a particular racial or ethnic group. (Israel treats Jewishness as a religion, ethnicity, and/or race in various contexts.)

you contradict, they will fling at you a hundred more.

But here's the thing about me. All my life, I have been a stubborn, back-talking pain in the ass to every parent, teacher, boss, and authority figure I encounter. When I see hypocrisy and injustice, it sticks in my craw. I find it impossible to shut up when I encounter a pile of lies and hypocrisy and injustice as big as Zionism. The fact that Israel claims to be doing its awful deeds "for me," because I'm Jewish, only provokes me further!

I'm like an alligator, locking jaws on its prey. The more Zionism thrashes—the more I've had insults and death threats thrown at me, the more I've lost personal relationships and professional opportunities—the harder I bite down and barrel roll, dragging Zionism down in the muck of the bayou with me. I can't let it go—even if I drown myself in the process!

I can't tell you how many times over the past year I've told myself, "Take a day off from videos, Sim, for your own mental health!" But then I'll see some new atrocity or receive some fatuous comment that loops in my brain until I make a video about it. I planned to take two months off from content creation when my baby was born in February, but I only made it three weeks before the psychological anguish of watching a genocide and saying nothing about it became more than I could bear. I can't rest, because the outrage won't quit.

And I'm also lucky in that I have the privilege of time to devote to this struggle, and the financial backing of a supportive spouse. For the last several years, my spouse has made enough money so I can be a full-time author and stay-at-home parent. While the parenting responsibilities do not, of course, budge, I've been able to give up writing science fiction for writing scripts for TikTok essays about Palestine. As I write this book, I'm pausing every half-a-paragraph to feed my baby, change a diaper, or retrieve a toy that's rolled maddeningly out of her grasp. I film my videos while she naps. It's been doable, in this way, to be a full-time activist for the past year.

Ope! Speak of the cutie-pie, there she goes, wailing for something.

BRB.

Ok, back. It was a pee diaper.

Advocating for Palestinian Liberation, like having a baby, takes a serious toll on your career. For both of these "lifestyle choices," you may find professional opportunities evaporating all around you, but rarely will you be

11

told the reason why. Did that editor, in fact, reject my manuscript because it's "not a fit for the market right now," or was it because they saw my Canary Mission profile when they googled me? Why did a major trade publication decline to review my latest novel, when they've reviewed all my previous books? Was *The Free People's Village* just not good enough to be short-listed for any awards—even in niche genre categories—or did the judges not want to deal with backlash for nominating a sci-fi novel that features Palestinian resistance and says in its last chapter, *From the river to the sea, Palestine will be free!*?

Being an author is largely a lonely grind of sitting at your laptop for months on end. A couple times a year, though, I used to go to a convention, or do a reading, or be on a panel. On those rare occasions, I'd get to geek out with other authors over the sci-fi that inspired us, or bitch with them about the trials and tribulations of the publishing industry. And then there's meeting fans, people who'd actually *read* my books, who'd cried along with my characters, asking insightful questions that made me consider my own work in ways I'd never thought of. Ach! Nothing beats it!

But the fun of those events is gone. Now the thought of advertising where and when I'm going to be somewhere, posting that information online, and encouraging strangers to come *find* me?! That's fucking terrifying. I was supposed to do a book tour around my home state of Texas back in November, during the worst of the dogpiling I was getting from Christian MAGA Zionists. My notifications, DMs, and even email inbox were flooded with hate mail and death threats. Scary in a different way are the fans who've developed a parasocial relationship with me and started expressing their "love" inappropriately. I've since learned it's just as important to block these folks, the moment the vibes feel off, as it is to block the haters.

I'm far from the only author who's faced hate and professional backlash this past year. The first high-profile aftershock came just a few days after October 7th, when the Frankfurt Book Fair announced it would be declining to present a planned award to Adania Shibli, a Palestinian author who wrote *Minor Detail*, a novella about the 1949 rape and murder of a Palestinian girl by Israeli soldiers.[11] My editor, Hannah Moushabeck, has experienced far more censorship and hate than anything I've gotten. She's had numerous school events for her heartwarming picture book *Homeland: My Father*

Dreams of Palestine abruptly canceled, with the reasons given including that she's a "known antisemite," "a threat to Jewish children," and that "Jewish parents felt uncomfortable about a plan to highlight a Palestinian voice." A Zionist couple even checked out her book, along with other Palestinian children's books, from New York Public Libraries and publicly vowed never to return them.[12] Hannah used to work for Simon & Schuster, until she was told to keep quiet about her Palestinian identity, prompting her to quit. At a peaceful vigil she organized, someone shouted, "The Moushabecks are indoctrinating you!" and someone spray-painted the word "Hamas" on her front lawn. While Palestinian authors like Moushabeck and Shibli faced the worst censorship within the publishing industry, even some of the US's most celebrated non-Palestinian authors—including Ta-Nehisi Coates, Viet Thanh Nguyen, and Naomi Klein—have been maligned by Zionists for expressing solidarity with Palestinians.

Knowing that I was facing this backlash in good company didn't make it any less scary.

By November, my visibility had exploded from a net following of around 50K to a net following of over 400K, and I had no idea how to judge my relative safety. I couldn't stop thinking about Salman Rushdie, the author of *The Satanic Verses,* who'd been stabbed the year prior at a book event. In 1989, the supreme leader of the Islamic Republic of Iran, Ayatollah Khomeini, issued a fatwa calling for Rushdie's assassination, and for thirty-three years, Rushdie had continued writing, publishing, and appearing in public without incident. By 2022, he probably wasn't all that stressed about it anymore; the fatwa was old news! But it just takes one nutjob.

And look, I fully understand I am not anywhere *near* Salman Rushdie's level—not in terms of renown, or in my caliber as an author or thinker. I also know that getting a DM from "User123456789" saying, "I'm gonna put you on the other side of the ground" is not anywhere near as serious a threat as having the supreme leader of an authoritarian theocratic regime call for your assassination.

But still. It only takes one nutjob. And I had plenty of those in my comments.

Maybe I would've gone through with the tour if I hadn't been pregnant. Let's say I did get stabbed—I might've survived, but my baby probably wouldn't have. As unlikely as it was that I would face a violent attack, I just couldn't get the idea out of my head, and I canceled the rest of my book tour.

Nowadays, I've gotten more used to my level of online visibility, but I still don't know whether my fears of appearing in public are reasonable or paranoid. I started seeing a therapist in the hopes that she would help me overcome my agoraphobia. But after telling her about my situation, she seemed even more scared for my safety than I was!

I've done a few stealthy book events this year, showing up to a panel or reading without advertising it on my socials. Everything went fine at those events, and I had a lovely time once I relaxed. But I dreaded those appearances for weeks in advance and showed up to them shaky with fear. All of these author gigs are unpaid, so I can't work out whether the risk and distress is even worthwhile. But without these rare moments of in-person connection, my entire career will just be me, alone in my office, writing for readers I'll never get a chance to meet.

Obviously, these are itty-bitty grievances compared to the horrors of the massacres, bombings, starvation, dehydration, lack of sanitation and medical care, and psychological and physical torture that Palestinians in Gaza have faced every day since October 7th, 2023. So I don't go around feeling too sorry for myself.

I should share that the impact of speaking out on Palestine hasn't been all bad. While I've lost some opportunities, I've gained others. While I might've sold a few dozen copies of *The Free People's Village* on my canceled book tour, *thousands* of my new followers have bought the book in solidarity. A certain digital privacy company cares more about the size of my following than my political beliefs, and I make one-minute ads for them, each of which pays better than the advances for my first three books combined. (Granted, these were tiny indie-press advances). While I was rejected from *almost* every book festival I applied to last year, I was embraced by the awesomely radical Bay Area Book Festival, which paid for me to stay an extra night in Oakland, just so I could meet up with their local Jewish Voice for Peace chapter. My latest novel did not sell to a big-five publisher,* but I was approached by

....

* The big five are Penguin/Random House, Hachette, Harper Collins, Macmillan, and Simon & Schuster. Together, these five corporations (themselves owned by even-larger media conglomerates) capture an estimated

Interlink to work on this book instead, and there's no publisher I could be more honored to work with in this historical moment.

And that brings me to the greatest boon I've earned from a year of rabble-rousing for Palestine: I am doing hands down the most fulfilling work of my life.

Over the past year, my followers have raised over half a million dollars for families and mutual aid efforts in Gaza. The first family we supported were able to evacuate to Rafah before Israel destroyed the border crossing, and they are living in safety in Cairo. For the families we've helped who are still in Gaza, I've been able to organize medical care and shelter and support their daily expenses from afar.

I've received hundreds of messages from folks saying that my videos inspired them to become an anti-Zionist, or a leftist, or an activist for the first time. And I have found a strong community of anti-Zionist activists to draw strength from and collaborate with.

And perhaps the greatest honor of my life was hearing from Bisan Owda, who said she "so appreciated my content" and "never missed a video." There is no one on this Earth I admire more than Bisan, who has relentlessly, brilliantly, and courageously kept reporting from the ground in Gaza over the past year, where every day she reminds the world that she is still alive to tell the story of a people facing genocide.

The thought that Bisan has watched my videos from Gaza and felt any amount of solidarity or comfort in them—that's infinitely more valuable to me than any starred book review or publishing award.

You see, all I've ever wanted for my life was to be *helpful*, and capitalism makes it so hard!

I remember having my first, the-world-is-fucked, how-can-I-go-on existential crisis in 1999. I was in eighth grade, home sick with the flu, watching *Animal Planet* all day, because it was the only TV that wouldn't make me nauseous. This was back when *Animal Planet* was wall-to-wall thirty-minute educational episodes featuring different species of animals. And by the seventh or eighth episode, I realized that every show ended the same

....
(continued) 80% of the US book market. Any publisher, like Interlink, that is not owned by these five corporations is considered "Independent."

way—"pollution, habitat destruction, and global warming are threatening this species' survival." And all at once, I just *got* it. That every single ecosystem on Earth was in decline. That we were fucking over our one and only planet, irrevocably, suicidally, and Captain Planet was not coming to save us.

For Gen-Zers, who have grown up amid wildfires, floods, heat waves, and open political discussion of climate change, this might seem like a painfully obvious realization. But back in the '90s, the pre-9-11 US was still high off the falling of the Berlin Wall, Bill Clinton was playing jazz saxophone on *Arsenio Hall*, and the Western world was partying like it was literally 1999 because neoliberalism* had defeated the Soviets. History had ended, and we would all keep enjoying our SUVs and Big Macs and ever-accelerating consumerism forever and ever without any repercussions. So I felt extremely alone with my epiphany. No politicians were saying the words "climate change," and every adult I tried to talk to about my fears gaslit me into feeling like some kooky, killjoy environmentalist who needed to calm the fuck down.

I became very depressed. Sometimes my climate grief would get so overwhelming, I couldn't operate, and getting out of bed was a struggle. But the rest of the time, I worked relentlessly at school, determined to graduate top of my class, so I could become either a politician or an environmental scientist who would change things. I had wanted to be a fantasy author up to that point—I had been a dragon-obsessed kid, playing Magic the Gathering and tearing through pulp fantasy series. But there was no time for such frivolity now. I had to save the world from mass extinction!

Once I got to college, though, I quickly realized I didn't have the temperament for either scientific research or electioneering. I decided science communication was equally important. There was plenty of climate research showing the trajectory we were on, but people weren't connecting to it on a human level! I wanted to write a thrilling, young adult climate fiction novel, as wildly popular as *she-who-will-not-be-named's* book series. An unputdownable adventure that would spur a new generation of readers into becoming climate activists! So I majored in creative writing.

....
* *Neoliberalism* is the belief that society should definitely be capitalist—
  we need to have billionaires with multiple mega-yachts at the same time as
  homeless people dying in the streets—but we can make capitalism *seem* nicer
  by allowing for a constitutionally limited democracy and a few social
  welfare programs, as a treat.

But then I graduated, slammed face-first into "the real world," and took a teaching job to pay the bills. I thought I could write my novels during summer breaks, but I never found the time. And as the years went by, I thought maybe my little way of making the world a better place would be through teaching. But I was teaching at one of these "high-performing" charter networks in Houston, and the culture was extremely toxic and cultlike. No matter how much I tried to be the best teacher I could be for my students, I was complicit in a school district that, at its core (and like all school districts in the US), was ableist, racist, and existed to indoctrinate future generations into accepting a violent status quo. I kept accepting leadership promotions to try and change things for the better, until I found myself interacting regularly with the board of trustees. They were a group of right-wing, white male oil and gas executives who saw our schools as a justification of their beliefs about the laziness of Black and Brown* kids and public-school teachers. Their work on the board was charity they did to help themselves sleep at night, balancing out, in their minds, the evil deeds of their salaried jobs in the petrochemical industry.

I was already disgusted and fantasizing about quitting, when I became disabled by the birth of my first kid, and the district refused to provide me ADA accommodations. So, as the 2017 school year started, I found myself jobless with a newborn, recovering from a botched postpartum surgery. That's when I finally decided to write my YA climate fiction novel. And I did. I wrote it, like this book, in between naps and diaper changes. But my publishing career has not been a Cinderella story. With my first few books, I clawed my way into a career with indie publishers, accepting advances that wouldn't even cover my groceries for a month. My YA book sold only a few dozen copies in its first year.

....
* In this text, you'll see me capitalize Black and Brown as identity labels, but not the word white. This convention is becoming increasingly mainstream; the Associated Press began capitalizing Black as an identity label, but not white in 2020. For many people, the terms Black or Brown represent a shared identity and lived experiences, including discrimination based on skin color, and should be capitalized, just as an ethnicity would be. Whiteness, on the other hand, is used here as a term for describing those who are most privileged in a white supremacist society. Historically, whiteness has often, but not always, been determined by skin color, and is highly variable depending on time and place. Later, we will explore how very pale Irish and Jewish people in the early modern period were excluded from whiteness. So, to my mind, "white" works more like the term "elite" than a proper-noun identity label.

Writing and staying at home with the kid afforded me a bit more time and bandwidth, though, to get involved in organizing. I had mostly put volunteer energy into electoral politics in the past, block-walking and phone-banking for Barack Obama, Wendy Davis, and Bernie Sanders in turn. But when the DNC sabotaged Bernie's presidential campaign for a second time, I started to realize that the Democratic Party would *never* deliver the kind of change that was desperately needed to halt or reverse climate change.

In college, I'd had friends who were self-described communists and anarchists.* Mostly these were white guys who were also Jewish. We'd be playing Star Wars Battlefront on PlayStation 2 in some trust fund kid's apartment, the walls decorated with Grateful Dead tapestries and posters of Che Guevara. Some guy would take a gravity bong rip off a two-liter of Mountain Dew, then launch into a Marxist rant. And while I appreciated their acumen on the icy battlefields of Planet Hoth, I would always roll my eyes at their outsider political beliefs.

Much the way liberal critics dismiss me now!

But then came the 2016 election, when the DNC cheated progressive Bernie Sanders out of the nomination, despite his massively popular grassroots movement, in favor of widely disliked, center-right Hillary Clinton. Bernie's candidacy had been the closest thing to hope I'd felt for our country since Obama turned out to be a war criminal and fracking magnate. With his defeat, I suddenly wanted to know what those stoned Marxists had been on about.

So I started reading leftist books, and the way the world worked started making more and more sense to me. I particularly found clarity in Black

---

* *Communists and anarchists* both believe that there should not be billionaires with multiple mega-yachts while homeless people starve in the streets. Both believe humanity should get it together and *share*. Both dream of a classless world without elites, where workers control the means of production, resources are shared sustainably and equally, and everyone's needs are met.

However, these groups differ in their attitudes towards hierarchy and authority. Communists think a little power imbalance is essential. How can they defeat capitalist states without a strong central state of their own? Anarchists, however, see authoritarianism and capitalism as equally insidious threats and seek to remake the world without imbalances of wealth or power.

But members of both groups famously struggle to agree on definitions of these terms! Many books have been written seeking to define them in greater clarity, and this is just a footnote. So, grain of salt!

radical thinkers like Cedric Robinson, who wrote *Black Marxism*, and the writings of Ruth Wilson Gilmore and Françoise Vergès anthologized in that book's follow-up, *Futures of Black Radicalism*.

I started to understand why phone-banking for Democratic Party candidates would never end forever wars, or secure universal health care, or deliver the climate solutions the world so desperately needed. Voting blue-no-matter-who couldn't even stave off fascism,* as the DNC has claimed they were doing in each election of my lifetime. Because those same Democrats were simultaneously pursuing fascist policies like mass deportation, mass incarceration, criminalizing protest, and building the cop cities that are taking us ever further into an authoritarian state.**

Between 2016 and 2021, I waffled about in leftist spaces and among various ideologies, trying to figure out where I fit in "the movement." I organized at times with groups focusing on abortion rights, environmental justice, anti-war, anti-racism, education, and housing rights. I cared about all the things, and I was trying to show up for all the causes, all the time. As a result, I had very little impact anywhere. I would go through spurts of trying to make every meeting and action, then get burned out, pull back from all the work I was doing, and feel deeply ashamed for being such a flighty bitch who wasn't worth their carbon footprint. This pattern kept repeating, until I found my way to anti-Zionist organizing.

I had read some books about Palestine at this point and had started showing up for local protests organized by the Palestinian Youth Movement. But there was no Jewish Voice for Peace chapter in Houston for me to organize with. Not until 2021, when my friend Hannah Thalenberg and I, along with a few others, started a local chapter, and I finally committed to JVP as my organizing home.

....

* A *fascist* government is a capitalist government without the nice window dressings of neoliberalism. Traditionally, this looks like a one-party-system, ruled by a dictator-for-life, whose total power is not limited by a constitution or checks and balances.

** An *authoritarian* state is a government where obedience to authority is maintained with a whole bunch of violence. In my humble opinion, all existing states are authoritarian, but there are more and less extreme examples (North Korea vs. Iceland, for example). Authoritarian governments may be capitalist, as in Nazi Germany, or communist, as in the Soviet Union.

Founding that JVP chapter, like so much of my work this past year, was motivated by equal parts spite and love. A few months earlier, I'd been invited to a Zoom call of "Anti-racist Houston Jews." That first call was organized by a liberal Jewish boomer. Let's call her Deb.

Deb had been deeply troubled by the police killing of George Floyd. Deb was embarking on her "anti-racist journey," was "doing the reading," and wanted to bring the wider community of Jewish Houstonians along with her.

Deb's call to action took place in the spring of 2021, during the escalation of violence in Sheik Jarrah, Jerusalem, which was the run-up to the Zionist massacre that would be called Operation Guardian of the Walls. But of the fifty Houston Jews who signed on to that first Zoom call, only two of us wanted to talk about Palestine. Me and Hannah. (Not the editor of this book, Hannah Moushabeck. Different Hannah! All the best people are named Hannah!)

Hannah was someone I'd known for a while, from seeing them around the internet, and they were one of the few other millennials on the call of mostly Gen Xers and baby boomers.

Our insistence on talking about Palestine derailed the ever living fuck out of Deb's hopes for that first call.

And the second one.

After that, Deb sent out an email stating that no further mention of Israel/Palestine would be tolerated within the group. Theirs would be an organization that would only discuss anti-racism *within* the US. (She did not mention whether we could discuss anti-racism towards Palestinians in the US, but I assumed that was a no-go as well.)

I wrote a reply-all email saying:

> If this group cannot take a firm stance against Israeli apartheid as a starting point, it has no moral standing to work towards anti-racism in the US. For US Jews to confront anti-racism necessitates confronting the ways in which we benefit from racial apartheid in the US and Israel.
>
> Deb, you once told me that your worst fear is that this group would be a book club that lets white Jews feel good about themselves, like they're "doing something" about racism, without

actually confronting the structural privileges we experience as beneficiaries of institutional racism. If we cannot take a strong stance in support of Palestinian liberation, that's exactly what this group is, and I won't be a part of it.

I went on to—surprise, surprise—recommend some Palestinian books for my fellow Jews to read, and then I described my experience at a recent demonstration for Palestine organized by the Palestinian Youth Movement.

> With two other Jews, we carried signs identifying ourselves as Jews in support of a free Palestine, and we experienced zilch antisemitism—only heartfelt, sometimes tearful thank-yous from Palestinians here in Houston. I could not say "You're welcome," though, because it felt like the bare minimum for us to be there. Instead I said, "I'm sorry there's so few of us." Everyone in this group—we ALL should have been there.

A short while after I hit "Send," Hannah wrote back another reply-all.

> Sim, thank you for articulating so clearly what I haven't had capacity to say to this group ever since I realized it's not one I want to be part of. I look forward to (un)learning and organizing with you and everyone who agrees that there can be no racial justice without decolonization and reparations, including in Palestine.
>
> On that note, I'm planning to show up in solidarity again at a demonstration for Palestinian liberation that's taking place this evening. If anyone else wants to join, please reach out at the phone number in my email signature!"

At the demonstration that night, Hannah and I showed up with our signs that read, "This Jew says *Free Palestine*." We were approached by a few other folks who introduced themselves as Jewish anti-Zionists. Together, we established a Houston chapter of Jewish Voice for Peace.

And Hannah has become one of my closest friends!

So, no, October 2023 wasn't the first time I'd gone head-to-head with

Zionists, and it wouldn't be the first time I'd get exiled from Jewish community for doing so. Still, talking about anti-Zionism with *the whole entire internet* was a way more intense undertaking than breaking up with fifty Jews I knew from a Zoom call.

So I was scared and hesitant and reluctant when I started posting videos about Palestine back in October. But I also had this strange feeling of destiny. It's a little like the night I hooked up with my would-be spouse for the first time. Even before we kissed, I had this funny feeling we would wind up getting married. In a weirdly similar way, deep down, I think I've known for years that once I got going on it, dismantling Zionism would become *the* struggle that would define the rest of my life.

I never wonder, any longer, if I'm making the most of my time on this earth. I've "found my why," and I didn't have to pay some life coach thousands of dollars to do it!

I've shared this story of how I got here, because it was all so unintentional, you see? I've been effective at this work because of some combination of my identity, my life history, my personality, and the whims of the algorithms. Becoming an "Influencer for Palestine" has been terrifying, emotionally harrowing, and disastrous for my career as a fiction author. But I've stuck with the work, because my obstinate ass doesn't know how to quit!

And while it is traumatizing to bear witness to the horrors of genocide, there is peace of mind in standing firmly rooted, ten toes down, in the struggle against empire. You might think I'd sleep worse, given all the dead bodies I've seen this year in my Instagram feed. But for the first time in my life, I'm not plagued by insomnia. I sleep soundly, tired out, and knowing that I'm doing something important with my life. I've lost lifelong relationships with some Jewish family members and friends. But I've since forged truer relationships, with anti-Zionist Jews (like Hannah Thalenberg!) and Palestinians (like Hannah Moushabeck, editor in chief! Can I keep all these exclamation marks and parentheticals?!)

These relationships are grounded in shared values and sacred work, and there are no people on this earth I'd rather have as comrades than those who stand in principled solidarity against genocide.

Part II.
Answering Hasbara

Hasbara is the Israeli term for propaganda. Hasbara is the mountain of bullshit Israel piles on top of its bloody history in order to confuse you about some very basic facts: Israel stole the land from Palestinians. Israel has been ethnic cleansing Palestinians for over seventy-five years. Israel is an apartheid state, doing genocide. Genocide bad.

Confronting and dismantling this Hasbara is vital work in support of liberation. But believe me, I get that arguing with Zionists can be… overwhelming. My advice is to start by just picking a lie—any lie—and correcting it.

That's what I started to do back in October, and it's what I continue to do one year and hundreds of videos about Palestine later. I started identifying patterns of Hasbara in my comments and taking them on, one TikTok video at a time. I don't argue in the comments, as the individuals repeating these claims may be bots, committed Zionists, or even salaried Hasbara employees—all of whose minds are equally impossible to change—or they may be well-intentioned bystanders repeating what they've heard from Zionist sources. Arguing with them one by one is a futile task and a colossal waste of energy.

But if I see a hundred similar comments, I can make a video addressing all of them at once, to an audience of people who may be uncommitted or questioning. And through that one video, I might help dozens, or hundreds, or even thousands of people untangle truth from fiction, depending on how effectively I communicate and whether the algorithm cooperates.

When I started arguing with Hasbara, I felt like I was trying to flatten this mountain of bullshit by standing on the peak and chucking pebbles off one by one. I'd hold up a stone to the light, say, "Look, it's bullshit"—and chuck it over the side. But for every lie I revealed, the Zionists in my comments would hurl a hundred more back at me. This labor, you can imagine, is not the most pleasant thing I could be doing with my time. It felt tedious, impossible, overwhelming, and it meant spending my days wading through bullshit.

But soon the movement for a free Palestine took off on social media, and suddenly there were thousands of others all over the internet, helping expose Zionist lies along with me. And I learned that for most people, folks who were unengaged on Palestine before October 7th, you don't have to expose *all* the lies for them to realize the mountain is bullshit all the way down. Three or four major corrections might do the trick! Five or six and they might join you in the task of flattening Bullshit Mountain.

This book is designed to help you in this bullshit-exposing, mountain-flattening enterprise. I've found that, even though there's a mountain of Hasbara out there, the mountain is composed of just a few different *types* of bullshit. And when you learn to spot those types, and how they function, you get better at exposing them. In the chapters that follow, I identify the nine most frequent types of Hasbara I encounter, I explain why they're bullshit, and I offer various strategies for responding to them.

Again, I don't recommend using these strategies to argue with strangers in internet comments because that is a waste of your precious time on this earth. You could very well be arguing with paid Hasbarists and invested Zionists who will never change their minds. However, feel free to take these ideas to make your own original content, which might reach a wider audience of the uncommitted or Zio-questioning folks. Even better, use these arguments to have those difficult, face-to-face conversations with friends, loved ones, and coworkers that are the most effective way of doing the world-altering task of changing peoples' minds.

1. "Who Are You to Speak on Israel?"

A primary goal of Hasbara is to get you, a supporter of Palestinian liberation, to shut the fuck up. In order to win the world over to supporting the Zionist project, all dissenters must be silenced. If you do start criticizing the actions of Israel, or even share a tepid recognition of the humanity of Palestinians, some Zionist is going to come along and ask for your credentials to do so.

They might ask, "What does Palestine have to do with you?" or "Have you even set foot in the region?" They might co-opt social justice language, saying, "Americans should stay in their lane," or "Listen to Israelis."

They might use whataboutism to shame you into silence, a tactic of silencing one accusation by bringing up another one. Zionist whataboutism sounds like, "Why are you so focused on Gaza and not [insert other humanitarian crisis]?" or "The US is a colonial state too! Give back your own country first!"

Inevitably, if you are standing up for Palestine, Zionists will challenge your right to say anything on the topic. Whatever your level of education or expertise, it will never be enough. And whatever your identity is—whether you're white, Black, Jewish, Muslim, Arab, queer, disabled, etc.—they'll insist you're not the right mix of marginalizations to give an opinion on Palestine.

When Zionists question your credentials to speak out on genocide, they are expecting you to play by the rules of "deference politics." Understanding the mechanisms of deference politics—and why we should embrace a constructive politic instead—will prevent you from getting derailed by questions like "Who are you to speak on this?"

In *Elite Capture: How the Powerful Took Over Identity Politics (And Everything Else)*, philosopher Olúfẹ́mi O. Táíwò defines "deference politics" as "an etiquette that asks people to pass attention, resources, and initiative to those perceived as more marginalized than themselves."[13] Basically, deference politics asks you to look around a room, figure out who is the most oppressed person there, and just ... do whatever they say. "Center their voice" and "follow their lead." Táíwò sees deference politics as the result of the "elite capture" of *identity politics*, which was originally a far-left political project.

Táíwò uses the term "elites" (as I will for the rest of this book) to mean anyone who hoards wealth and power. In a global context, "elites" are billionaires, politicians, CEOs, shareholders, board members, and A-list celebrities—rich motherfuckers, basically. You don't have to be uber-wealthy to be an elite, though. In the context of your workplace, your boss, who might be making barely more than minimum wage, is an "elite." Whether we're talking globally or locally, elites tend to do things that will increase their hoard of wealth and power. "Elite capture" is the process by which elites invariably hijack the political projects of the masses, twist them, and weaponize them to serve elite interests.

No conspiracy is needed for elite capture to take place (although, do the wealthy get together sometimes and plot how to foil the impoverished masses? Absolutely!) But whether intentionally or not, whether emerging from secret meetings in shadowy board rooms or not, whether funded by the CIA and enacted by paid infiltrators or not—elites are going to capture! Your boss is going to try to foil your plans to unionize. Corporate is going to try to hide its crimes against humanity with social-justice-y charity work. Táíwò calls elite capture "a kind of system behavior ... an observable, (predictable) pattern of actions."[14] Hijacking leftist projects is just what elites *do*.

One of those hijacked political projects is "identity politics," a term coined by Black feminist lesbians of the Combahee River Collective in the 1970s. These women felt that neither the civil rights movement, nor the feminist movement, nor the gay rights movement were listening to their unique priorities as Black lesbian women. To them, identity politics was about asserting their right to pursue "a political agenda based in their full experiences and interests, rather than positioning them as white women's tokens or as Black men's secretaries, and one that incorporated the full complexity of their values, rather than a degraded and misshapen caricature of them."[15] Identity politics was about asserting their right to speak from the intersection of being

Black, women, and lesbians—all at the same time! But the Combahee River collective never meant for identity politics to be used to silence anti-imperial voices or fracture solidarity among the left. Thanks to the process of elite capture, though, the rhetoric they developed has been weaponized by elites to do just that. This perversion of identity politics is what Táíwò calls deference politics, and he makes a compelling argument that the left must abandon deference politics in favor of constructive politics.

When we're told we're not allowed to be anti-genocide, because some of the people doing the genocide have historically been marginalized—that's deference politics. When the Israeli military brags about being one of the most LGBT-friendly in the world, they're trying to distract you from the fact that their military is flattening entire apartment blocks full of families with deference politics.[16] When Kamala Harris shut down anti-genocide protesters at a campaign event by saying, "I'm speaking,"[17] she was invoking the rules of deference politics. A major (failed) strategy of her presidential campaign was to bank on her gender and Black and South Asian identities as credentials that must be *deferred* to, in order to silence dissent on Palestine.

Deference politics tokenizes people—reducing them to the sum of their marginalizations—rather than valuing their input based on the quality of their ideas. When you're asked to defer to the most marginalized person *in the room*, it's easy for elites to control the conversation by controlling who gets access to that room. That "room" might be a boardroom, classroom, or the Oval Office. It might be a TV studio or the offices of the *New York Times*. It takes enormous privilege—*elite* privilege—to access any of those rooms. Gatekeepers can easily ensure that the only visibly marginalized people they allow into those spaces are ones who will carry out their agenda.

And what is the agenda of deference politics? Protecting empire, enriching rich people, and preserving the status quo. As a result, deference politics focuses the precious, limited energy of activists on meaningless, symbolic victories so we don't have time to make transformative change. Deference politics asks us to defer to social justice "leaders" whose main agenda is tearing down solidarity between different identity groups on the left. Deference politics will have us spend all our energy shaming imperfect allies, rather than targeting *literal war criminals*. Deference politics asks us to boycott creators, organizations, and events that are working towards collective liberation, all because of semantics—because they said something that didn't quite get the *wording* right. And deference politics will ask us to support genocide, because a Black woman presidential candidate supports it, and because Black, gay, Jewish IOF soldiers are the ones mass murdering children.

Táíwò urges the left to abandon deference politics for constructive politics, which is all about building power and making radical change. "A constructive political culture would focus on outcome over process—the pursuit of specific goals or end results rather than avoiding complicity in injustice or promoting purely moral or aesthetic principles."[18] Rather than deferring to the person in the room who looks the most marginalized, constructive politics focuses on "building and rebuilding rooms" to include those who don't already have access. Those "rooms" might be physical spaces or signal chats. But IRL or digital, they're places where people can gather and build power. They're unions, student encampments, "peoples' universities," and anti-imperial coalitions. Constructive politics dreams big, keeps in mind a planetary perspective, and aims to "totally revamp our global social system—to rebuild the house we all live in together."[19]

When you start speaking out against Zionism, you will be immediately confronted with deference politics designed to shut you up. If you're not Jewish, Zionists will tell you to shut up and defer to Jews, because of the supposedly incomparable marginalizations we experienced during the Holocaust. If you *are* Jewish, like me, Zionists will tell you to shut up and defer to the *right* Jews—to Israelis. If you're an anti-Zionist Israeli Jew, they'll produce some Jew who has one more marginalization-token than you do—maybe they have darker skin, or they're queerer or more disabled than you—and they'll tell you to shut up and defer to that Zionist.

The best response to these comments is to recognize that deference politics sucks and *keep talking about Palestine!* If you want to address the question "Who are you to speak on Palestine?" simply share your honest reasons for talking in this space.

I've said things like, "As a US citizen, my government sends billions of my tax dollars to Israel every year, for the purpose of genociding Palestinians. They claim to be doing this 'in my name,' because I am Jewish. But I do not support genocide. In fact, I think genocide is bad. Like, it's literally the worst possible thing humans can do to one another. And those billions of dollars would be much better spent on health care, education, or literally anything besides mass murder."

After a year of genocide, many folks in the Free Palestine movement are no longer silenced by claims that their activism is "antisemitic," because we've heard that charge so often and in such bad faith as to render it meaningless. But many of us still get tripped up when deference politics come at us from the left—from our own side! Elite capture has us wielding deference politics against each other, eating our movement from within.

Recently, I've gotten much better at spotting this phenomenon—especially since reading Táíwò's book. But I'm sorry to say, over the past year, I've allowed myself to get derailed by deference politics more than once.

Last November, I put together a live-streamed event called *All I Want for Hanukkah Is a Free Palestine,* made up of Jewish content creators who had emerged as consistent anti-Zionist voices in the social media landscape after October 7th. At first, I invited a few creators I'd already forged connections with—Katherine (Katie) Bogen, Daniel Maté, and Jude Shimer. I asked those creators who else I should reach out to, and on their recommendation I invited a few more creators I wasn't yet mutuals with, including Mira Stern and Hadar Cohen.

As soon as I announced the event, I started getting DMs from several different Instagram accounts claiming to be Palestinian organizers. They told me, "Sim, I love your content, but this event is *not it."* Some said, "Sim, Jewish voices should not be centered right now. Cancel this event." Others approached me claiming to have insider information on why I shouldn't platform this or that panelist because they were "problematic." They accused several of my fellow panelists of clout-seeking and trying to "profit off Palestinians' pain." But the majority of the criticisms focused on Hadar Cohen, our only Israeli panelist, and the only Arab Jew among us. These accounts claimed Hadar was a "Zionist settler" and a "normalizer" and that it was an insult to Palestinians everywhere to include her in the event.

Again, I wasn't familiar with Hadar's work yet—hadn't been following her before putting together this event—and these criticisms really shook me. I had been trained in deference politics, and I was supposed to "listen to Palestinians" and "follow their lead"—without stopping to realize that their "lead" in this case didn't make much sense. I handled the situation badly, breaking solidarity among an emergent group that could have been a powerful anti-Zionist Jewish coalition over the year to come.

Despite the fact that the overwhelming response was excitement and gratitude, from hundreds of Palestinian and anti-Zionist Jewish folks, I deferred to those few critical accounts in my DMs. I approached the other panelists about the general criticisms of the event I was hearing, and I wondered if we should cancel altogether. I also approached Hadar individually about the criticisms focused on her, showed her screenshots of what these accounts were sending me, and basically asked her to defend her anti-Zionist bona fides. I regret the way I put her on the spot like that—especially now that I've gotten familiar with her work and have developed great respect for her consistent, courageous activism.

Hadar explained that these criticisms were nothing new to her. She had been organizing as an anti-Zionist Arab Jew, in Israel and the US, for many more years than I'd been out here. She had learned that facing criticism from *all* sides is just part of the landscape, and the best response is to just keep on keeping on, and let your work speak for itself. But, if that was what the group wanted, Hadar offered to bow out of the event to appease our critics.

In the group chat, Mira and Daniel saved us from total dissolution. They correctly identified that these calls for us to cancel the event and break solidarity only served Zionist interests. Daniel spoke about the necessity of building anti-Zionist Jewish spaces, and Mira stressed, in particular, the vital importance of including Hadar. *Because* she was Israeli and *because* she was an Arab Jew, Hadar's perspective was uniquely threatening to Zionism—and that's why the criticism she faced was so much more intense than what was launched at any of the rest of us.

I apologized to Hadar, in private DMs and the group chat, and Hadar graciously agreed to rejoin the event—which we went ahead with. Thousands of people tuned in for the live stream, and the response on the day-of was overwhelmingly positive and thankful. But I think the poor way I handled things soured the experience for everyone, and I lost confidence in my ability to build a community of anti-Zionist Jewish content creators. After the event, the group chat fell silent, and while some of us have collaborated on individual projects since then, we haven't had another major collaboration like that since.

Only in the aftermath of the Hanukkah event did I realize just how unserious all that criticism of Hadar had been. The same accounts that had approached me, saying things like, "Love your content, but this event is a terrible idea" started devoting their energy to smearing *all of us* who had participated in the panel—including me. They took some comments made by Katie Bogen, who works as a doctoral-level researcher of sexual violence, completely out of context. Katie had been talking about the importance of taking care of one's physical needs in a time of extended crisis—from drinking water to working out to having sex—but these accounts clipped her audio talking about masturbation as a form of self-care in the context of the COVID-19 epidemic, one sound bite in an hours-long event. They accused her of "getting off on genocide," and a year later, Katie is still referred to in some online spaces as a "Jewish slut" or "the girl who sexualized genocide." Daniel, who's gone on to become one of the hosts of the excellent and hilarious podcast Bad Hasbara, gets accused of being a Zionist because he occasionally expresses empathy for Israelis who've been brainwashed by genocidal propaganda all their lives. They accuse me of being a "normalizer" because I organize with Jewish Voice for Peace, which they claim is in fact a Zionist organization (despite all those rabbis you've seen getting arrested for saying "Free Palestine" at JVP actions). To this day, there are "pro-Palestine" accounts whose whole deal is sharing graphics and reels urging pro-Pal folks to block me and any other anti-Zionist Jewish content creators for our various "problematic" sins.

I'm ashamed to say that it was only when they went after *me* that I truly realized what a complete and utter schmuck I had been to give their concerns any weight whatsoever. I have often wondered if those accounts were actually run by Hasbara operatives. We know for a fact that Israel employs people to manage sock-puppet accounts* to sway public opinion on social media.[20] Did our anti-Zionist Jewish Hanukkah event get on their radar? Are those "Palestinian" critics really Israeli sock-puppet accounts? Or were they actually Palestinian activists who earnestly believe that silencing Jewish anti-Zionist voices is helpful to the movement?

....
* A sock-puppet account is a fake online identity that's used for deceptive purposes. Give your account an Arab name, make your profile pic a Palestinian flag, and suddenly David Cohen from Tel Aviv can be a "Palestinian influencer," sowing discord among the left!

31

The best thing about Táíwò's framework is that it frees me from having to figure out the answer to those questions. Because intentions don't matter. Whether our critics were Hasbara operatives or real Palestinians is immaterial—they were using deference politics to serve Zionist interests. We were engaged in a constructive project—building a space where anti-Zionist Jews could gather, celebrating our ancient traditions and defying empire at the same time. The effort to cancel that event and fragment our community would only strengthen the core Zionist narrative that Israel speaks for all Jews.

Now don't go throwing the identity-politics baby out with the deference-politics bathwater. Táíwò isn't saying *don't* listen to marginalized people. I'm not saying *don't* listen to Palestinians. Of course we should take cues from Palestinian organizers in the movement to free Palestine! But Palestinians are not a monolith. They are human beings with different motivations and ideas on which goals, strategies, and work we should focus on. So even if you want to "listen to Palestinians," you're going to have to figure out which ones.

And we live in a world where people are marginalized for all kinds of identities—so how do you know which oppressed group to prioritize over another? What's more, there are paid infiltrators in these streets! Particularly in the social media streets! CIA, Hasbara, and neo-Nazi operatives are out here, using sock puppet accounts on social media to turn us against each other. And for every one of them, there's a bunch more well-intentioned leftists who do the same work of empire, eating the left from within because they're naïve, or ego-driven, or misguided, or simply too exhausted to learn new ways of relating. So in deciding who to listen to, you're going to have to employ some critical thinking. Here are some helpful questions to ask:

Is this person building community, or tearing it apart?

Is this person more focused on building power, or on *appearing* morally pure?

Is this person prioritizing life-and-death issues, or are they prioritizing feelings, wording, and symbolic victories?

Is this person focusing on radical transformation, or on preserving the status quo?

Is this person centering the good of the movement, or centering their own ego?

Those of us standing against genocide, we want to be good people! We don't want to be bigoted in any form! So charging pro-Palestine activists with hatefulness is one of the most effective silencing tactics of Hasbara. When you're accused of being racist or anti-Jewish or even anti-Palestinian in your activism for Palestine, it can send your ego reeling. Those of us on the left who've grown up steeped in deference politics have heard "Listen to this group" and "Defer to that group" for so long that some of us need to relearn how to listen to *ourselves*—and trust our gut on moral issues as fundamental as Genocide bad.

So when you face such accusations, take a beat to reflect. Constructive politics is not a license to be a racist, sexist asshole in organizing spaces. Don't go quoting Táíwò to shut down criticism of abusive behavior or dangerous rhetoric. But consider who is leveraging the criticism, and whether or not their criticism is shared in good faith or to get you to shut up or give up on the fight for liberation.

We live steeped in a deeply unequal and oppressive society, so we are *all* capable of perpetuating bigotry. At the same time, charges of hate are a very common silencing tactic of Zionists. In fact, in the first six months of this genocide, one of the most common DMs I received came from followers privately telling me that they wished they could speak out, but they were afraid of being called antisemites. During the election, that concern shifted— towards people telling me they were afraid to criticize Kamala Harris's support of Israel, out of fear of being called racist.

Hasbara will keep evolving, will keep finding new ways to use deference politics to convince you that you're unqualified to say "Genocide bad." We must recognize the patterns, refuse to play by their rules, and focus more on building alliances and power than on tearing each other down.

And when we inevitably falter, because we are flawed and human and steeped in toxic systems, when we hurt a comrade or handle something less than productively, I hope we can extend to each other the kind of grace that Hadar Cohen has shown to me. Conflict is inevitable, and our allies are not disposable. We need to fess up to mistakes when we make them, and apologize when we've hurt someone, but we also need to abandon a culture of resorting to public humiliation, exile, and shunning of anyone who slips up.

Hadar gave me a second chance last year when she agreed to sign back onto our Hanukkah event, even after I'd tried to cut her out because of baseless, anonymous accusations. She took the time this year to read this chapter and offer notes. And she floated the brilliant idea to get the gang back together for a one-year reunion of All I Want for Hanukkah Is a Free Palestine. Mira, Katie, and Daniel have also offered their notes on this chapter, and they've agreed to join onto that event as well. We are back in cahoots, constructing anti-Zionist Jewish spaces, and I'm really looking forward to lighting some candles and reflecting on a year of activism with my esteemed Jewish comrades.

Take that, deference politics!

2. Marginalized Human Shields

Zionists claim that Israel is "the only Democracy in the Middle East," and that it provides a lone oasis of tolerance in the region, where Jews, women, LGBTQ+ people, and ethnic minorities are safe from those awful Arabs!

According to Hasbara, all Arabs, including Palestinians,* are a monolith of violent, misogynistic, ISIS-like tyrants who want to throw every Jew, queer, and sexually active woman off a building.

Because I am visibly queer and identify as nonbinary, Zionists in my comments say things like, "Go to Gaza. They will throw you off a building for your haircut!" Zionists frequently tell me their fantasies of how "Arabs" in Gaza would beat me, behead me, stone me, and burn me alive, etc. for my pronouns.

According to Zionist logic, anything that Israel does to "defend itself" is justified, because if the IOF stopped brutalizing Palestinians for even a moment, all the poor, helpless queers and women of Israel would be swept away by bloodthirsty Arab hordes!

And you don't *hate* gay people. Do you?!?!?

Using marginalized Israelis to justify committing war crimes against Palestinians is a specific kind of deference politics I call "using marginalized human shields." The term *human shields* refers to a military strategy in which the presence of civilians is used to deter attacks on military targets and is recognized as a war crime, even by the US military. Israel routinely accuses Hamas of using human shields, claiming Hamas has hidden military

---

* Mainstream Israeli media almost always uses the term "Arabs" rather than "Palestinians" in their reporting. This rhetoric has the effect of erasing Palestinians' unique identity and their ties to the land.

targets within civilian infrastructure, whenever the IOF blows up Palestinian schools, hospitals, and apartment buildings full of people. However, after bombing over 200 schools[21] and dozens of hospitals over the past year, Israel has yet to produce convincing proof of Hamas strongholds in those locations.

(Not that it would be okay to bomb schools full of children and hospitals full of patients, even if there was military equipment hidden within them. You don't bomb hospitals and schools, *period.*)

There's a useful refrain I will keep coming back to: Every Zionist accusation is a confession.

The Israeli military *has* routinely used human shields in combat situations. In the past year alone, Israeli soldiers have forced Palestinian prisoners to enter tunnels and buildings they believe to be booby-trapped.[22] Israeli soldiers have also forced Palestinian children and families to surround their tanks to prevent attacks—at times, while the children and their caregivers were handcuffed, blindfolded, and stripped to their underwear.[23] And in an extremely literal example of human shielding, in June 2024, Israeli forces in the West Bank city of Jenin were caught on video having strapped a wounded Palestinian man to the hood of their Jeep.[24]

So the Israeli military uses human bodies to shield themselves from literal attacks. And their Hasbarists use marginalized peoples' identities to shield the military from any rhetorical attacks or international criticism.

Look at us! cries the Zionist media. *Look at our Black soldiers (#BlackLivesMatter)![25] Look at our #girlbosses invading Lebanon![26] Look at these gay soldiers holding hands when they're not mass-murdering Palestinians![27]* Israel insists that their queer, multiracial, multi-gendered fighting force is proof of moral authority, proof that Israel exists to defend the rights of marginalized groups from the threat of an intolerant (imaginary) Arab horde.

Thus, Zionists position themselves as an anti-hate authority while *actually* inciting hatred of Arab, Muslim, and Palestinian people. They claim to be preventing a hypothetical future genocide of marginalized peoples in Israel while *currently* perpetrating an *actual* genocide of Palestinians. It's so fucking insidious, but we're not going to buy into this kind of weaponized deference politics anymore, are we? We're not going to be deterred by their marginalized human shields.

Pinkwashing: A case study in marginalized human shields

Using queer folks, specifically as marginalized human shields, has been dubbed "pinkwashing," and as one example of how to combat this kind of Hasbara, let's pick apart the many layers of bullshit underlying Israel's claim that violence against Palestinians is in any way justified by a support for queer rights. We'll consider the following four pillars of Israeli pinkwashing:

1. The notion that genocide is OK if the people being genocided, or their leaders, are anti-queer
2. The claim that Palestinians make a habit of killing queer people
3. The claim that Israel is a haven for queer rights
4. The erasure of queer Palestinians and their human rights

Let's start with the first claim, because it renders the rest of these points moot. I live in Texas. My governor and state legislators are anti-queer and anti-trans. Last year they tried to pass an anti-drag performance law that would've criminalized my ability to appear in public as a queer author. They're banning my books. They're trying to make being a trans person illegal and impossible here.

And it's not just our political leaders who are hateful. A lot of my fellow Texans, once you get outside the inner loop of our major cities, are also anti-queer and anti-trans. When I'm out in the boonies, they give me funny looks and make me feel unsafe. And yet I can easily say that I stand against the genocide of Texans!

Even if Gov. Greg Abbott of Texas passed a death penalty for queer people, I would stand against the genocide of Texans. Even if that law was voted in by a referendum, and a majority—nay, a consensus—of Texan voters agreed to the Bill, I'd *still* be against the genocide of Texans!

Even if I, myself, a queer person, was not a Texan, I would still stand against the genocide of Texans.

Because genocide bad!!! Under every circumstance!!! What a concept.

Now let's turn to the bullshit claim that Palestinians as a whole, or even Hamas specifically, are going around killing LGBTQ+ people as a matter of policy, something I've been informed of approximately fifty thousand times in my comments by Zionists.

Many of these commenters, if pushed for evidence, will refer to the 2022 murder of Ahmad Abu Markhiyyeh, who was beheaded in the West Bank.[28] May he rest in power. A suspect who was an acquaintance of Abu Markhiyyeh has been arrested, but not indicted.

This murder was a horrific act that should absolutely be condemned. But it was not carried out by Hamas. Hamas does not even operate in the West Bank—that would be the Western-backed Palestinian Authority. And there is zero evidence the PA had anything to do with Ahmad's murder. This was a crime that seems to have been committed by a lone suspect. We don't even know for sure that it was a hate crime, although it may well have been.

Unfortunately, I also live in a country where people are murdered for being queer. Last year, in a town not far from me, Akira Ross was shot in front of her girlfriend at a gas station by a man shouting homophobic slurs.[29]

Such hate crimes occur in Israel too. In 2015, a sixteen-year-old girl named Shira Banki was stabbed in broad daylight at a Pride parade in Jerusalem.[30]

Now I've never been to Palestine or Israel. I can't say comparatively how much better or worse anti-queer hate is in those places compared to Texas. What I know is that things for queer people are shitty, pretty much everywhere, and I wish they were better. But again, no matter how bad they are, I don't think people *anywhere* should get genocided for having hateful neighbors.

Extrajudicial killings of queer people are not, contrary to what Zionist commenters suggest, official Hamas policy. So what is the official stance of Palestinian state leadership towards LGBTQ+ people?

In the West Bank, under the Palestinian Authority, homosexuality has been decriminalized since 1951. In Gaza, under the leadership of Hamas, homosexuality between two men is criminalized and results in jail time (not beheading). But that criminalization began, not with Hamas or any Palestinian leadership, but with the British! Male homosexuality was first criminalized in Palestine under the British Mandate Criminal Code Ordinance of 1936.[31] Hamas has merely failed to decriminalize it.

And sure, I still think that's bad. I'll even condemn it!

Here I go: "I condemn the criminalization of male homosexuality, anywhere, by anyone!"

Even if Hamas is anti-queer, keep in mind that the beliefs of Hamas do not necessarily reflect the opinions of the majority of Ghazawis. There has not been an election in Gaza since 2006. Only an estimated 7 percent of the current population of Gaza participated in that election and voted for Hamas.[32]

It's worth noting that the outcomes of elections in the US also don't reflect the will of its people, given the electoral college, gerrymandering, unlimited corporate spending, and constraint to a center-right/far right two-party system. For presidential elections, only 0.05 percent of the population, swing state independent voters, decide who will lead the executive branch.[33]

So sure, there are queer-hating Palestinians in positions of power, just like there are queer-hating politicians just about everywhere. Right now, anti-trans hate is a central platform of right-wing parties in the UK, the US, and all other Western countries. And yet I don't support genocide in any of those places!

Personally, I have experienced far more anti-queer hate from Zionists than I have from Palestinians. Among the Palestinian organizers in my network, and at the dozens of pro-Pal protests and actions I've attended, I have never witnessed an iota of anti-queer hate. Among my hundreds of thousands of online followers, many of whom are Palestinian or non-Palestinian Muslims or Arabs, I am overwhelmingly affirmed and supported any time my queer identity comes up.

Of course, not everyone in the movement for Palestinian liberation is equally down for LGBTQ+ liberation. The main, like, micro-*annoyance* I would say (not micro-aggression, because 99 percent of the time, I don't think it comes from a place of "aggression," but rather oversight) is people using she/her pronouns to refer to me in my comments, rather than they/them. This error is so ubiquitous among my followers, across all races, ethnicities, and genders, that I don't think folks from Arab countries misgender me any more than queer USian liberals do.

Once in a great while, I get a comment from a Muslim follower telling me that while they appreciate my content, they think I'm misguided in my gender or queerness, and that they are praying for me to read the Quran and reform my ways.

And that sucks. I sometimes block or mute those people, depending on how obnoxious the comment is. Most often I don't, as they usually seem well-meaning, taken in the context of their worldview and life experiences, which are very different from mine.

But oh my goodness, the vast majority of anti-queer hate I receive online comes from Zionists. And this is true of both Israeli Jewish Zionists and USian Christian Zionists. They will call me all kinds of straight-up slurs, in English and Hebrew, and verbalize their fantasies about my violent death for being queer. Because that's what they're really doing when they say, "Go to Gaza. You'll get beheaded for your haircut!"

For the record, I would feel totally safe traveling to Gaza, haircut and all, were it not for the fact that Israel has dropped over 70,000 tons of bombs on Gaza over the past year at the time of writing.[34]

All this anti-queer hate coming from Israel's most stalwart keyboard warriors should clue you in that—no, actually, Israel is not some haven for LGBTQ+ rights. An apartheid state can *never* be a haven of LGBTQ+ rights, because any queer people suffering under their apartheid system will be met with violence. Queer Palestinians are massacred, imprisoned, raped, and tortured by the IOF, regardless of whether or not they're queer.

But Israel isn't even a haven of queer rights for rich, white Jewish Israelis! Netanyahu came to power in the last election by embracing the support of openly anti-queer and racist Likud party members.[35] Israel has not legalized same-sex marriage. Israel does recognize same-sex marriages that happen abroad, but only because it'll do about anything to attract more white, Jewish settlers to move to Israel and bolster its colonial project.

Just like in Texas, queer white Israelis live in a country where, in some urban centers, they may be able to live openly, in relative safety. But head to rural areas, and they may experience some very nasty anti-queer hate and even violence. They do not have equal rights. And powerful members of their government are openly hostile to them because they are queer.

And what about all the queer Israelis who aren't white Jews? How's Israel for their LGBTQ+ rights? Well, for them, regardless of whether they're queer or straight, Israel violates their human rights because that is what a white supremacist* ethnostate does.

Because Israel has painted itself as a haven for LGBTQ+ rights, in the

....
* *White Supremacy* is the belief that white people are superior to other races and should have control over them. Very important note: "whiteness" is a social construct, and what constitutes whiteness has changed across varying places and times. Lots more on this in the next chapter, "But Israel Is So Diverse!"

past few decades, a small number of queer Palestinians have moved there to seek asylum for being queer. But because they were Palestinian, they were denied the protections of other asylum seekers. They were forced to live in poverty, without official documentation, access to medical care, or other social services. Only exploitative, under-the-table working conditions were available to them, including sex work. A detailed 2021 report in +972 Magazine details the discrimination faced by these queer Palestinians. In one interview, a queer man named Muhammed says of living in Israel, "I would have rather died in the West Bank than live here like this." [36]

Muhammed's story contradicts the final pillar of Israeli pinkwashing: the erasure of the existence of queer Palestinians. News flash: queer people are everywhere, and queer Palestinians exist! (The book you're reading was edited by one, the fabulous Hannah Moushabeck—Hello again, Hannah!)

Some of the most engaged, hard-working Palestinian activists I've met in the diaspora are queer folks. Within the state of Israel, there are queer Palestinians like Muhammed and those interviewed by +972 Magazine. And there are queer people in the West Bank and Gaza too. And when they're not being actively genocided, some of these queer people have been organizing for queer rights. In 2019, the West Bank tried to ban LGBTQ+ groups, but there was such a backlash—a massive grassroots protest led by the Palestinian queer rights group Al Qaws—that the PA rescinded the ban. [37]

While many queer people in Gaza kept their queerness private, some of their stories were shared around the world in October 2023. Queering the Map is an app where LGBTQ+ folks living stealthy lives can post anonymously with a rough geo-tag, letting others in their area, and around the world, know that queer people live there, without giving away their identities. In the wake of October 7th, Queering the Map stories out of Gaza went viral as queer folk facing bombardment shared heartbreaking posts like these:

"Idk how long I will live so I just want this to be my memory before I die. I am not going to leave my home, come what may. My biggest regret is not kissing this one guy. He died two days back. We had told how much we like each other and I was too shy to kiss last time. He died in the bombing. I think a big part of me died too. And soon I will be dead. To younus, i will kiss you in heaven. [38]"

Of course there are queer people in Gaza, in the same proportions as there are queer people anywhere. Prior to October 7th, these queer Ghazawis were *not* being massacred by Hamas. But they're sure as shit being massacred by Israel now. As high-tech as the Israeli military is, they don't have bombs that only hit straight people.

The only state that is mass murdering queer people in the Middle East is the exact fucking state that claims to be a "haven" for queer people.

Don't buy into Zionist pinkwashing, or any other use of "marginalized human shields." Israel is also NOT a safe haven for women, or disabled people, or even for Jews!

"Marginalized human shields" Hasbara underscores why it's so important for anti-Zionist organizing spaces to be proactively inclusive. Pitting straight folks against queer folk, or any marginalized group against another, is a tool of empire that will only ever benefit the ruling, warmongering class. If you say "Free Palestine" but only mean that for straight people—then no, you don't really mean it.

At the same time, we need to move away from a deference politics that weaponizes our identities against one another. We can't be dissuaded from criticizing war crimes just because they're committed by Black, Jewish soldiers or queer, female politicians. When you practice constructive politics, you realize that the race, gender, and sexual orientation of people committing genocide are irrelevant, as are the political attitudes of the people being genocided.

Genocide bad—in all circumstances. Don't let the fuckers divide us!

3. "But Israel Is so Diverse!"

If you call Israel a white supremacist society (which it is), you're going to get Zionist commenters all-caps screaming at you things like, "ISRAELIS ARENT WHITE. ARE YOU INSANE. THEYRE BROWN AND BLACK AND WHITE AND DIVERSE YOURE WILDLY OUT OF LINE."

On my first video about Palestine that got millions of views, I said, "Western media is extremely white supremacist, and that is how racism works: Israelis get to be white. Palestinians are non-white. And they are therefore *not people.*"

The MAGA T-shirt salesman clipped just part of that statement. He showed his millions of followers me saying, "Israelis get to be white. Palestinians are non-white," and then he mockingly cited the percentages of Black and Brown Israelis.

That same stitch was then used dozens or even hundreds of times by Zionists. They'd show the clip of me saying, "Israelis get to be white," and then cut to a Black IOF soldier saying, "Do I look white, bitch?" Or the inverse—they'd stitch the part of my video saying, "Palestinians are non-white," cut to a picture of a blonde-haired Palestinian, and say, "They sure look white to me, you [insert ableist slur]."

By now, you can probably recognize the deference politics at play here, which go like this: Because I am white, my argument (that Israel is a white supremacist society) can be discarded as long as a Black Zionist is willing to contradict me. It's not the argument or ideas that matter, but the identity of whoever happens to be speaking.

Táíwò, our philosopher who coined the term *deference politics*, sees this phenomenon as a weaponization of identity politics. But in their responses to me, these Zionists demonstrated an incredibly superficial understanding of identity politics. They've mistaken *colorism* for racism. So we're going to have to clarify those terms before we can explain why Israel is a racist state, despite the fact that, yes, some Israeli Jews do have dark skin! And, also yes, some Palestinians have pale skin!

Those facts do not negate the fundamental white supremacy of Israeli apartheid. To understand why, we're going to need to move beyond an elementary-school definition of racism.*

Colorism is discrimination based solely on the darkness of your skin color.

Racism is a social, economic, and legal construct that sorts people into categories of more- and less- human, in order to justify the exploitation and oppression of racialized groups.

In a *white supremacist* society, certain types of people get to be "white," and these people are afforded more wealth, privilege, and civil and human rights than those who are "non-white." Whiteness may be determined by colorism alone, but other factors such as ethnicity, religion, or class may be of equal or even greater importance, depending on that society's rules for who gets to be white.

I did not pull these definitions out of my butt. I learned them from Black Radical thinkers like Cedric Robinson, who wrote *Black Marxism*. In that book, Robinson critiques Karl Marx's assertion that "the history of all hitherto existing society is the history of class struggles." Robinson argues that Marx, being a white German dude from the nineteenth century, had a big-ol' blind spot when it came to race. So Robinson builds on Marx's ideas about class struggle, which he finds solid, but adds analysis of how racism was *also* a driving force of history from the early modern** period onward.

In terms of my political analysis, reading *Black Marxism* felt like filling

---

* Widespread ignorance of these terms is why critical race theory absolutely *should* be taught in schools, folks!

** The *early modern* period in Europe took place roughly between the sixteenth and eighteenth centuries, in the time span between the Middle Ages and the Industrial Revolution. When I was in school, these centuries were referred to as the Enlightenment and the Renaissance (a French word meaning "rebirth"). I don't use these terms anymore, as they are Eurocentric and loaded. If you were being colonized or ghettoized by Europeans during these times, you were not undergoing "rebirth," and there was nothing "enlightened" about that experience.

in the last missing piece of a jigsaw puzzle. When you start looking through a Black Marxist lens, world history and US politics start to make a lot more sense.

If you only view the world through the lens of class, you'll forever be baffled as to why poor white people in the US vote against their own class interests. (Hint: it's because racism!)

And if you only have a racial understanding of the world, but lack a class analysis, then you wind up at neoliberal politics. And you're going to think silly things like: the solution to racist policing is to have more Black cops. Or the solution to racial income inequality is to have more Black CEOs. But as Dr. Ruha Benjamin said in her 2024 commencement address at Spelman College, "Black faces in high places won't save us ... just look at the Black woman's hand, ambassador at the UN, voting against a ceasefire in Gaza."[39]

In *Black Marxism*, Robinson argues that capitalism evolved in the early modern period simultaneously with white supremacy, which is why scholars in the Black Radical tradition often use the term "racial capitalism" to emphasize the fact that white supremacy and capitalism are inextricably intertwined. Capitalism and racism are two peas in a pod, and there has never been a version of capitalism that was not white supremacist.

The sixteenth century was the beginning of what scholars term the early modern period, which saw the end of medieval feudalism and the emergence of racial capitalism. It's no accident that this century witnessed the ghettoization of minority populations across Europe. Robinson claims that racialized "others" at this time—including Jews, the Irish, and Romanies—began to be systematically constrained to certain areas and economic activities, so they could be used as a captive pool of cheap labor. Early modern elites dehumanized these groups to justify their exploitation.

Racism divided the laboring classes into white and non-white groups. The white group—those in the religious or ethnic majority—now saw themselves as more allied with the nobles who were robbing them of their wealth than they were with their fellow non-white workers.

This same dynamic explains the popularity of billionaire real estate mogul Donald Trump among the white working class, even though those voters have far more in common *materially* with unhoused Black people and undocumented immigrants from Central America.

But back to sixteenth-century Europe. Racial capitalism emerged as ghettoization of minorities spread in several areas at once. In the 1500s, Great Britain re-colonized Ireland, and the entire island served as an Irish ghetto. Meanwhile, throughout continental Europe, Jews were ghettoized in walled-off slums within cities. The first Jewish ghetto was established in Frankfurt in the fifteenth century, and the sixteenth century would see the establishment of many more, in cities that were powerhouses of early-modern trade, including Venice, Florence, Rome, Prague, and Vienna. (More on this history in Chapter 8).

Were these ghettoized Jews in early-modern Europe non-white? According to Black Marxist thought, absolutely. The paleness of Irish or Ashkenazi Jewish skin was irrelevant to their non-whiteness. Jews experienced structural racism because they were confined to a ghetto, where their economic activity was limited to scrap work, secondhand trade, and banking, and when they left the ghetto, they were forced to wear an identifying "Jewish badge." Thus, Jews and the Irish, along with darker-skinned minorities such as Romanies, were segregated, kept impoverished, and were discriminated against by law. According to Black Marxist thought, that means they were all non-white.

But what about Jews today? Are we still not white?

As Europeans exported their way of life around the globe through colonization, colorism became the defining method of sorting people into racial hierarchies. Unlike a Jewish badge, you can't take off your skin color or facial features and assimilate into whiteness. So colorism was easier to enforce than the Jewish badge had ever been.

Colorism remains one of the most important determining factors in global racism. If you are a Black or Brown Jew, whether you are in Israel or the United States, you are non-white.

But what about fair-skinned Ashkenazi Jews like me? Are we white?

Short answer: Yes. As long as we pass for Christian.

In the United States, white Ashkenazi Jews possess *conditional* acceptance into white supremacy. We get to be white, as long as we dress and act white. In order to be truly white in the United States, you have to be Christian—and not a visibly different offshoot of Christianity like Mennonites or Amish people. Ideally, you're a tiny-gold-cross-wearing, Christmas-loving, Protestant kind of Christian.

Thus, white Jews lose their conditional acceptance into whiteness when we look too Jewish. For example, Orthodox Jews, who wear traditional ethnic and religious garb, aren't really white in the context of the United States because their dress serves as a "Jewish Badge" that marks them out as *other*.

Similarly, when Jewish people gather in community or ritual, we lose our conditional whiteness. When white Ashkenazi Jews gather in a synagogue, they become non-white, because synagogues are targets of racial violence. When my Jewish Voice for Peace chapter gathers at Buffalo Bayou on Rosh Hashanah to blow the shofar and do tashlik, we become visibly Jewish and lose our conditional whiteness.

But 99 percent of the time, if you're an Ashkenazi Jew like me who doesn't wear religion on their sleeve while going about daily life in the United States, you're going to be perceived as white and benefit from white supremacy.

If you have a very Jewish sounding name or are regularly told you "look Jewish," you may experience some amount of discrimination for these qualities, but you are not experiencing structural racism on the level that Black and Brown people face. Particularly when it comes to economic racism.

Ninety-two percent of Jews in the US identify as non-Hispanic white,[40] and these white Jews have a much higher household income level than the average US citizen.[41] To illustrate just how well we're doing, 23 percent of US Jews report family incomes of $200,000 or more, compared to just 4 percent of all US adults.

Many Ashkenazi Jews have grown up with stories of the poverty and discrimination our grandparents and great-grandparents faced when they first immigrated to the United States. But, statistically speaking, those experiences are not the reality of most Jews in the US today. Colorism has trumped anti-Jewish hate, and pale Jews of European ancestry have been folded into white supremacy.

But what about in Israel, a country with a non-white majority? Of 7 million Israelis, only 25–30 percent are Ashkenazi Jews with European ancestry. Another 35–40 percent are Mizrahi Jews—Jews from Arab countries such as Iraq, Yemen, or Morocco; 2.2 percent are Black Ethiopian Jews, and 20 percent are Palestinian citizens of Israel.[42] "How can such a diverse nation be white supremacist?" Zionists will ask.

You might explain to them that white people don't have to be in the majority for a country to be white supremacist. If there's one category of people that's "white," and they're at the top of the economic and political ladder, then that country is white supremacist. In Israel, whiteness is claimed by Ashkenazi Jews.

As proof, you might cite the huge income and education gap between white Ashkenazi Jews and non-white Mizrahi Jews, a gap that is only worsening over time.[43] You might look at the Knesset, Israel's version of Congress, which is overwhelmingly made up of white men. You might point to the poverty among the Ethiopian Jewish community and their experiences facing widespread racism, discrimination, and routine police harassment.[44] You might bring up the fact that for years, Ethiopian Jewish migrants to Israel were routinely sterilized without their knowledge, cutting their birth rate in half compared to the general population.[45]

And that's just racial discrimination among *Jewish* Israelis!

Colorism does not trump anti-Palestinian hate in Israel. Yes, there are pale-skinned, blue-eyed, blond-haired Palestinians, but all of them live under racial apartheid. Amnesty International has found Palestinians experience "massive seizures of Palestinian land and property, unlawful killings, forcible transfer, drastic movement restrictions, and the denial of nationality and citizenship to Palestinians ... all components of a system which amounts to apartheid under international law."[46]

In Gaza, Israel is exterminating a captive population of 2 million Palestinians, through bombing, white phosphorous attacks, starvation, dehydration, withholding of medical supplies, and the rape and torture of prisoners. Nothing is more racist than genocide!

That thundering sound in the distance you hear? That's a stampede of whataboutists coming to derail you with "BUT THE US IS RACIST TOO!"

Yes, dudes, we know. But we're still talking about Israel right now.

Back to my video that got stitched a zillion times.

I didn't say, "All Israelis are white." I said, "Israelis *get to be* white." And the stitchers cut out what I said the sentence before—that they get to be white *according to Western media.*

As we've learned, whiteness is an artificial construct that shifts over time.

Ashkenazi Jews in seventeenth-century Europe were *not* white. But Ashkenazi Jews in Israel today are the definition of white.

In Western media, Israelis are consistently portrayed as white, while Palestinians are consistently portrayed as non-white. We know this because Israelis are humanized by Western media coverage, whereas Palestinians are dehumanized. When you look at the way Western mass media outlets covered October 7th and the ensuing genocide, there is a stark difference in the treatment of Israelis and Palestinians.

The Intercept analyzed over 100 articles written during the first six weeks of the assault on Gaza and found that Israeli deaths were mentioned at a rate sixteen times higher than that of Palestinians.[47] Journalists used highly emotive words and employed the active voice to describe the "slaughter" and "massacre" of Israelis, whereas they more often used the passive voice to describe Palestinians "dying." *The Intercept* also found asymmetry in the way news outlets emphasized the toll on children. Despite the assault on Gaza being one of the most deadly genocides of children in modern history,[48] very few mass media outlets mentioned the death toll of Palestinian children. Some stories about the prisoner exchange in November referred to "Israeli *children*" and "Palestinian *minors*" in the same article.[49]

US media outlets report on the murder of Israeli Jews like they're human beings whose individual deaths are a tragedy. At the same time, our media treats Palestinian people, regardless of the color of their skin, as inhuman, and the violence against them as inconsequential. Anything Palestinians do to defend themselves—from telling their stories, to peaceful protesting, to armed resistance—is portrayed as unjustifiable and "antisemitic." In the eyes of the Western world, the only thing Palestinians are allowed to do is die silently.

And that's fucking racist!

4. "But the Holocaust!"

Deference politics begs the question—which marginalized group should we defer to when there's disagreement? Should I listen to Jews or Palestinians about this *mishigas** in the Middle East? Zionists answer this question with: Jews, because the Holocaust. We have suffered like no other people in history have suffered, and therefore, by the rules of deference politics, we are the ultimate moral authority.

Zionists remind us endlessly of the six million Jews killed in the Holocaust, and they insist that those deaths give them permission to enact whatever violence they wish upon Palestinians. They claim that the state of Israel somehow protects not just Jews in Israel, but all the Jews of the world from another Holocaust. And they claim that this secondary Holocaust is sure to break out the moment Zionism fails.

However, if you (correctly) bring up similarities between the ideologies of Zionism and Nazism, or between the Holocaust and the ongoing genocide in Gaza, Zionists will clutch their pearls and cry, "How dare you!" They use the Holocaust as a rhetorical trump card that only they are allowed to play.

It doesn't matter if whoever's speaking is a descendant of a Holocaust survivor, or a survivor of the Shoah** themselves. Anti-Zionist Jews, who see the Holocaust as precisely the reason we must stand against the genocide of Palestinians, get shouted down and called self-hating Jews for daring to learn from our own history.

....
*   *Mishigas* is Yiddish for craziness, nonsense, tomfoolery, or, in this case, a big fucking mess.

**   *Shoah* is a Hebrew word for "calamity" and refers specifically to the six million Jews killed under the Nazi regime, as opposed to the more general term "Holocaust," which refers to all eleven million victims.

My advice is to ignore the pearl-clutching and reject the idea that you're not allowed to draw similarities between the Holocaust and other genocides. Drawing comparisons is how we learn from history! How are we going to ensure "Never again" if we refuse to see "again" when it's staring us in the face?

Something that's truly taken me by surprise this year is realizing just how much Jewish historiography* about the Holocaust is intertwined with Zionism. So much of the funding for Holocaust memory-keeping projects comes from the Israeli government or private Zionist sources. From online databases to storytelling projects to Holocaust museums, these institutions that claim to exist to prevent future genocides are, by and large, only financially viable because of the Israeli state and its ongoing genocide against Palestinians.

Since October 7th, Holocaust museums across the world have lain bare their hypocrisy by pledging unwavering support to Israel, even after the International Court of Justice (ICJ) found Israel to be plausibly committing genocide.[50] Holocaust museums have also silenced voices raised in support of Palestine, condemning protesters[51] and disinviting Shoah survivors[52] and other Jewish speakers who have dared to condemn genocide.[53]

The irony of a Holocaust museum taking the mic from a Holocaust survivor who is protesting a modern-day holocaust reveals the deep, irreconcilable schism in the global Jewish community.

Zionists' takeaway from the Holocaust seems to be: Never again ... *will Nazis kill us, because we will become the Nazis!*

And anti-Zionist Jews who believe: Never again, *FOR ANYONE!!!*

I've been told by Zionists so many times, in so many ways, that I am shaming my ancestors by speaking out for Palestinian liberation. I could not be more certain they are wrong. If anyone's ancestors are rolling over in their graves, it's theirs. In fact, their ancestors are probably crying, screaming, puking, shitting all over Sheol** at the shonda*** of watching their great-grandchildren become exactly the kind of monsters who tormented them.

I've come to believe there is something deeply wrong with Jewish

----

* *Historiography* is the study of the way we write history.

** *Sheol* is the realm of the dead in the Torah.

*** *Shonda* is a Yiddish word for a shame, embarrassment, disgrace.

history-making, if the memory of our persecution can serve as justification to persecute others. We focus too exclusively on our own victimhood, rather than seeing our suffering reflected in others. We study the Holocaust stripped of context—both the context of the centuries of anti-Jewish persecution that led up to it, and the context of the many other genocides enacted by white supremacist colonial capitalism around the world, before and since.

And if we fail to look at genocide through a Black Marxist lens, we fail to realize how wealth, power, and race factor into every genocide. The Holocaust was motivated by racism, nationalism, and capitalism, as much as it was motivated by religious persecution. Anti-Jewish hate was not the driving force of World War II, but a *tool* wielded by power-, wealth-, and land-hungry elites. Just as anti-Muslim and anti-Arab hate are tools wielded by power-, wealth-, and land-hungry elites in Israel and the US today.

So, as anti-Zionist Jews, we must take back our historiography and change the way we teach our history, including the Holocaust, to future generations. We must stop fetishizing our victimhood, look outside our own community, and embrace solidarity with all those who have been persecuted like us, and whom we have in turn persecuted.

I can't remember when I first learned about the Holocaust, because there was never a time in my memory when I didn't know about the genocide of our people. I assume the same holds true for most Jews. I remember certain moments when my understanding of the Holocaust deepened, like when I was seven years old, and my parents made me watch all three hours of *Schindler's List* with them. Or the time my dad took me to visit Michael Kern in Brooklyn, the only still-living member of our family who had immigrated from Stanislawa, Poland, and I heard firsthand his stories of anti-Jewish persecution in the old country.

Jewish holidays served as periodic reminders of our victimhood. There's a running joke that every Jewish holiday is "They tried to kill us. They failed. Let's eat!" And that's a pretty accurate summation. At Passover seders every year, we are reminded of the (bogus) story of our enslavement and exodus from Egypt.* At Hanukkah, we remember our persecution under the Seleucid king Antiochus (and we gloss over the Jew-on-Jew violence of the Maccabean

....
* For a deep dive into this myth, see Chapter 9.

revolt). On Purim, we remember how smoking-hot Esther saved us from annihilation at the hands of the Achaemenid Empire. And on each of these nights, and on Holocaust Remembrance Day, we take a beat to reflect on the more recent horrors of the Shoah.

Like many Jewish kids, I developed a fascination with the Holocaust, spurred by self-preservation. "Never again!" had been drilled into me. To me, this meant not that I needed to stand in principled solidarity against genocide, but rather that I needed to read every book about the Holocaust I could get my hands on, so I could learn the best strategies for hiding from Nazis. I kept at the serious business of this research, planning out hiding spaces in my house, until I gave myself recurring Nazis-at-the-door nightmares. From talking to other Jews, I've gathered that this is a pretty common experience. By the time we're twelve years old, a lot of us have at least a master's-degree-level-knowledge of the Holocaust and are carrying around a good deal of self-inflicted, secondhand Holocaust trauma.

So it was unthinkable to me when, one day in my first year teaching seventh grade English, I referenced the Holocaust and was met with utterly blank stares from my students.

"Have you heard of World War II?" I asked.

No response.

"You know, the Nazis?"

Blinks and crickets.

"Jews???"

One student raised his hand and offered, in a hopeful voice, eyes bright, just wanting to supply the right answer since I seemed so upset: "Weren't Jews the people who killed Jesus?"

Children, of course, aren't to blame for their ignorance. In Texas, kids are forced to take Texas history in both elementary and middle school, but they receive no world history instruction until their sophomore year of high school. My school was 99 percent Latine, probably about 95 percent Mexican-American, with a few kids from El Salvador. Most of the students were Catholic, with a handful of evangelical Christians. I taught over a thousand students during my ten years teaching in that district, and for the vast majority of them, I was the first Jew they'd ever met.

Given that role, I felt obligated to teach my students the lesson of "Never again." Every year thereafter, I taught a novel set during the Holocaust. Students who graduated from my class would know a little bit about World War II, Nazis, Adolf Hitler, and the Holocaust, and they would be able to offer a better definition of Jews than "the people who killed Jesus."

We spent six weeks out of every year in the Warsaw ghetto, reading Jerry Spinelli's *Milkweed*, or in the attic with Anne Frank's diary. We studied maps and timelines, so they'd get a cursory sense of World War II. We learned about famous Jews like Albert Einstein and Ruth Bader Ginsberg (still a living Supreme Court justice), so they wouldn't just think of Jews solely as victims of genocide. Basically, I provided a middle school crash-course in twentieth-century geography, world history, and Jewish studies.

My efforts were more and less successful. I'll never forget one teacher-fail moment. We were reading an article about Jesse Owens, the Black USian runner who humiliated Adolf Hitler by winning four gold medals at the 1936 Berlin Olympics. Halfway through the reading, I asked students to make a prediction about what would happen in Owens' race, and one kid raised his hand and said, "I predict Hitler is going to win the race."

I had learned, by this point in my career, to investigate kids' confounding answers rather than shooting them down. So rather than say, "Hitler isn't actually *running* in the Olympics," I said, "Tell me why you're thinking that."

He replied, "Because Hitler only has one race!"

Ah ... the whole time we'd been talking about Nazi ideology, and Hitler's focus on *racial* purity, my student had thought we were talking about "race" as in footraces. Running. Like Jesse Owens. A perfectly reasonable mistake for a sixth grader, because I never defined which type of race we were talking about. Whoops!

Another time, I noticed a line of sixth-graders who were in the other teacher's reading class, whispering and giggling outside my classroom.

"Y'all need something?" I asked.

"Miss, are you *Jew*?" one asked.

"I'm Jewish, yes," I replied.

Their faces went white as a sheet. "Were you in the Holocaust?" the student whispered.

"No," I explained, drawing a quick timeline on the board to show the gap in time between the Holocaust in the 1940s and my birth in the 1980s.

By the time we reached the end of our books, most of these large misunderstandings would be ironed out. In *Milkweed*, the people of the Warsaw ghetto are loaded onto boxcars headed to the gas chambers at Treblinka. In the *Diary*, Anne and her family are discovered by the SS. The afterword explains that they were sent to Bergen-Belsen, where she would die of typhus, two weeks before the camp was liberated by US forces. On these days, all of my students would be uncharacteristically somber and soft-spoken. Some would cry, and I would be gratified by their tears, assured I had fulfilled my duty to teach them the horrors of genocide.

One year, I chaperoned an eighth-grade class trip to Washington, DC, and we visited the Holocaust Museum. Because the museum paces your entry, each teacher went through the exhibits with a group of about eight students. With my group, we read every placard, contemplated every display. We started crying together when two of the girls—twins—learned about Dr. Mengele's horrific twin experiments. By the time we got to the boxcar—like the train cars that had shipped all our beloved characters from *Milkweed* to the gas chambers of Treblinka—the girls were all sobbing and hugging each other.

When we finally emerged from the museum, blinking away our tears in the blinding afternoon sunshine, we learned that the rest of the chaperone groups had all rushed through and exited the museum fully an hour and a half earlier. We'd made everyone late for lunch, but no one had wanted to come inside and rush the sole Jewish teacher.

I wasn't a bit sorry. To the core of my being, I believed that learning traumatic history is part of the painful, necessary work of ensuring the next generation doesn't grow up to be Nazis. I assumed that, now that they knew the shape of genocide and had empathized with its victims, my students would be on guard for the rest of their lives against hate. My most sacred job as an educator was nothing to do with teaching comma rules or subject-verb agreement, but to ensure my students joined team "Never Again."

But if I were still a teacher, I would teach those units very differently now.

If Israeli Zionism teaches us anything, it's that memorializing genocide won't prevent you from doing one. Apparently, many Jews in Israel studied the history of Nazi war crimes and, rather than ensuring such evil acts were never repeated, took notes on how to exterminate Palestinians.

I've come to believe it is a grave error to make the Holocaust as precious as we do, to study it in isolation and to insist that it cannot be compared to other genocides. The reality is that, even as I was teaching middle school between 2009 and 2017, I was woefully ignorant about other genocides that have occurred around the world and throughout human history. This hyperfocus on the Holocaust gave me a skewed view of the world, which Zionists share. I believed that the suffering of Jews was something unique in the human experience. I believed Jews had been so persecuted because we're *special*—because we are uniquely peaceful and have a uniquely profound reverence for life and education.

Fucking *LOL*.

But if you've only consumed stories of Jewish persecution from the time you were very small, then it's hard to see it when Jews are the ones doing the persecuting. Even when Jews are the ones with tanks and nuclear weapons and all the wealth and power. Even when a Jewish soldier, wearing body armor and carrying a machine gun, is facing down a *child* with a *rock*, you might get confused as to who is the oppressor.

So if I were teaching sixth-grade reading now, I might still teach *Milkweed*, but I would teach a unit on the Holocaust only in the context of other genocides, including the ongoing, genocide in Palestine. Rather than insisting that my students care only about the genocide of *my* people, I would connect the history of my people with their own, and we would study the genocide of Indigenous people in Central America at the hands of conquistadors. We would learn that Jews have not only been victims, but perpetrators of enslavement and genocide, reading about how Jews, alongside Christian Europeans, profited from and participated in the transatlantic slave trade at every level.

We would seek commonalities across different places and times. We would learn that, while the foot soldiers of genocide are often fueled by hate, the architects of genocide are focused on seizing land, power, and wealth. We'd learn that hate is only pretext and justification, manufactured by people in power. And we'd learn that hate can be manufactured *by* anyone *about* anyone. It can be manufactured by or about Jews. It can be manufactured by a Black woman pledging that, if elected president, she would continue a genocide of Palestinians and "crack down" on immigrants, like my students' families, at the border.

Young Adult Fiction About Genocides That Aren't the Holocaust

1 *Winterkill* by Marsha Forchuk Skrypuch — the Holodomor, the Soviet starvation of Ukrainians, 1932–1933
2 *Burn My Heart* by Beverly Naidoo — the Mau Mau rebellion in Kenya, 1952–1960
3 *Never Fall Down* by Patricia McCormick — the Cambodian genocide, 1975–1979
4 *The Night Diary* by Veera Hiranandani — the India-Pakistan partition, 1947
5 *The Honey Jar: An Armenian's Escape to Freedom* by Joan Schoettler — the Armenian genocide, 1915–1923
6 *Under the Hawthorn Tree (Children of the Famine)* by Marita Conlon-McKenna — the Irish famine, 1840s
7 *A Long Walk to Water* by Linda Sue Park — the Second Sudanese Civil War and the Lost Boys of Sudan, 1985
8 *Inside Out and Back Again* by Thanhhà Lai — the US War on Vietnam, 1975
9 *Bamboo People* by Mitali Perkins — the ethnic cleansing of Karen people in Myanmar, 2000s
10 *War Brothers* by Sharon E. McKay — the Uganda Bush War, 1980s
11 *Four Faces of the Moon* by Amanda Strong — the genocide of the Michif, Cree, Nakoda, and Anishinaabe peoples, 1800s–present

Maybe all that's a tall order for a sixth-grade reading class, but we would try.

It would take a lot of proactive work to put such a unit together, however, because this myopic fixation on the Holocaust is reflected across children's publishing. As I sat down to write this chapter, I realized that I could think of dozens of children's literature titles about the Holocaust off the top of my head, but I couldn't think of any middle-grade or young adult books about other genocides.

A browser search instantly led me to a list of 184 kid-lit titles about the Holocaust provided by the Jewish Book Council.[54] [55] But I searched for an hour and found comparatively few titles about other genocides. I took to Instagram and TikTok, where I have many librarian, publisher, author, and teacher followers, and asked for recommendations of books I might have taught instead of *Milkweed* that met the following criteria:

Middle grade or young adult books

Memoir or historical fiction

About a genocide other than the Holocaust

Many of the titles suggested to me weren't actually for children or weren't about genocide, but the ones here fit the criteria.

For the most part, I could only find one title about each of the genocides listed here, compared to the 184 titles about the Holocaust that were instantly available. Katey Flowers, a children's bookseller who sent me a few of these recommendations, said, "I get the sense that genocide is largely deemed 'not age-appropriate' but that the Holocaust is the exception."

Why is the Holocaust remembered and read and taught so exceptionally? Why did I do that as a teacher? And why do kid-lit publishers hold it sacred to learn about the genocide of the Jews in Europe, but not those committed by European colonizers in the Global South?

In the US, we may focus on the Holocaust more because more people in the US feel a personal connection to it. This genocide happened in recent memory. There's a large Jewish population here whose families were directly impacted. And an even larger portion of USians have family members who fought in World War II.

Now, granted, even *more* USians' families were involved in the genocide of Indigenous peoples and the genocide and enslavement of African peoples. But those genocides make white people feel bad about their families and country. Whereas the story of US soldiers triumphing over Nazism and liberating concentration camps—well, that makes us white folk feel good! About our grandparents, and our nation! And since publishing is overwhelmingly dominated by white people, is it so surprising that the focus is on this rare historical moment when their ancestors were liberators rather than oppressors?

Perhaps another reason why the Holocaust is seen as teachable to middle schoolers, but not other genocides, is that it has had more of a resolution. The genocide of Indigenous and Black peoples in the US at the hands of the white ruling establishment never ended. These genocides continue, through ghettoization, mass incarceration, police brutality, and stochastic terrorism.*

Ashkenazi Jews after the Holocaust, on the other hand, have been accepted into whiteness in the US, at least conditionally. And Ashkenazi Jews in Israel became the definition of whiteness. So, with the Holocaust, we can tell adolescents a myth of progress, a fantasy of evil defeated conclusively and relegated to the past, in a way we just can't do with the genocides of Black and Indigenous peoples. For the global majority, the nightmare continues, and that's a heavier story to tell a child.

When I've brought up this discrepancy in attention to various genocides, some people argue that it's not racism, it's just that the Holocaust is exceptionally well-documented. We still have hundreds of thousands of living Shoah survivors, still telling the stories of their experiences. And since the Nazis kept detailed records of their crimes, the identities of most those who were killed have been accounted for and are part of the public record. And the stories, artifacts, and locations of the Holocaust have been

....
* *Stochastic terrorism* occurs when hate speech delivered by public figures instigates hate crimes. You can't always say who's directly responsible for outbreaks of hate crimes—like the rash of violence targeting Palestinian and Arab children in the US over the past year. Only the murderer of Wadea al-Fayoume, six years old, stabbed twenty-six times by his landlord, will face arrest for that crime. But *stochastic terrorism* introduces the idea that the many journalists and politicians, including Joe Biden, who repeated the lie that "Hamas beheaded forty babies" and routinely demonized and dehumanized Palestinians in public speech, all bear some responsibility for inciting Wadea's murder.

preserved through billions of dollars in funding for Holocaust memorials and museums.

For most of my life, I believed the intentions of such memory-keeping were pure, and that these institutions existed solely to prevent future genocides. But when Holocaust museums turn their backs on their stated mission, a third of Holocaust survivors in Israel live in poverty,[56] and Holocaust survivors in the US are arrested for protesting genocide,[57] then it's clear that all this funding comes with a big ol' string attached:

We're only allowed to remember Jewish history in ways that are convenient to Zionism.

No other genocide can compete with the kind of funding Zionists put up to position the Holocaust as the worst atrocity in human history. Zionist organizations like PJ Library exist to start this conditioning in childhood, through children's books. PJ Library buys large print runs of children's books about Jewish themes and distributes them for free in order to ensure that those books are successful, and that the children who read them grow up with the right (Zionist) values. In a feature in *Hadassah* magazine in 2017, "industry insiders" reported that a successful children's book will sell between 5,000–10,000 copies, whereas PJ Library usually purchases 25,000 copies of a book to distribute, "giving [PJ Library] the power to effectively shape the market."[58] PJ Library also hosts an annual "Author Israel Adventure," taking a group of children's book authors and illustrators on an all-expenses-paid trip to Israel, to encourage them to write more Jewish (Zionist) stories. When authors are wined and dined, and taken to the World Holocaust Remembrance Center* in Jerusalem, and assured a bestseller if they write about Zionist-approved Jewish themes—is it any wonder that there are hundreds more books about the Holocaust than any other genocide?**

....

* This museum stands a mile and a half away from the remains of Deir Yassin, a Palestinian village where Zionist paramilitaries massacred over 100 residents in April 1948. There is no mention of the Deir Yassin massacre at the site of the World Holocaust Remembrance Center.

** I'd just like to point out the absurdity here of accusations that I support Palestine "to help my author career." PJ Library is just one cog in a Jewish publishing apparatus that nearly guarantees success for Jewish authors—as long as they toe the Zionist line. I have stomped all over that line. The Jewish Book Council will not be selecting this title for their book clubs or marketing grants, and no nonprofit will be buying 25,000 copies of my books to give away for free!

Holocaust remembrance institutions have been so effective that, as recently as yesterday, someone commented on my post about this topic, "But the Holocaust was the largest true genocide in history."

True genocide?

What's not true about the Belgian genocide in Congo under King Leopold, which also killed between eight and ten million people?[59]

What's untrue about the genocide of Indigenous people in the Americas, where European colonizers may have killed as many as 175 million people?[60]

Back when I was teaching, before I embarked on a self-taught decolonial education, I might have said something similar to that commenter's remark. I did not think of the mass killing of Africans or Indigenous people in the Americas as examples of genocide in quite the same way as the Holocaust.

Now I wonder, did I see the Holocaust as a more *true* genocide, because I saw its victims as more truly human?

Under white supremacist capitalism, we use skin color, ethnicity, religion, class, education, health, gender, sexuality, age, and body size, among other metrics, to sort people into a hierarchy of more-and-less human. Part of what the Western world finds so horrifying about the Nazi Holocaust is that the evils of colonial occupation were visited upon pale people! Europeans, no less! Many of its victims were educated or even wealthy. Some were those hyper-religious rural Jews, sure, but some were urban, secular Jews—business owners, doctors, and lawyers! It is much easier for white Westerners to view educated, wealthy, and above all *pale* victims as fully human and deserving of empathy. The genocide of impoverished, dark-skinned people in the Global South just doesn't stir their emotions in the same way.

Some of these factors also explain why, in 2024, European victims of Russia's invasion of Ukraine get far more empathy and attention from Western media than Palestinians do. But we must also confront those factors that explain why Palestinian victims of genocide receive far more attention than victims of concurrent genocides in Congo and Sudan.

One may point to a greater personal connection between the Western world and Israel and Palestine. Billions of our taxpayer dollars in the US are directly funding the Israeli military that is carrying out the genocide in Gaza. In the US, 7.5 million Jews have had our identities dragged into this conflict, whether we like it or not, and in response, a small fraction of that

7.5 million—but a fraction that amounts to thousands of us—have organized in student encampments and with groups such as Jewish Voice for Peace to stand in protest. There are also over 170,000 Palestinians[61] living in the US who are leading the movement for a free Palestine, in contrast to only 70,000 Sudanese-USians[62] and fewer than 20,000 Congolese-USians.[63] And there are fully ten million Christian Zionists in the US who see Israel's existence as the fulfillment of a divine promise, a gathering of Jews in the "Holy Land" that will kick off their fantasies of Armageddon—aka genocide-by-God.[64]

The genocide in Palestine is also extremely well-documented, compared to the genocides in Congo and Sudan. We see the daily atrocities in Gaza on our smart phones, because many Ghazawis have cell phones and social media, whereas enslaved Congolese people working in artisanal cobalt mines generally do not. The irony is that those cell phones cannot be manufactured without the cobalt mined by enslaved people in Congo.

These are powerful explanations for why the movement for a free Palestine is so large compared to outcry over the African genocides, but racism, classism, and educationism are also likely contributing factors.

Because of social media, Westerners have learned that many Palestinians don't look like the racist caricature of an Arab terrorist that Zionist media makes them out to be. A lot of Palestinians look as white as me. Some are blonde-haired, blue-eyed, rosy-cheeked children. They speak English, and they're some of the most literate and highly educated people in the world.[65] We are deeply conditioned, in the West, to therefore see their lives as more valuable than the lives of Black people in Sudan.

I've been sitting with these factors lately and trying to unpack these biases in myself. I still feel more called to speak on Palestine, because of how my identity as a Jew is *figuratively* weaponized against Palestinians. And because, as a US taxpayer, my wealth is *literally* weaponized by my government to supply bombs to Israel. The US is also absolutely financially invested in messing with Sudan and Congo's stability, but in less overt ways. Congress isn't authorizing multi-billion-dollar aid and arms shipments to Sudan and Congo every few months, like it does for Israel.

For these reasons, I think it's okay to keep the bulk of my advocacy focused on Palestine. But I'm trying to move in solidarity with organizers focusing on the genocides in Sudan and Congo and to keep learning from them.

And while I don't teach middle school English anymore, I have been trying to take a more comparative-history approach to Jewish history, both as a book influencer and an author.

On TikTok and Instagram, I've been encouraging folks to read widely about other genocides besides the Holocaust. We should all learn about the persecution of the Romani people, who faced exile and genocide alongside Jews throughout centuries of our history in Europe, and yet whom Jews largely erase from our history-making. A good place to start reading is *We Are the Romani People*, by Tim Hancock, and *The Roma: The History of the Romani People and the Controversial Persecutions of Them Across Europe*, by Charles River Editors.

I've also encouraged my fellow USians to really confront the scope of the genocide committed against Indigenous people here in the United States, which is hardly touched upon in our formal schooling. To fill this gap, I recommend *Bury My Heart at Wounded Knee: An Indian History of the American West*, by Dee Brown, *Our History Is the Future: Standing Rock Versus the Dakota Access Pipeline, and the Long Tradition of Indigenous Resistance*, by Nick Estes, and Roxane Dunbar-Ortiz's *An Indigenous People's History of the United States*.

Many people still think that the Holocaust, with its six million Jews killed, was the largest single genocide of any ethnic group in history. But that's just not true. Under King Leopold in the Congo, somewhere between eight and ten million people were killed in slave labor camps. And to learn that very relevant history, check out *King Leopold's Ghost: A Story of Greed, Terror, and Heroism in Colonial Africa* by Adam Hochschild. Then, to connect that history to the genocide occurring in Congo *now*, which has killed at least 6 million people since 1996, folks can check out *Cobalt Red: How the Blood of the Congo Powers Our Lives*.

After the fall of Bashar al-Assad's regime in Syria, which occurred in the last days of finalizing this text, I was shocked and horrified that some individuals in the Free Palestine movement were willing to defend the genocide Assad committed against his own people, because they believed in a simplistic narrative of "Western Imperialism=bad, therefore, any regime Western Imperialists don't like=good." In the comments of a video I made in solidarity with Syrian people celebrating the fall of Assad, the genocide apologia from some of these commenters ranged from tepid disapproval of Assad's torture dungeons (while asserting he was a "strategic necessity" for Palestinian resistance because he allowed the flow of arms from Iran to Hezbollah to pass through Syria), to outrageous, ahistorical claims that Assad was a committed anti-Imperialist and friend to the Palestinian people. These commenters need a reminder that GENOCIDE BAD, even when the "enemies" of the US and Israel do it.* To them, I recommend researching the history of Syrian aggression under Assad towards Palestinians, and I particularly recommend *The Shell: Memoirs of a Hidden Observer* by Mustafa Khalifa, who was imprisoned and tortured for 13 years by Assad's tyrannical regime. Sit with Khalifa's experiences before you tell us how they were a "strategic necessity." Anyone who believes a tyrant operating torture dungeons is going to give them their liberation is not only incredibly wrong, I think they're incredibly dangerous.

Finally, of course, read about the ethnic cleansing of Palestine! To start with, you can try Ilan Pappé's *The Ethnic Cleansing of Palestine*, Rashid Khalidi's *The Hundred Years' War on Palestine*, and Phyllis Bennis's *Understanding Palestine and Israel.*

As an author of fiction, I have also been trying to shift Jewish historiography with my forthcoming novel, *The Ba'al Shem's Traveling Apothecary.*** I see this book as part of a tiny, but growing, body of anti-Zionist Jewish fiction, even though the story takes place in the mid-seventeenth century, more than two hundred years before the invention of Zionism.

Ever since reading *Black Marxism*, I had wanted to write a book set in this early modern period, when Robinson sees racial capitalism emerging from

....

* I put "enemies" in scare quotes, because my personal opinion is that the Islamic Republic of Iran or Russia are "enemies" of the US and Israel the way that the owners of rival football teams are "enemies." But in this case, the game is war, and the people are the players. The owners of the opposing teams want the war to be controlled and never-ending, because war is what makes them wealthy and powerful. The leaders of Western and anti-Western regimes share class solidarity and authoritarian solidarity. As long as the war continues, the people lose, and the tyrants stay wealthy and powerful. So to my mind, a more useful axis for understanding global power is people vs. tyrants, rather than some version of North vs. South or East vs. West.

** Working title, but whatever it's called, it'll be published Spring 2026!

the ghettoization of Jews, Irish, and Romani people. As I started to research, I quickly discovered that Jews everywhere in Europe were not suffering under equal levels of persecution at this time. While throughout the Holy Roman Empire, Jews were ghettoized, discriminated against, and forced to wear an identifying Jewish badge, the Polish-Lithuanian Commonwealth at this time was known as a *Paradisus Judaeorum* or "heaven for Jews."[66] Here, under the Jagellonian monarchy, Jews and Romanies experienced far more civil equality and religious tolerance than anywhere else in Christendom. Meanwhile, in cities in the Ottoman Empire, many Jews were able to rise into the upper class, amassing exorbitant wealth and power, which they used to enslave others.

Up until reading this research, my naïve ass had thought that, post-Bible-days, Jews had never kept slaves. Because every year on Passover we have a whole weeklong holiday about how evil and terrible slavery is! When will I learn that just because we fixate on our own persecution, doesn't mean that's going to keep us from persecuting others?

In researching this novel, I learned that many upper-class Jews in the Ottoman Empire enslaved teenage Slavic or Hungarian girls as domestic workers. These girls were kidnapped from their families in Tatar raids, sent to special schools run by Jews where they were taught to keep kosher homes and forced to work for Jewish families for a period of ten or more years before they would earn their "freedom." Throughout this time, they were legally required to be sexually available to their enslavers, and many wound up becoming second or third wives to their Jewish enslavers after they were "freed." Jewish enslavers of the Ottoman Empire prided themselves on their humanity for recognizing the sons born of these raped, abducted teen girls as legitimate heirs, as long as the boys got circumcised.[67]

This is such an important piece of history for everyone, not just Jews, to study, because it demonstrates how wealth and power—not faith or ethnicity—determines who is the oppressor and who is the oppressed. At this time, many Jews across the Holy Roman Empire were being exiled, ghettoized, and massacred and were far too impoverished to enslave anyone else. In the Americas, white-skinned, blonde-haired people imposed the horrors of chattel slavery against Black Africans. But in the Ottoman Empire, maybe the closest thing the early modern world had to neoliberal capitalism, people of all faiths and ethnicities could get rich and own other people. And white-skinned, blonde-haired Slavic teen girls were among those trapped in slavery to Jews, Christians, and Muslims alike.

Everyone should sit with that history, until it makes you an anarchist.

In *The Ba'al Shem's Traveling Apothecary*, I don't shy away from any of these complexities. My characters travel around Central and Eastern Europe, demonstrating how the conditions of Jews varied. From Jewish scrap workers in the Florentine ghetto to Jewish slave-traders in the city of Buda, I show how Jews oppressed others and were oppressed in turn, depending on where they fit into the racial and class hierarchy of the region. I also don't shy away from portraying how, within Jewish communities everywhere, women and queer folk were routinely silenced, exploited, oppressed, and faced sexual violence.

I tried to be unflinching in showing the harm Jews have done to their own and to others—and that's what makes the book, in my mind, "anti-Zionist." Such a narrative disrupts the perennial victimhood narrative that Zionists manufacture to bolster support for the Israeli state. Even just exploring this time period—outside the Holocaust—felt revolutionary. I had to dig into scholarly databases, relying on friends to circumvent academic paywalls, in order to find research on Jewish life in early modern Central Europe. There's so little scholarship on the Polish-Lithuanian Commonwealth during its time as a "heaven for Jews" in the seventeenth century, compared with heaps of scholarship about the suffering of Jews in that region once it came under Russian imperial control.

I found my research frustrations echoed by Shlomo Sand in *The Invention of the Jewish People*: "When we consider the tremendous effort that the memory agents in Israel have invested in commemorating [our ancestors'] dying moments, compared with the scanty effort made to discover the rich (or wretched, depending on one's viewpoint) life lived in Yiddishland before the vicious massacre, we can draw only sad conclusions about the political and ideological role of modern historiography."[68]

History-making is always political. Zionists have dominated Jewish history-making for far too long, pouring billions of dollars in funding to universities, museums, and historical foundations so they will remember *only* our genocide. They have fetishized our victimhood and weaponized our grief, so that the global Jewish community would cosign their own bloody, genocidal project against Palestinians.

As anti-Zionist Jews, we must take back our history. If you are a Jewish teacher, educator, writer, artist, historian, or curator—make sure the politics behind your history-making are rooted in collective liberation. Building a new anti-Zionist Jewish historiography means airing all our dirty laundry. We must examine the evils Jews have perpetrated as openly and thoroughly as we examine the evils done to us. For Ashkenazi Jews, we must embrace our deep ties to the European continent, not see our millennia of residence there as an unfortunate way station that brought only misery. We must care as much about how our ancestors lived as we care about how they died.

And when it comes to the Shoah, we must learn to see it in a historically accurate context—not as some uniquely evil aberration, but as one genocide among the hundreds that European colonizers inflicted upon Indigenous peoples around the globe. We must include the five million other victims of the Holocaust in our history-making—Romani, disabled people, queer people, communists, and other political dissidents—in order to truly understand the nature of fascism.

And we must make crystal clear that our takeaway from studying the Holocaust is not "Never again, for Jews," but rather, "Never again, for anyone!"

5. Bogus History

Zionist pseudo-intellectuals have produced an alternate-reality history of Israel, more extensive, detailed, and utterly based in fantasy than J.R.R. Tolkien's *Silmarillion*.* And Zionists will attempt to trip you up with their encyclopedic knowledge of these bogus factoids.

For every event in Israeli history that makes them look bad, Zionists have cooked up an alternate version that posits themselves as victims, underdogs, or heroes. And given that Israel has pretty much always acted like oppressors (because they're a settler-colonial apartheid ethnostate), there's a *lot* of this bogus history.

These commenters might try to shut down your arguments with ahistorical claims that "Israel has only ever defended itself from hostile Arab neighbors," or "There was no such thing as Palestine before 1948," or even something as trivial as "Israel invented the cherry tomato."

Committed Jewish Zionists have been indoctrinated since birth with this ahistoric lore, and taking them on can be as daunting as challenging a fluent Elvish speaker to a *Lord of the Rings* trivia contest.

Just as elementary students across the US spend their formative years coloring in cute cartoon pictures of slave-owning, Indigenous-people-genociding "founding fathers" like George Washington and Thomas Jefferson, Israeli kids are taught to lionize land-grabbers and ethnic cleansers like Golda Meir and David Ben-Gurion. They are incredibly fluent in fantasy-based Zionist history, and if you're not as well-read in the

----
* The *Silmarillion* is a whole-ass encyclopedia of lore and backstory that Tolkien wrote as a supplement to *The Hobbit* and *The Lord of the Rings*. It even includes vocabularies for two distinct dialects of his fictional Elvish language.

reality-based history of Palestine, they will trip you up with an avalanche of false historical claims.

The only way to counter Zionist historical misinformation is to become equally well-versed in Palestinian history. This means reading. A lot—and from actual, published books written by Palestinians and actual, professional historians and journalists. Only when I'd read about ten books on the topic of twentieth-century Palestinian history did I start to feel competent going toe to toe with these Zionist armchair historians.

One of the most helpful books I've read for dispelling Zionist bogus history is Rashid Khalidi's *The Hundred Years War on Palestine: A History of Settler Colonialism and Resistance 1917–2017*. In October and November of 2023, Khalidi's book hit the *New York Times* Best Sellers list for nonfiction. I hadn't read it yet, so I picked up a copy to see what everyone else was learning about Palestine.

From the first few pages, I could tell Khalidi was both a principled historian of *factual* history and someone who was equally familiar with (and exhausted by) Zionist *bogus* history. If you know Zionist narratives about Israel's founding, as you're reading *The Hundred Years' War*, you'll appreciate how Khalidi anticipates each of these myths and demolishes them with irrefutable primary-source documentation, insightful analysis, and dry wit.

For example, let's take the Six-Day War of 1967. The Zionist version of this history goes something like this:

Israel was a helpless widdle baby of a country, a total underdog in the region. Then suddenly, Israel was attacked on all sides!!! By antisemitic Arab neighbors, who hated Israel just because it was a Jewish state!!! But then, in a move that surprised everyone, like David beating Goliath, the Israeli army defied all odds and destroyed the Arab armies.

Khalidi's telling of the Six-Day War dismantles this narrative piece by piece. As for the underdog claim, Khalidi demonstrates that neither US nor Israeli officials ever seriously thought they were in danger of losing a regional war. Khalidi quotes US president Lyndon B Johnson, who said of the Israeli forces before the war, "All of our intelligence people are unanimous . . . you will whip the hell out of them," and five Israeli generals who gave interviews after the war "[stated] in different venues that Israel was not imperiled by annihilation."[69] The Israeli army had been funded for decades by the US and the UK, and its military was far more powerful than the surrounding militaries of Egypt, Syria, and Jordan combined.

Khalidi also clarifies a basic fact—one that online Hasbarists lie about all the time—that this was no defensive war. Israel launched a "long-planned preemptive strike" on June 5, 1967, bombing the airfields of the Egyptian, Syrian, and Jordanian armies, giving "Israel complete air superiority, which, in that desert region, in that season, provided an absolute advantage to its ground forces."[70] In six days, Israel conquered the Sinai Peninsula, Gaza Strip, West Bank (including East Jerusalem), and Golan Heights. As the government of every involved nation had predicted, Israel had always been Goliath.

Israel seized on an Egyptian act of military theater as a pretext for launching its offensive strike. Earlier in 1967, Palestinian resistance fighters based in Syria attacked Israel in guerilla raids. In response, Israel attacked Syria. Khalidi explains that "the Egyptian leadership felt obliged to answer this challenge to maintain its prestige in the Arab World," so Egypt moved troops and planes into the Sinai Peninsula, closer to Israel's border.[71] Again, neither Israeli nor US intelligence thought that Egypt was actually going to attack Israel. Egypt at the time was bogged down in the North Yemen Civil War, and Egyptian intelligence officials knew as well as those of the US that its army could not compete with Israeli forces.

It's true that Egypt, Syria, and Jordan at this time did not recognize Israel's borders, but not because of anti-Jewish hate. Rather, these countries were demonstrating solidarity with the large numbers of Palestinian refugees who now lived within their borders—ever since Israel had stolen the Palestinians' land and expelled them during the Nakba of 1948.

Tensions between the Arab states and Israel were also heightened by the Cold War. The communist USSR was allied with Syria and Egypt, whereas Israel was backed by the capitalist US and the UK. So the Six-Day War was also a proxy war between the two Cold War imperial powers.

These tensions caused Israel to be sure to seek US permission for their strike. Back in 1956, Israel had invaded the Suez Canal without such approval, and the USSR had threatened to use nuclear weapons in retaliation. In response, US officials threatened to end economic aid to Israel if it didn't pull out of Suez. So in 1967, Israel wanted the green light from the US before launching an attack on Egypt. Meir Amit, the head of Israel's intelligence agency, approached US Secretary of Defense Robert McNamara with his plan to start a regional war. As Khalidi recounts, "According to Amit, McNamara replied 'All right,' said he would tell the president, and asked only how long the war would last and what Israeli casualties might be."[72] Thus, with a shrug, the US gave Israel permission to start a preemptive invasion of three different nations and another mass theft of Palestinian, Jordanian, Syrian, and Egyptian land. Even worse, Khalidi reports that "in the run up to the war … [US Ambassador Goldberg] had conveyed to Arab ambassadors that the US was mediating with Israel to defuse the crisis and would refrain it from attacking."[73]

But, oh well. Shrug. Johnson and McNamara changed their minds. And six days after that fateful "All right," Israel had seized control of the Sinai Peninsula, the Golan Heights, Gaza, and the West Bank, and would soon erect one of the most violent, oppressive, and blatantly racist apartheid systems in history.

A year ago, I was heartened to see Khalidi's *The Hundred Years' War on Palestine* on bestseller lists, but I also worried that many of the people purchasing the book would not persist in actually reading and internalizing the content, cover to cover. From my years teaching middle school and high school English, I am well aware that more than half of USians read below a sixth-grade level,[74] and Khalidi's book is a college-level text.

To help readers along, I created a series of TikTok videos on Khalidi's book, going chapter by chapter, summarizing key points from the text as clearly and entertainingly as possible. I believe this video series was one of the most impactful forms of activism I've done over the past year, as many of those videos amassed hundreds of thousands of views, and commenters thanked me for helping make the text more accessible.

After the completion of my series, in December 2023, the group Librarians and Archivists for Palestine arranged a live-streamed event, where I got to chat with Professor Khalidi for an hour and a half. During that talk, he shared a piece of advice that has guided my activism throughout the past year, and throughout the writing of this book.

When asked what was the most important practice for activists in combatting disinformation, Khalidi responded simply, "Inform yourselves more." He went on to clarify what he meant, saying, "It doesn't just mean reading histories or watching stuff you can see on social media. It also can mean looking at literature and looking at poetry and looking at things that reveal the lived experience of an entire people, and that are now accessible in English." Khalidi chuckled and admitted, "I'm a historian, and I'd love for people to read history, but there are so many ways today that people can get access to that other narrative that was so invisible for so long. One of the things I try to do, and I think people should be trying to do, is give people access to those kinds of resources ... Be as well informed as you can be and try and puncture some of these myths."[75]

On Khalidi's marching orders, I have continued to inform myself more. I keep reading and learning about Palestinian and relevant Jewish history, and I have shared what I learn on social media and in this book. And Khalidi's point has proven true time and time again—the more informed I become, the more effective I am as an activist.

At the same time, we can't afford to wait until we're all fully equipped to go toe-to-toe with the most committed Zionists in order to *act*. People starving to death in Gaza, facing bombardment, don't have time for you to read ten books on their history before you speak out. Don't let Zionists' bogus histories intimidate you, like I let them intimidate me for years before 2021.

At any given moment over the past year, Israel has been enacting apartheid, stealing Palestinian land, torturing prisoners, destroying cultural sites, and mass-killing Palestinian people. It doesn't take a doctorate in Palestinian history to say, "Genocide bad."

6. "But Hamas!"

When you say "Genocide bad," Zionists will counter, "But Hamas [did something terrible]."

"But Hamas" comments try to derail you from talking about Israeli violence by asking you to first address the violence of the Palestinian resistance.

Comments might sound like, "Do you condemn Hamas?" or "But Hamas started this!"

They may share facts, such as, "Hamas abducted children," lies such as, "Hamas beheaded babies," or—trickiest of all—partial truths, like, "Hamas calls for a genocide of Jews in its charter."

As I'm writing this chapter, Israel has just invaded Lebanon, and this familiar refrain on cable news networks has shifted to, "But Hezbollah!" If Israel continues expanding its regional war, Hasbarists will continue responding to any criticism of Israel by asking you to *first* condemn any local populations daring to take up arms and resist their own extermination.

It's up to you whether you want to get derailed here. Because sometimes we *do* need to talk about Hamas. We need to talk about the important distinction between violence that comes from imperial colonizers versus violence that comes from Indigenous people defending their homes. Though if you start down that road, you're going to have to define what you mean by "colonizers" and "Indigenous," and you'll get drawn into debating the meaning of Indigeneity.*

But notice—you were trying to say "Genocide bad," and now they've got you arguing semantics!

....
* See Chapter 9 for this very discussion.

We also need to contradict blatant lies about the Palestinian resistance, like the "Hamas beheaded babies" story. It's important to clarify that, no, they did not.[76] That story proved to be false. Israelis are the only military force that have *actually* beheaded babies over the past year, babies like Ahmad Al-Najr, eighteen months old, whose head was severed from his body in the bombing of a Rafah tent encampment on May 26, 2024.[77] The video of Ahmad's father, shaking his headless child's body, wailing in agony as people burned alive in the holocaust of tents behind him, was the worst thing I've ever seen, even after a year of this digitally broadcasted genocide.

So Israel beheads babies, not Hamas.

Remember: every accusation, a confession.

What's trickier and more time-consuming than contradicting outright lies is picking apart the strands of partial truths—but this is especially important work, as these half-truths, or truths-stripped-of-all-context can cause a lot of confusion. Take the example above, that "Hamas calls for a genocide of Jews in its charter."

The kernel of truth here is that Hamas's original 1988 charter defined its struggle as a "struggle against Jews," included a quote from the Quran about a prophecy of Muslims killing Jews, and decreed in Article 15: "In face of the Jews' usurpation of Palestine, it is compulsory that the banner of Jihad be raised."[78] However, in its 2017 revised charter, Hamas clarified, "Hamas affirms that its conflict is with the Zionist project not with the Jews because of their religion. Hamas does not wage a struggle against the Jews because they are Jewish but wages a struggle against the Zionists who occupy Palestine." Hamas also explicitly condemns anti-Jewish hate in its revised charter: "Hamas rejects the persecution of any human being or the undermining of his or her rights on nationalist, religious or sectarian grounds. Hamas is of the view that the Jewish problem, anti-Semitism and the persecution of the Jews are phenomena fundamentally linked to European history and not to the history of the Arabs and the Muslims or to their heritage."[79]*

You might also take the time to unpack the anti-Muslim hate and panic that informs Westerners' understanding of the word "jihad." Many USians

....

* I happen to agree that antisemitism is a phenomenon fundamentally linked to European history, not Arab or Muslim history. See Chapter 8 for lots more on that topic.

think "jihad" is a synonym for suicide bombings or genocide. When they hear "jihadist" they picture ISIS fighters storming their suburb to enact Sharia law. In reality, the word just means "struggle" or "fight," and is often used in Arabic in nonviolent contexts, such as a struggle for self-improvement or what a Christian might term "wrestling with your faith."

But if you get into all of that, not only are you now miles away from whatever point you started off making (genocide bad), now a hundred Zionists in your comments are *still* going to insist, "BUT HAMAS BEHEADED BABIES!" And you're back where you started.

If you give a Zionist a cookie, they're going to ask you to condemn Hamas.

And maybe, in fact, you *do* want to condemn an action of Hamas. Maybe Hamas has done something that violates your moral code, and it's important for you to make sure your audience knows that, because otherwise you fear you'll lose credibility with them.

For example, I am staunchly against abducting children. I don't think children should be taken from their parents at gunpoint, under any circumstances. So yes, I condemn Hamas's abduction of thirty children from their families on October 7th.[80] I'll also condemn the abduction, rape, torture, and killing of *any* civilians.*

But consider—why am I asked to condemn Hamas for abducting children *first*, when every year, Israel abducts an estimated 500–700 Palestinian children at gunpoint?[81] Since October 7th, at least 640 children in the West

----

* Some anti-Zionists object to the notion that *any* Israelis are civilians, because all Israelis participate in and benefit from settler colonialism, and because Israel has a policy of mandatory military service. However in 2020, the Jerusalem Post reported that fully a third of Israeli youth do not enlist, and neither do people who move to Israel from other countries. Civilians in many countries, including the US, benefit from and are complicit in violent colonial systems, and you can point out this complicity without conflating those people with active duty soldiers. I find the flattening of the distinction between Israeli people who may or may not have served a tour in the military at some point in the past with currently-employed military and security forces to be imprecise and dangerous. Eroding the distinction between civilians and active combatants benefits people who commit genocide, not their victims. And echoing this kind of rhetoric gives credence to Zionists who say things like, "there are no civilians in Gaza." So I will be preserving that distinction, and when I say "Israeli civilian" in this text, I mean Israelis who are not *currently* employed by the IOF or security forces.

Bank have been arrested by the IOF, many facing medical neglect, abuse, and even torture in Israeli prisons.[82]* Furthermore, before October 7th, Israel had killed forty-one Palestinian children in the West Bank,[83] taking them from their families forever. Between October 2023 and July 2024, the Lancet, a leading international medical journal, estimated that 186,000 deaths "could be attributable to the current conflict in Gaza."[84] And because 47 percent of the population of Gaza are children,[85] 87,420 of those killed by Israel may be children. Though even that's likely a conservative estimate, as children are more vulnerable to violence, famine, disease, and medical neglect, so the number of Palestinian children killed by Israel's genocide may be even higher.

For whatever action you're being asked to condemn Hamas, the IOF has done something similar, more extremely and more frequently, to more people, for a longer period of time—and they fucking started it.

So sure, *sometimes* we need to talk about Hamas, but most of the time, we should avoid this derailment tactic that sets us on a defensive footing, apologizing for the actions of an impoverished, besieged Indigenous resistance rather than attacking one of the most powerful and violent colonial militaries in the history of the world.

That's why, 99 percent of the time, I shut down people asking me to condemn Hamas with, "Forget Hamas! My tax dollars don't fund Hamas."

^^That's where I ended this chapter when I first drafted it. With a tidy soundbite that let me avoid going too deep into my thoughts and feelings on armed resistance—which are unsettled at best. I'm way out of my depth on this topic. And armed resistance is a very loaded topic to discuss, because if I misstep, I risk, on the one hand, being exiled from the Free Palestine movement for the crime of normalization,** or, on the other hand, landing

---

* Before the whataboutists come for me, let me be clear: Yes, I absolutely condemn the police abduction (arrest) of 250,000-plus children in the United States every year!

** The BDS movement (Boycott Divestment Sanctions) defines *Normalization* as: "dealing with or presenting something that is inherently abnormal, such as oppression and injustice, as if it were normal. Normalization with/of Israel is, then, the idea of making occupation, apartheid, and settler colonialism seem normal and establishing normal relations with the Israeli regime instead of supporting the struggle led by the Indigenous Palestinian people to end the abnormal conditions and structures of oppression."

on a government no-fly list for being a radical terrorist sympathizer.

Or ... worse. There are worse things that have happened to authors who are proponents of armed anti-colonial struggle.

So you can see why I hesitated to get too deep into my thoughts. But since completing that first draft, I watched on my phone—on my little handheld magic window into war crimes—the last moments of Yahya Sinwar, chairman of Hamas's political bureau, before he was killed by a gunshot to the head.[86] I suspect he was killed by the Israeli drone that filmed his last moments, although that detail has not been confirmed.

Now I have more to say about Hamas, although it's all kind of a mess in my head. Forgive me that what follows is fragmentary and won't come to a tidy resolution.

You should watch the video if you haven't seen it.

The clip begins as a disembodied viewpoint swooping over an apocalyptic landscape. From the abrupt, robotic adjustments of the flight path, you can tell this is drone footage—and a very expensive drone at that, delivering crystal-clear HD images. I had to remind myself, in those first moments, that I wasn't watching the intro to some Hollywood movie. The demolished city was no multi-million dollar set or CGI creation, but the very real ruins of thousands of homes in the Tal al-Sultan neighborhood in Rafah, a refugee camp—and now a graveyard for countless people who died beneath the rubble.

In 2017, the sci-fi series *Black Mirror* aired a chilling episode called "Metalhead," which follows a woman as she flees through an abandoned landscape from a pack of dog-like, four-legged armed drones. Throughout the tense, forty-one-minute episode, she is mostly silent, because the drones are attracted by noise. After surviving several near-death encounters with the metalheads, she is wounded and takes shelter in an abandoned home. In the final shot, an aerial drone pans away from the house, showing a dozen of the killer robot-dogs closing in on her location, and we presume she is done for.

"Metalhead" was a cultural phenomenon in the US—the kind of TV that got everyone in the teacher's lounge at my school insisting, "You *have* to watch it." "Metalhead" left such an impression on me that I included police drone-dogs in my 2023 sci-fi novel, *The Free People's Village,* the cover of which features a masked punk smashing a Metalhead-like drone with a baseball bat.*

But in Gaza in 2024, there's nothing futuristic about armed robots hunting down human beings—that nightmare has become a part of everyday life. One evening last June, that reality came crashing into my own cushy life in the imperial core. I was in Berkeley, California, attending the Bay Area Book Festival to promote *The Free People's Village.* I was walking towards an author meet-and-greet event, wearing my keffiyeh, because I had vowed to bring Palestine with me onto every stage I was afforded. Still, I was trying to compartmentalize the genocide, for the moment. I was having fun. My kids were back at the hotel with my spouse, and I was looking forward to a free drink ticket, cheese plate, and schmoozing with other authors, feeling swept up in the glamour of the rare chance to travel for my author career.

Halfway to the event, my phone buzzed with a notification—it was my friend Mohammed in Gaza.

Throughout the spring, I had been using my TikTok platform to fundraise for pregnant and postpartum people in Gaza who were trying to evacuate to Cairo. I had used a random number generator to select Mohammed's campaign from a list of hundreds of such fundraisers. By raffling off signed copies of my book, I had raised the nearly $100,000 in bribe money that Mohammed's extended family needed to pay off Egyptian officials and evacuate. But in June, before any members of Mohammed's family were able to evacuate, Israel had destroyed the Rafah border crossing—the last route for Gazans to escape from genocide.

Though their plans to evacuate had fallen through, Mohammed, his wife, Shahd, and I had stayed in touch. Their baby, Heba, had been born just a few days after my own baby. We started chatting regularly, sending each other baby pictures and updates on our kids' milestones. I learned about how Mohammed had visited my state of Texas as a teenager, on a foreign-exchange student program, staying on a ranch where he'd fallen in love with the USA and horses and wide-open spaces. I learned that they were both doctoral students in biomedical engineering, still somehow taking exams and writing papers between bombardments and diaper changes. By June, I loved baby Heba like a niece, and I considered Mohammed and Shahd to be friends.

....

*   That stunning cover was done by revolutionary Egyptian street artist, Ganzeer, who also designed and illustrated the cover of this book!

So that evening in Berkeley, my heart dropped into my stomach as soon as I saw the notification. It was the middle of the night in Gaza, so something must be terribly wrong.

Mohammed texted me that an armed quadcopter was patrolling the street outside the building in Rafah where they were then staying. A dog right outside their window had just barked at the drone and been shot dead. Mohammed was terrified, because there was no glass in the window. Only a thin curtain separated his sleeping family from the quadcopter, which would attack anything that made a noise. What if baby Heba woke up and started screaming?

I slumped against the side of a building, the horror of Mohammed's reality shattering that balmy northern California evening. Couples strolled past me on the sidewalk, chatting in soft tones or laughing with their heads thrown back. I was holding my breath, hoping a robot didn't massacre this precious family on the other side of the world.

I could do nothing for Mohammed but be there with him, digitally at least. I could bear witness as he stayed awake through the long watches of the night, tensed to comfort Heba at the first sign of movement. I texted some pitiful banalities, like, "That's so terrifying. I am praying for you." And even though I'm not religious, it was true.

They got lucky. Heba slept soundly. The quadcopter moved on. My friends have survived, to the day I am writing this. And Heba's mother, Shahd, has written a powerful letter to you, dear reader, which you'll find on the final pages of this book.

So of course I was thinking about that quadcopter when I watched the video of Sinwar's last moments. I wondered if the drone stalking him was the same make and model of machine that had killed a dog outside the window where baby Heba slept. I wondered about all the people who built these machines, and what they got paid for their labor. I wondered what it cost the Israeli military to buy a drone like that. And I wondered who profited the most from their sales.

In the video of Sinwar's last moments, the quadcopter zooms into the bombed-out side of a building, where everything is thickly dusted with rubble. It takes the viewer—and the drone—a few moments to recognize that a man is sitting there on an overstuffed sofa. He's camouflaged by the asbestos-filled dust that coats his skin as thickly as everything else in the room. But if your eyes can't pick him out, don't worry—the drone's AI software soon identifies the human form, tracing a helpful red line around his head and torso.

Like *Predator*. Like *Terminator*. Except wait—you must remember! You're watching real life, not a movie.

At that moment, you might notice that the man is missing a hand, and the blood leaking from the stump of his arm has darkened the armrest of the sofa. He holds very still, like he is hoping the drone will not spot him. But we viewers have already seen the red identifying line, foreshadowing the man's death. We have seen the caption of the video—"Sinwar's last moments!" Time flattens; in the video, the man is alive and hoping to survive, but we in the future know he is doomed.

Growing up, my older brother was obsessed with *Star Wars*. He had *Star Wars* bedsheets, a collection of the original 1970s action figures, and dozens of tiny plastic ships that he would arrange in elaborate formations on the carpet before acting out space battles, making the laser beam sounds with his mouth. *Pew-pew!* Because I idolized my big brother, I absorbed an encyclopedic amount of *Star Wars* trivia. To this day, tons of information on the military hardware of a fictional space empire is still stored in my brain—I can tell a Tie Bomber from a Tie Fighter, and an AT-AT from an AT-ST. Among our small collection of VHS tapes, we had all three *Star Wars* movies, which meant—in those days before streaming services—that we watched them over and over.

I must have watched *The Empire Strikes Back*—my brother's favorite—about a hundred times. Burned into my memory forever is the image of Luke Skywalker as he clutches a catwalk above a windswept abyss, filthy and bleeding from his forehead and the stump where Darth Vader has just cut off his hand with a light saber. Luke screams in defiance, "I'll never join you!" and lets go, plummeting into a seemingly bottomless void.

Luke Skywalker is one example of a classic sci-fi archetype—the plucky resistance fighter taking on an evil empire. Katniss Everdeen in *The Hunger Games*, Paul Atreides in *Dune*, and Evey Hammond in *V for Vendetta* are other examples. All are stories that mirror anticolonial resistance movements throughout history, with one crucial change: in the Hollywood versions, the rebels engaged in violent struggle are all white.

Hollywood raised my generation on stories of young people who take up arms against an imperial army full of robots despite overwhelming odds. These heroes are *violent*. They carry light sabers and blasters and fly bomber spaceships. They mow down soldiers by the dozen. They blow up space stations, presumably staffed with at least *some* civilians. And they destroy capital cities full of wealthy-but-otherwise-innocent bystanders.

Hollywood taught me that their violence was justified.

What was Hollywood thinking?

According to Western journalism, only white people representing colonial empires are allowed to do violence in "self-defense." Black and Brown people who fight back are engaged in "terrorism."

So when these film franchises were in production, did the multimillionaire elites who owned the studios think that we'd pay more attention to Luke Skywalker's white skin than his material conditions? Did they think, when presented with the stark difference between the wealthy revelries of the Capitol and the starving laborers of District 12, that we would not see parallels to income inequality between the imperial core and the Global South? Were they counting on us to dehumanize Black and Brown people that much?

When you watch the final moments of Yahya Sinwar, you are not seeing Luke Skywalker. But you *are* seeing a man with a bleeding stump where his hand should be, facing down a killer robot. You will recognize familiar tropes. You will have been trained, by countless sci-fi shows and movies and video games, to identify which character is the plucky resistance fighter and which character is the imperial droid. And even if you have never watched *Star Wars* or read *The Hunger Games*, even if you know absolutely nothing about the man in the overstuffed chair, you will recognize that he is human. He is a member of your species, and the thing that is hunting him is decidedly *not*. On a primeval, ancient, lizard-brain level, you are going to root for the human being over the killer robot that hunts him.

Unless, of course, you *don't* see the man in the chair as human. Maybe you've been indoctrinated since birth to see men like him as monsters. Well, then you're going to cheer on his demise, the way movie theaters full of parents will laugh and applaud, even beside their very young children, when the villains of Disney movies meet with a violent death.

In the footage—which, remember, is not a Disney film—Sinwar realizes he's been spotted, and we see a blur of movement. The red outline appears again, tracing the shape of something in his hand. Is it a gun? A sword? No, just a piece of wood—a splintered bit of framing blown off the wall at some point in a year of relentless bombardment. Sinwar tests the stick's weight, readying it to throw. With what must be the last of his strength, his lifeblood gushing out the stump of his arm with every heartbeat, Sinwar lobs the stick over his head.

You already know how this ends. You've read the caption. And from the moment the stick leaves his hand, you can plainly see the trajectory is off and that it will fall short. And yet you can't help hoping that somehow, miraculously, his aim will prove true. That a simple piece of wood will take down a sophisticated robot. That human will defeat machine.

The drone pivots to track the arc of wood through the air—a moment of distraction—and if this were a Hollywood movie, that's when Sinwar would get up, sprint across the rubble as bullets graze past his ankles, launch himself out the blasted-out wall of the apartment building, and plummet toward the streets below, only to be rescued at the last second by an allied hovercraft.

Or maybe a team of his comrades would burst through a back door, blasting the drone out of the air in its moment of distraction. A Steadicam from another angle would capture Sinwar turning to his battle-buddies with a grin, saying, "Took you long enough."

But this is not a Hollywood movie, I can't stress that enough. It's a snuff film of a man's death, released purposefully by the Israeli military, in what has to be one of the worst Hasbara blunders in history.

The video abruptly ends. Sinwar died from a gunshot to the head, but we don't see that part.

On Israeli television, the on-air personalities—in their brightly lit studios, in thousand-dollar suits, with their perfect hair and teeth—played this clip and then passed around sweets, one journalist chewing with relish and licking his fingers.[87] Their food-based celebration may strike you as in particularly bad taste if you know, or care, that Israel is intentionally starving two million Palestinian people as a tool of genocide.

You will recognize the tropes. If you have seen *The Hunger Games*, the twentieth-highest-grossing film franchise of all time, you will correctly identify which of these characters lives in the Capitol, and which character lives—well, *lived*—in District 12.

Unless—unless you were raised in the Capitol, and you've been taught since birth that War is Peace, Freedom is Slavery, and Jews are Indigenous to Palestine—then you might be so blinded by hate for the man with the stick that you fail to see how enormously sympathetic he appears in that video, regardless of how one feels about Hamas.

The global film industry is worth upwards of $136 billion, and people pay all that money to watch actors, with no firsthand experience of war, *pretend* to have the kind of courage in the face of certain death that Yahya Sinwar displayed in the last moments of his life.

And Israel released that footage to the world of its own volition.

Whoops! Big ol' PR blunder.

A representative of the Islamic Republic of Iran described Sinwar's death to the UN as follows: "When Muslims look up to Martyr Sinwar standing on the battlefield—in combat attire and out in the open, not in a hideout, facing the enemy—the spirit of resistance will be strengthened. He will become a model for the youth and children who will carry forward his path toward the liberation of Palestine."[88]

Yeah. I don't doubt it. If there were any teenagers out there, waffling about whether or not to join the armed resistance, I don't doubt that watching the footage of Sinwar's last stand might have swayed their decision.

Israeli and Western media scrambled to regain control of the narrative in the twenty-four hours after the snuff video's release. Every major USian news outlet ran a profile on Yahya Sinwar, reminding their audiences that Sinwar was the architect of October 7th, the top terrorist we're all supposed to fear and loathe these days, now that Saddam and Bin Laden are gone.

Even riddled with Zionist distortions, these articles all painted a pretty sympathetic picture of Sinwar. I had known vanishingly little about the man before his death. I had heard his name mentioned as the "head of Hamas." I'd heard that he'd taken over ceasefire negotiations after Ismail Haniyeh's assassination, but that was about it.

From the flurry of media after his death, I learned that Sinwar had been labeled a "psychopath" by Israeli officials.[89] Then I learned this diagnosis was made by Shin Bet agent Michael Koubi, a man who had *interrogated* Sinwar for 180 hours over the course of Sinwar's twenty-two years in Israeli prisons. Forgive me if I don't take professional torturers at their word when it comes to diagnosing the mental health of their victims.

The idea that Sinwar was primarily motivated by a hatred of Jews—as Koubi attests—also doesn't square with the fact that the year Sinwar assumed command of Hamas was the year that Hamas revised its charter as discussed above—specifically to clarify that Hamas's beef was with the *Zionist occupation of Palestine*, not the Jewish people.

Sinwar had reasons for his grievances against the occupation. He was born into a refugee camp in Khan Younis, the child of parents whose home had been stolen by Zionists during the Nakba.* In 1967, when Sinwar was four years old, Israel took command of the Gaza Strip after the Six-Day War. Thereafter, Sinwar and his family were subjected to the daily humiliations of life under Israeli occupation.

In his young adulthood, he was detained by Israeli forces multiple times for involvement with student political groups, and by his early twenties, Sinwar was involved in armed resistance. According to Israeli courts and Western reporting, in this period of his life, he tortured and killed people—including two Israeli soldiers and twelve Palestinians whom he suspected of collaborating with Israel.[90] Now once again, I'll condemn torture. Genocide bad; torture bad. Bear in mind, however, that the information that led to Sinwar's conviction was also extracted by Israeli "interrogation." Meaning torture. Israeli forces torture Palestinian prisoners.[91]

Sinwar spent the following twenty-two years in Israeli prisons, where he taught himself Hebrew, studied Jewish history, wrote a novel, and once led a hunger strike of 1,600 prisoners. In 2011, his brother had him freed through a hostage swap in which Israel traded *one* Israeli soldier for over 1,027 Palestinian prisoners.[92] A hostage swap. That's as deep as I'm going to dive into Yahya Sinwar's biography, because I have absolutely no qualifications or additional information with which to dig deeper. But even from these surface-level facts, reported by every mainstream Western outlet, you can understand Sinwar's logic when it comes to October 7th. He got free through a hostage

---

* The *Nakba*, Arabic for "catastrophe," is the 1948 ethnic cleansing of Palestinians, in which Zionist paramilitary forces (you might also call them terrorists) stole the homes and lands of 750,000 Palestinian people at gunpoint. Israelis call this their "War of Independence."

deal, so maybe another one could free his 5,000 Palestinian comrades who were still being held in Israeli detention on October 7th, 2023. He was trying to pay it forward. It doesn't take Sherlock Holmes to figure out that Sinwar was more motivated by a desire to *free his people* than to kill a bunch of Jews.

But Hamas did do that. We don't know exactly how much of the slaughter of October 7th was carried out by mob violence, and how much was planned and intentionally executed by Hamas fighters. But those Hamas fighters certainly killed people on October 7th, and they abducted over 250 people, most of them civilians, including those thirty children—acts I've already condemned.

So do I condemn Hamas? Do I condemn Yahya Sinwar?

I mean truly, who the fuck needs my opinion here? Let me tell you something else I understood watching the footage of Sinwar's end: I understood the depths, the *profound* depths of my own cowardice.

Ghassan Kanafani was a Palestinian author of short fiction and an advocate of armed resistance, writing in the 1960s and '70s. I read Kanafani's *Palestine's Children* last spring, when I was trying to sort out my feelings on armed resistance.

In the climactic scene of his short story, "Return to Haifa," Kanafani's protagonist proclaims, "A man is a cause." And I didn't really *get* what that meant when I read it last spring. Because most people I know—most of us in the West? We are not a cause. Most of us are a bundle of anxieties and materialistic aspirations wrapped in flesh.

But Yahya Sinwar was a cause. He was willing to die for his people, and for liberation.

And that's the kind of shit I've only ever seen in movies. All my life, I've watched these little fantasy stories, just for the rush—just for that sweet ache in my heart when Katniss makes the sign of the Mockingjay, when Luke lets go of the catwalk, when Aragorn, at the gates of Mordor, cries, "There may come a day when the courage of men fails, when we forsake our friends and break all bonds of fellowship. But it is not this day!"

Something inside us needs these stories of people who are a *cause*—something that is starved by Western civilization.

So I've watched these fictions about white characters, written by white authors, acted out by white actors on soundstages in Propaganda City in the heart of a white supremacist empire. And meanwhile, I have led a charmed, white, middle-class life in the wealthiest nation on earth. I wasn't born in a refugee camp. I've never gone hungry. I've never stared down the barrel of a gun that's pointed at me. I've never heard a bomb explode. I've never spent so much as a night in jail, because I always dip out of the protest when the cops pull out their zip ties. I have zero firsthand experience of war—only those images I've seen through my phone screen.

And all the peace and comfort I've enjoyed throughout my life has been purchased in blood—blood that I've never had to get on my hands. The US sits at the pinnacle of a global economy founded on the enslavement of the entire Global South. Western empire exports endless violence around the world to ensure obedience to its core project: funneling ever more wealth and resources and human blood and entire ecosystems into the foundries of capitalism—all so we can make rich people richer and richer and richer until there's nothing left of life on earth.

And because I was born as the right race, in the right place, at the right time, I'm supposed to sit back and enjoy my little comforts near the tippy-top of this system. Being white in the US affords me air conditioning, and my own car, and a dozen streaming services to distract me from the horrific cruelty that makes my society possible. And I can choose from a zillion flavors of booze to numb the pain of watching the rapidly approaching collapse of the planetary systems that sustain carbon-based life on Earth.

Oh, I make my little TikToks, and I write my little books, calling for a more just and sustainable world, but I have never come close to putting my life on the line for a cause. Not really.

What kind of credibility do I have to sit in judgment of a man like Yahya Sinwar? A man born beneath the crushing weight of that same empire, whose life experiences were so radically different from mine? And the same question goes for all these Western journalists who open every interview with a Palestinian or Palestinian-sympathetic guest with the question, "Do you condemn Hamas?"

What a farce. What clown shit—for those of us in the Capitol to pass judgment on the resistance fighters in District 12.

Honestly, it's clown shit that our most enduring myths of principled resistance, within the US, are children's stories written by other privileged white people like George Lucas and Suzanne Collins, people who have never experienced war, occupation, or colonization firsthand. And though these creators became exorbitantly wealthy off their whitewashed stories of anti-imperial struggle, they have not reinvested that wealth into supporting anti-imperial struggles in the real world.

As a Jewish USian, the only real-life stories of armed resistance that I grew up with were stories of the Warsaw Ghetto Uprising. In the spring of 1943, Nazis began the final phase of liquidating the Warsaw Ghetto—shipping 265,000 Jews in crowded cattle cars to the extermination camp of Treblinka, where they were immediately herded at gunpoint into gas chambers and killed with a rat poison called Zyklon B. On April 19th of that spring, around 750 young Jews of the Warsaw Ghetto took up arms and fought back. Vastly outgunned and outmanned, the resistance held out for twenty-seven days, taking out Nazi troops using guerilla tactics, until finally the Nazis burned the entire ghetto to the ground and hunted down the resistance fighters still hiding among the ruins.[93]

These days, I feel like the whole world is in pretty unanimous agreement that the Warsaw Ghetto Uprising was justified, and Jews celebrate its fighters as heroes. No one cries, these days, over dead Nazis. Now I'm not saying October 7th provides a parallel to the Warsaw Ghetto Uprising—that would not be an apt comparison, in part because the Jews of the uprising did not target civilians. But when Hamas fighters are trading fire with the IOF among the rubble of Gaza City and Rafah—as they have throughout this past year—the parallels are striking, especially considering that the IOF have admitted to learning from Nazi tactics during the Warsaw Ghetto Uprising. In 2002, a senior Israeli military officer told Israeli newspaper Yediot Ahranot, "the Nazi campaign to subdue the Warsaw Ghetto uprising in 1943 required careful study as an example of successful urban combat."[94]

On the much-celebrated twenty-fifth anniversary of the Warsaw Ghetto Uprising, a former combatant named Yitzhak Zuckerman said, "I don't think there's any real need to analyze the uprising in military terms. This was a war of less than a thousand people against a mighty army, and no one doubted how it was likely to turn out. This isn't a subject for study in military school … If there's a school to study the human spirit, there it should be a major subject.

The important things were inherent in the force shown by Jewish youth after years of degradation, to rise up against their destroyers, and determine what death they would choose: Treblinka or uprising."[95]

At the time he gave this speech, Zuckerman was living on the Kibbutz Lohamei HaGeta'ot, which translates to "the Ghetto Fighters," a settlement he and his wife founded north of Haifa, on stolen Palestinian land. If Zuckerman ever spoke publicly about Palestinians, I haven't found it. Did he foresee that someday Palestinian youth, "after years of degradation" at the hands of settlers like himself, would "rise up against their destroyers, and determine what death they would choose:" Israeli drone, JDAM missile, or Hamas?

Over the past year, I have witnessed glimpses of the Israeli degradation of Palestinians. I have not smelled the blood. I have not felt my bones rattled by the explosions. But through my magic window into war crimes, I have seen countless precious children with their skulls smashed open, their mouths ajar, their blue skin and lifeless limbs. I have seen babies, with their sweet milk-breath, choked with the poison dust of rubble. I have seen toddlers, whose hands should be so chubby, shriveled to skeletons from weaponized starvation. I have seen kids no larger than my own seven-year-old carrying the corpses of their younger siblings on their backs, or in pieces in a backpack, or in plastic bags full of loose meat. I have heard the wails of parents clutching their children and grandchildren in a last embrace, and I have heard the wails of children realizing they have just been orphaned—left without any grown-ups to love them in an unfathomably cruel and heartless world. I have heard the shouts of those trapped beneath the rubble, and the anguished cries of those above, of the men who shred their palms digging through concrete with their bare hands, trying to free the people below. I have fundraised for pregnant moms, trying to get them out of harm's way before they had to give birth, only for Israel to blow up all the crossings, trapping two million people between concrete walls and Israeli tanks and the sea. I have cried as one of those babies was born alive—miraculously—only to die that very night, because there was heavy bombardment nearby, and her little heart couldn't take the fear. Her name was Manal Mattar, and she died of terror. Of Israeli terrorism. She lived to be not one day old.

I have watched extermination. I have watched a holocaust.

The more real-world violence I've seen in this life, the less I can tolerate fantasy violence. I used to love a good first-person-shooter video game as much as the next millennial, but after decades of mass shootings in the US, I can't bear to play any game that involves guns. A guy I dated once convinced me to buy a gun for "home defense." But after living with it for a while, and deeply contemplating what it would be like to shoot another person, I decided I'd rather be murdered than kill anyone, and I got rid of it.

But that feeling changed after I had kids. If anyone was about to do to my children the things I have seen done to the children of Gaza, I wouldn't hesitate to pull a trigger, not for a second. And come to think of it, I don't think I would hesitate to pull a trigger to save my spouse or my parents or my friends either. In fact, alone in an alley, if *anyone* was about to do to *anyone else* the kinds of things I have seen done to the children of Gaza, I'd pull that trigger.

So I'm not sure I believe in self-defense, but child-defense? Other-people-defense? Genocide-defense? That's easy math for me.

And that's why anyone pretending to be baffled by the existence of violent Palestinian resistance is full of shit.

But it's also why Israel's reaction—in collectively punishing millions of people for the deaths of 1,200 Israelis, including children—was totally predictable. Not *justified*, of course not—GENOCIDE BAD. But it was predictable, because Zionist Israelis truly believe that Palestinians want their mass extermination, that Palestinians hate them just because they're Jews, not because they are being violently oppressed under racial apartheid. Israel's genocidal reaction was predictable even to me, on the other side the world, because throughout Israel's brief seventy-six years of existence, it has never passed up a good excuse to further the ethnic cleansing of Palestinians.

Sinwar knew Israel would retaliate disproportionately, and yet he was involved in the planning of Operation Al-Aqsa Flood. I don't know what exactly Hamas's marching orders were that morning. And again, given the Hannibal Directive, I don't know how many of the 1,200 Israeli victims were killed by Hamas and how many were killed by the IOF to prevent more hostages being taken captive. As for the abduction and killing of Israeli children—I don't know if Hamas leadership intended to target children, or were apathetic about targeting children, or if they'd actually given orders to *avoid* targeting children, but individual fighters broke protocol or made mistakes in all the chaos.

Gun to my head, if I had to guess, I'd bet it wasn't the first one. In the last interview he ever gave, Sinwar spoke with Vice News about why Hamas fires rockets at civilian areas.

"Israel," he says, "which possesses a complete arsenal of weaponry, state-of-the-art equipment and aircrafts, intentionally bombs and kills our children and women. And they do that on purpose. You can't compare that to those who resist and defend themselves with weapons that look primitive in comparison. If we had the capability to launch precision missiles that targeted military targets, we wouldn't have used the rockets that we did. We are forced to defend our people with what we have. And this is what we have. What are we supposed to do? Should we raise the white flag? That's not going to happen. Does the world expect us to be well-behaved victims while we're getting killed? For us to be slaughtered without making a noise? That's impossible. We decided to defend our people with whatever weapons we have."[96]

I can't begin to understand what it's like to be Yahya Sinwar, but I can understand that logic. According to his own words, it sounds like Sinwar would've preferred to only strike military targets. Perhaps, similarly, he would've preferred to only take Israeli soldiers hostage on October 7th, if Hamas had had the firepower to do so. But Sinwar and the rest of Hamas leadership made the decision to carry out an attack that would include civilians among their targets, thus provoking one of the most powerful militaries in the world from a nation founded on the erasure of Palestinians. Not only that, on October 7th, Hamas killed and kidnapped Israeli *kids*.

It's not in any way fair that imperial powers like Israel can mass-abduct and mass-murder Indigenous Palestinian children, as they've done throughout their 76-year history, and still be considered a respectable nation in the eyes of the world. Meanwhile, impoverished resistance fighters using homemade bullets and mortars are held to much higher standards of military decorum. Israel can mass-murder hundreds of thousands of civilians and still participate in Eurovision and the Olympics; and calls for Israel to be banned from those events are labeled "antisemitic" by Western media. Meanwhile, Palestinian resistance fighters are vilified as terrorists for killing even a single Israeli. And anyone who publicly advocates for Palestinians' right to armed resistance will be dismissed as a terrorist sympathizer and face severe material consequences—up to and including assassination.

This double standard is not fair, but that's how Western empire maintains its dominion. International law and order have historically operated as a PR campaign for genocidal empires. The Geneva Conventions aren't to be applied to United States and its allies, but they provide a convenient pretext for the US to invade or bomb or orchestrate a coup in any nation in the Global South that doesn't bow down to US interests. And those interests require these nations to enslave their own people in the businesses of extracting oil or lithium, or cleaning rich peoples' houses, or providing them with beautiful beachfront resorts, so that all the wealth of these nations can be transferred to the Global North as cheaply as possible—maximizing profits for the West and maximizing poverty for the Global South. Any country that even just tries to protect its wealth and nationalize those resources will be accused of violating international law for some reason or other, and sanctions, assassinations, and drone strikes are sure to follow.

And for those who dare to violently *attack* a Western imperial power? Well, for them, the sky's the limit in terms of punishment. And that punishment will not be constrained by the Geneva Conventions or any UN resolution.

I wonder if Sinwar ever regretted October 7th, this past year. As the death toll mounted into the tens of thousands—as the estimated dead surpassed the violence of the Nakba several times over. Was he surprised when Netanyahu proved to give absolutely zero fucks about getting the hostages back, or even avoiding killing them in the bombardment? Of course, Sinwar had known Israel would retaliate for October 7th, but I wonder if he had any idea that it would hold *nothing* back. That it would pursue, in full view of the entire world, the extermination of the Palestinian people, dropping more tonnage on the Gaza Strip than the entire amount of explosives used in World War II in the bombardment of London, Dresden, and Hamburg combined.[97] I wonder if Sinwar ever had moments where he wished he could take it back, as Israel obliterated the hospitals and schools and refugee camps. As Israel found newly cruel and despicable ways to mass-murder and torture Sinwar's people with each passing day. Had he banked on more help from a callous world that has failed and failed and failed to put a stop to the genocide? Some of us common people have marched, and we've carried banners and dropped banners and chanted and held press conferences and written letters to the editor and gone to meetings and vigils, and those of us on social media have made our rabble-rousing little tweets and reels. College kids camped out. And some people vandalized private property about it. Some people went to jail about it. Not me—well, I had the convenient excuse that I was breastfeeding. But some of my more courageous comrades in JVP got arrested about it.

Aaron Bushnell made the ultimate sacrifice and set himself on fire about it.

But still, day after day after every day until this one, we have failed to end the genocide.

But at least we've been trying.

Most people haven't. Most people in the world haven't lifted a single finger or spoken a single public word in solidarity with Palestine. Either they were too scared, or they couldn't be bothered.

Stern speeches have been made in the UN, the General Assembly has passed resolutions, and the ICC has issued warrants for Netanyahu and Yoav Gallant's arrest. But that body, which is supposed to represent the sum total of global political leadership, has also failed to end the bloodshed.

And so I can't tell you how it affected me—to witness a man who actually *fought* for the people of Palestine, right up until the bitter end. Starving, hand blown off, riddled with shrapnel, he hurled a stick at a killing machine, defying empire to his last breath.

Do I condemn Hamas?

Do I condemn Yahya Sinwar?

Do I wish he *had* consented to be "slaughtered without making a noise?" After all, in 2021, the year he gave that last interview, Israel *only* killed 319 Palestinians—not hundreds of thousands. That year, Israel *only* stole 895 Palestinians' homes—whereas this year, the number of homes destroyed rose above two million.[98] If the members of Hamas had been "well-behaved victims," then maybe Israel would still be grudgingly allowing *some* Palestinian children to grow up with all their limbs intact. Maybe baby Manal's heart would still be beating, along with tens of thousands of other slaughtered kids. And sure, they would live out their lives trapped in the concentration camp of Gaza, drinking polluted water, malnourished, denied civil rights and any employment besides performing manual labor for the racist occupiers who stole their ancestral lands, under the constant threat of being randomly arrested, disappeared, tortured, killed in a bombardment, or shot for no particular reason by a bored Israeli teenager.

Without Operation Al-Aqsa Flood, the people of Gaza could've still had that status quo, instead of this full throttle genocide. And if every life is precious, is a universe unto itself—wouldn't that have been worth it? Parents who are now bereaved—who loved their children every bit as much as I love mine—they could've watched those kids grow up, and fall in love, and have babies of their own—to be subjected to lifelong Israeli occupation in their turn. At time of writing, Israel has exterminated all members of at least 902 families in Gaza—erasing those lineages from existence, and from participating in whatever the future may hold.[99]

If every life is precious, is a universe unto itself, and if October 7th triggered this mass death, then why won't I condemn Hamas?

In *The Hundred Years' War on Palestine*, Rashid Khalidi relates how, in the 1980s, the Palestine Liberation Organization asked an anticolonial resistance expert, Eqbal Ahmad, to evaluate its military strategy. Ahmad was no softhearted lib normalizer, okay? He "had worked with the Front de libération nationale in Algeria in the early 1960s, had known Frantz Fanon, and was a renowned Third World anticolonial thinker."[100]

After studying the PLO's situation, even though he was, "in principle a committed supporter of armed struggle against colonial regimes ... Ahmad questioned whether armed struggle was the right course of action against the PLO's particular adversary, Israel. He argued that given the course of Jewish history, especially in the twentieth century, the use of force only strengthened a preexisting and pervasive sense of victimhood among Israelis ... it unified Israeli society, reinforced the most militant tendencies in Zionism, and bolstered the support of external actors."[101] Perhaps in part as a result of Ahmad's advice, in 1988, the PLO renounced armed resistance as a strategy for Palestinian liberation ... until the Second Intifada.

Khalidi characterizes the First Intifada of the late '80s and early '90s—a mostly *nonviolent* uprising consisting of strikes, boycotts, demonstrations, and civil disobedience—as "the first unmitigated victory for the Palestinians in the long colonial war that began in 1917."[102] Precisely because Palestinians remained nonviolent, whereas Israeli forces responded with their typical brutality, "[international] television viewers were riveted by repeated tableaus of wrenching violence, which inverted the image of Israel as a perpetual victim, casting it as Goliath against the Palestinian David."[103] Khalidi argues that the nonviolent uprising unified Palestinian factions, spread the Palestinian narrative to a worldwide audience, and led to a "profound and lasting positive impact on both Israeli and world opinion" of Palestinians.[104]

The 2000 Second Intifada would be very different from the first.

Between the two uprisings, the Oslo Accords would be signed. US President Bill Clinton brokered this agreement between Israeli Prime Minister Yitzhak Rabin and PLO Chairman Yasser Arafat. Optimistic Palestinians hoped that the result of the process would be the creation of an autonomous Palestinian state, but they would hope in vain. Khalidi details how the US and Israel rigged the talks and frustrated the aims of the PLO, ensuring that the Palestinian delegation failed to secure any substantial material improvements for the Palestinian people.

In the final agreement, the PLO "recognized" the state of Israel, and Israel "recognized" the PLO—not as a state, but as a "representative of the Palestinian people." That's some tepid bullshit, but it was a big change from Israeli policy in the past. So why did Rabin break with tradition and give the PLO a shred of legitimacy? Khalidi argues it's because of "the lesson Rabin learned from the First Intifada: that Israel could no longer control the Occupied Territories solely by the use of force."[105] Through the Oslo Accords, Rabin essentially hired Arafat and the PLO to control the territories on Israel's behalf, as the rebranded Palestinian National Authority—now shortened to the Palestinian Authority, or PA.

What did Arafat get in return for agreeing to "recognize" Israel, even though Israel had not "recognized a Palestinian state or even made a commitment to allow the creation of one?"[106] Well, he got to live in Palestine, after years of exile in Jordan, Lebanon, and Tunisia. Now, he and the other members of the PLO could return to Palestine, and Israel had promised them they would live comfortably compared with other Palestinians, and they'd enjoy positions of authority. As Israel built an elaborate system of checkpoints and walls throughout the West Bank, "Arafat and his colleagues in the PLO leadership ... sailed through the checkpoints with their VIP passes" and "did not seem to know, or care, about the increasing confinement of ordinary Palestinians."[107]

The PLO had fallen prey to elite capture. At the time Khalidi wrote *The Hundred Years' War*, he characterized the PA as having "no sovereignty, no jurisdiction, and no authority except that allowed it by Israel ... its primary function, to which much of its budget is devoted, is security, but not for its people: it is mandated by US and Israeli dictates to provide security for Israel's settlers and occupation forces against the resistance, violent and otherwise, of other Palestinians."

In Yiddish, we have a word for what Arafat and the PLO became. Yiddish is a language rife with deliciously biting and fun-to-say insults like *schlemiel, schlimazel, alter cocker,* and *vilde chaya,* but the worst thing one Jew can call another—the most humiliating, degrading, and loathsome of all insults—is *kapo.* Kapos were the Jews who worked for Nazis in the ghettos and camps. Kapos were cops and snitches and prison guards who subjugated their own people in exchange for slightly less meager rations and a modicum of power, and the promise that they wouldn't be killed by the Nazis—for as long as they remained useful. Kapos didn't have to perform manual slave labor, because they became the overseers of their fellow enslaved Jews. Kapos made their cousins line up in the center of camp whenever the SS wanted to randomly execute someone. I get called a kapo all the time by Zionist Jews, not because it's a particularly fitting insult for me, but because it's the meanest thing they can think to say. A kapo is something so much worse than a rat or a pig or a motherfucker. A kapo incites rage.

Understandably, there was plenty of rage to go around as the consequences of the Oslo Accords set in. Palestinians had less control over their lands than ever, and now they were being harassed and brutalized, not just by Israelis, but by their own people in the Palestinian Authority. The backlash to the PA's new role allowed more militant groups—like Hamas and Islamic Jihad—to challenge the PA's authority amid the Second Intifada.

The Second Intifada was extremely violent compared to the strikes and boycotts of the first. Suicide bombers targeted crowded civilian areas within Israel, like buses, cafés, and shopping malls. The bombers traded their lives to inflict some of the pain and grief so familiar to Palestinians onto random Israeli people. Only a third of their Israeli victims would be members of the

Israeli security forces.[108] These attacks were planned by Hamas, Islamic Jihad, Fatah, and, eventually, even what remained of the PLO, as they tried to stay relevant with this new, more aggressive generation. But the largest portion of suicide attacks came from Hamas. And thus, the Western world was first introduced to Hamas as a group of suicide bombers who blew up buses full of Jewish people, including pregnant women and Holocaust survivors and children.

In Khalidi's estimation, the Second Intifada "constituted a major setback for the Palestinian national movement. Its consequences for the Occupied Territories were severe and damaging." In retaliation for the bombings, Israeli forces killed nearly 5,000 Palestinians and reoccupied what cities and towns it had evacuated after the Oslo Accords, "[shattering] any remaining pretense that the Palestinians had or would acquire something approaching sovereignty or real authority over any part of their land."[109] And on the international stage, "the terrible violence of the Second Intifada erased the positive image of Palestinians that had evolved since 1982 and through the First Intifada and the peace negotiations."[110]

Throughout 2024, a common protest chant at pro-Palestine demonstrations has been "Viva, Viva, Intifada!" And I know the protest leaders mean, like, the *concept* of intifada, an Arabic word that just means "rebellion" or "uprising." But given the stark difference and impacts between the capital-I First and Second Intifadas, when they chant "Viva, Viva, Intifada," I always want to ask, "But, like … wait, *which one?*"

Perhaps Hamas leaders realized the bloody strategy of the Second Intifada was hurting their own cause, because they largely quit suicide bombings in the mid-2000s and abruptly pivoted towards electoral politics. Hamas ran candidates in the 2006 parliamentary elections, in a campaign that downplayed its historical violence, conservativism, and religiosity, instead promising "reform and change"[111]—a slogan which would rhyme with Barack Obama's electoral promise of "hope and change" in the US presidential election a year later. In Palestine, Hamas won by a landslide, taking control of the Gaza Strip from Fatah, the largest political party of the PLO.

After the election, Hamas, Fatah, and other Palestinian groups tried to set aside infighting and come together in pursuit of unity, but Israel and the US were not going to let that happen. Israel vetoed the inclusion of Hamas as part of the Palestinian Authority, and the US Congress passed a bill to ensure US funding would never go to a Palestinian Authority that included Hamas. Numerous nonprofits that sustained the Palestinian people would be forced to shutter. Fatah leaders responded by trying to regain power in the Gaza Strip by attacking Hamas fighters. A bloody battle ensued between Fatah and Hamas in Gaza in June 2007, from which Hamas emerged victorious. From then until the present day, Hamas became the de facto authority in the Gaza Strip, operating independently from the Fatah-governed PA in the West Bank.

Israel responded to Hamas's triumph by imposing the siege of Gaza—walling off the Strip, closing the borders, restricting aid and fuel, and imprisoning two million people in a 140-square-mile concentration camp for the past seventeen years.

Long enough for an entire generation to grow up without a future.

What did Israel think was going to happen?

History does not repeat itself, but it does rhyme. In an echo of the First Intifada, the youth of Gaza attempted their own massive nonviolent resistance movement in 2018—the Great March of Return. Every Friday for a year, Palestinians in Gaza marched to the border wall separating them from Israel, demanding an end to the blockade of Gaza and the right to return to their ancestors' homes. Israeli forces responded to these nonviolent protests with mass murder, killing 266 people and wounding over 30,000.[112] Like the First Intifada, the Great March of Return highlighted the cruelty of the Israeli occupation for an international audience. I had been drifting away from Zionist thinking for a few years already, but 2018 marked the first year I attended a Palestinian demonstration, the year I started reading Palestinian books and calling myself an anti-Zionist.

Dear reader, if you don't already know, would you like to take a guess who orchestrated the March of Return? Well, *orchestrated* may not be the right word. Reporting is conflicting, but from what I can tell, the protests started as a spontaneous popular uprising, but were then absorbed and encouraged and sustained by Hamas.

And who do you think insisted that the march continue to be characterized by "peaceful resistance," and insisted that participants continue "avoiding the militarization of the demonstrations"?[113] Who showed up to march at the front of the crowds and gave speeches, even though he had been one of Israel's most-wanted targets ever since being released from prison in a hostage exchange and had taken over leadership of Hamas?

That's right, it was the man, the cause, the rebel fighter with a stick: Yahya Sinwar.

Everyone who participated in the Great March of Return has my deepest respect and admiration for that action. Week after week, for over a year, they walked into range of Israeli snipers on the border wall, risking their lives to highlight the Palestinian struggle to an uncaring world. And it worked—to an extent. The images of Palestinians linked arm and arm, mowed down by body-armored Israeli storm troopers, evoked the memory of Martin Luther King Jr. and the civil rights movement. The marchers' message reached some of us here in the US, and activated us—it activated me! But not enough of us before Israel started gunning down the protesters. And people can only be reasonably expected to march peacefully into live gunfire for so long. I wouldn't do it even one time. No way. I've already told you I'm a coward.

Yahya Sinwar was no coward. In another interview from 2021, he said about the prospect of his assassination, "The greatest gift the enemy and occupation can give me is to assassinate me, so I can go to Allah as a martyr by their hand. Today I'm 59 years old, and truthfully I prefer to be killed by an F-16 or missiles than die from Covid, or from a stroke, heart attack, car accident, or any other thing people die from."[114] Here, Sinwar sounds less like Luke Sykwalker and more like another beloved resistance fighter from *Star Wars*. At the end of *A New Hope*, Obi Wan Kenobi, the elderly Jedi, is dueling with Darth Vader and glimpses Luke running across the docking bay of the Death Star. Obi Wan taunts Vader, distracting him from his student, by saying, "If you strike me down, I will become more powerful than you can possibly imagine." He puts up his lightsaber, and Vader slashes—but Obi Wan's body vanishes into thin air. Vader prods the empty cloak where the Jedi just stood, as Luke and the gang make it onto the Millenium Falcon and escape. For the rest of the trilogy, during moments of great fear and crisis, Luke will see Obi Wan's ghost or hear his teacher's steadying voice in his mind, still guiding him from the afterlife ... or wherever Jedis go when they vanish from the mortal plane.

Yahya Sinwar did not vanish into mist at the moment of his death. Israel released a picture of his dead body—recovered one day after his final encounter with the drone. In the picture, five IOF soldiers stand over Sinwar's corpse, which is curled up and cradled by rubble, the blood of his gunshot wound dried and already coated with a layer of dust. The top-down angle distorts perspective, making the soldiers appear twice as large as Sinwar. Hasbarists clearly sought to humiliate Sinwar and demoralize the resistance by publishing the drone-clip and the photos of his corpse, but their publication had the opposite effect. The hashtag #Sinwar quickly racked up two million shares on Twitter, and pro-Palestine social media flooded with praise and mourning for Sinwar.[115]And I'm sure that there are millions of people all over the world who, like me, hadn't spared a thought for Yahya Sinwar before his death, but will be haunted by the footage of his last moments for the rest of our lives.

Eqbal Ahmad's assessment, back in the 1980s that due to the unique history of the Jewish people, armed resistance—particularly any that resulted in civilian casualties—served only to strengthen Israel, while weakening the Palestinian cause in the eyes of the world, seems to have been borne out by the events of the First and Second Intifadas.

But maybe not by October 7th. In the wake of Operation Al-Aqsa Flood, more people worldwide have rallied to Palestine's cause than ever before. Israel's retaliatory genocide, and the accompanying gleeful, sadistic content that countless Israelis have posted to social media over the past year, have laid bare the fundamentally racist nature of Zionism. Even among Israel's formerly most stalwart allies—US Jews—a sea change is occurring. Incredibly, a recent survey found that fully a third of teenage US Jews now "sympathize with Hamas."[116]

Meanwhile, op-eds claim that "Israeli society is unraveling."[117] And while I don't know the metrics for societal unraveling, recently a massive demonstration of over 750,000 people shut down Tel Aviv to protest Netanyahu's government. The war has cost Israel around $66 billion, its global credit rating has been downgraded, and numerous northern settlements have been abandoned, along with the port of Eilat.[118] New construction has ground to a halt because Israel relied on Palestinians for their hard, manual labor. The *Jerusalem Post*, in October 2024, exposed just how vulnerable the Israeli economy is—with less than 100,000 highly educated people in tech and medicine propping up the entire economy. These are the types of settlers who tend to possess dual citizenship with other countries, and, according to the head of the Shoresh Institute for Socioeconomic Research, many of those people "are giving up and leaving."[119] Their departure could cause Israel's economy to collapse.

The Israeli military, meanwhile, is running out of bombs. At the time of writing, Israel is fighting ground wars in Gaza, the West Bank, and Lebanon, air-striking targets in Syria and Yemen to boot, and being targeted by embargoes from principled anti-genocidal countries around the world. As a result, the IOF has begun rationing armaments—a development *Haaretz* credits for an increase in Israeli casualties.[120] It turns out that genocide, as the Nazis learned, is extremely costly and difficult to pull off.

I want to return to one statistic I mentioned earlier—that the Israeli forces have dropped more explosives on this tiny, densely packed area of the Gaza Strip in one year than the *entire amount of explosives used throughout WWII on the cities of London, Dresden, and Hamburg combined.* They've bombed Gaza as much as they possibly can. And yes, they've likely killed hundreds of thousands of people through this violence and the brutality of their siege. But there are still, surely, more than a million people in Gaza who've survived that unbelievable, historic bombardment. The IOF is trying its damnedest to exterminate Palestinians, but it's *failing*! Because Palestinians in Gaza are more resilient, resourceful, organized, and unified than they could imagine, *and*, at least in part, because for the past year, Hamas has continued fighting Israel's ground invasion of the Gaza Strip through urban combat.

It's hard to do a genocide! And if the leaders of Israel don't quit trying, they seem likely to destroy themselves in the attempt, just as Nazi Germany did.

Even Israeli soldiers are figuring out this war is futile. Their military is facing a crisis of defections. More and more soldiers are refusing to return to their deployments. In October of 2024, just after the one-year anniversary of the war, Israeli Hebrew media outlet Ha-Makom described the collapse of Israeli morale, publishing interviews with soldiers who kept being deployed to the same neighborhoods in Gaza they had previously cleared. "We are like ducks at the (shooting) range," one IOF soldier said, "we don't understand what we're doing here."[121]

Israel's loss of stature in the eyes of the world has had major consequences beyond its borders. In the US, the Democratic Party's association with the genocide likely depressed turnout and contributed to its historic losses in the 2024 election. A global movement of college students engaged in civil disobedience faced brutalization and arrest at the hands of police, finding themselves at odds with the administrators of their own universities. With striking uniformity across the Western world, the ruling class has responded to nonviolent, anti-genocide protests for Palestine with disproportionate police violence. Such brutality can be a radicalizing experience for young people. Just look what became of those kids who marched peacefully in Gaza in 2018.

In a zillion-jillion ways I couldn't possibly enumerate, the impact of Operation Al-Aqsa Flood has touched every corner of the world. It has likely forced everyone on earth with an internet connection to contemplate Palestine at some point over the past year, and its aftershocks have rattled an empire to its foundations. Because let's be real—Israel is a proxy for the US military. The IOF are Jews who've consented to be cannon fodder in exchange for proximity to whiteness and the privilege of brutalizing an Indigenous population. And if US empire in Israel can be defeated, then empire anywhere can be defeated. If Palestine can get free, then anyone, anywhere can get free. And a certain class of people are willing to burn down the world rather than let that happen.

Sinwar must have died understanding, to some degree, the extent of these impacts. And so maybe, staring down the barrel of a flying gun, he died with no regrets at all.

I've probably focused on Sinwar too much here. He's just one man—and the strength of an anticolonial resistance, like Hamas, relies on its decentralization. Israeli media described the killing of Sinwar as "cutting off the head of a snake." But that's a shit analogy for a guerilla fighting force like Hamas, and every Israeli and US military strategist *should* know that. Because an idea like "armed resistance to colonization" is not a snake that has a head to cut off. It's not an idea that can be killed! Anyone who was involved or responsible for the US's failed wars on Vietnam, Iraq, or Afghanistan should know that.

And I suspect they actually *do* know that. All these generals and politicians and Hasbarists. They know Hamas and Hezbollah will never be defeated through force. They just don't *care*, because the weapons manufacturers who own them will make trillions whether or not the US empire "loses" or "wins" its forever wars. All that matters is that the war against Indigenous people continues—somewhere, anywhere—forever. For war profiteers, 2023 was the most profitable year in history, with the global defense budget jumping to a record high of $2.4 trillion.[122] And if 2024 doesn't prove to be significantly higher, I'll eat my keffiyeh.

In mansions and palaces, from Western Massachusetts to Moscow to Paris to Shanghai, the people who own the means of producing bombs are watching this spectacle of armed resistance and genocide and are, I assume, cackling with glee as they bathe in swimming pools full of money, Scrooge-McDuck-style. Because for every maimed and mutilated human body, their wealth and power becomes more unassailable. Israel is running out of bombs? Cool. That's a guarantee they'll sell even more next year.

So *does* armed resistance actually gain ground against empire, or does it just play into the schemes of the billionaires who sell bombs, and extract the oil that makes the bombs, and pull the puppet-strings of empire? Was any of the last year *worth it?* When I think about baby Manal, whose first and only hours in this world were shattered by screams and hellfire and exploding shells so loud and violent that her heart just couldn't take it … When I think about baby Heba, sleeping a few feet away from a murderous drone, protected by nothing but her silence and a thin piece of fabric….

Was October 7th worth it? The questions of whether a military action is moral, legal, and/or strategic are not necessarily connected. The war crimes committed that day were illegal, according to international law, and immoral, according to my own subjective, privileged, never-remotely-put-to-the-test moral code. But was the operation *strategic?* Was Hamas's plan a foolish gambit that woefully underestimated what the scope of Israel's retaliation would be and banked on assistance that failed to materialize from its allies in the Arab world? Or was October 7th a calculated, accelerationist, 4-D chess move, designed to trigger such incredible violence that Israel would self-destruct in the process of meting it out? Do their intentions matter to the many tens of thousands of lives that have been destroyed in its wake?

Someday, if and when Palestine is free, future Palestinian historians may debate whether that liberation was a direct result of, or in spite of, the attacks of October 7th. I don't know the answer to that question. But my guess is, I doubt they'll come to a clear consensus.

Call me naïve, I still believe that words are more powerful than weapons. I think we do a great injustice to the memory of those who lost their lives in nonviolent struggles—in the First Intifada and the March of Return of 2018—if we don't recognize how those movements primed the world to react in the way it has to October 7th. For me personally—I first started reading Palestinian books in 2018, because of the March of Return. I, and a few other anti-Zionist Jews formed Houston's chapter of Jewish Voice for Peace in 2021, because we'd been activated by Palestinian journalists reporting on the Sheikh Jarrah protests. We were ready to respond on October 7th, as anti-Zionist Jews standing in solidarity with Palestinian people, because of the education that had already been spread around the world by earlier nonviolent movements. It wasn't killing and abductions that inspired me to say "Genocide bad" on October 8th. It was fucking *poems!* The poems of Mahmoud Darwish and Mohammed el-Kurd, and the prose of Hala Alyan and Raja Shehadeh, which I had only bought and read because nonviolent struggle had caught my attention from the other side of the world.

Khalidi, in a recent interview on the *Bad Hasbara* podcast, shared some historical evidence that this battleground of words—of public opinion—is at least equally important for an anticolonial struggle as the physical battlegrounds of armed resistance. He references several anticolonial struggles many point to as examples of the triumph of armed resistance, clarifying that, "[Algerian revolutionaries] won over huge segments of French public opinion, and that's why they won. You think they were winning in ... the mountains? They weren't winning. The French army could've gone on indefinitely if French public opinion hadn't turned against the war. The US Army could've gone on indefinitely in Vietnam or in Iraq if American public opinion hadn't turned against the war." Likewise, Israel may go on indefinitely killing people in Gaza, unless public opinion turns even more decisively against this genocide.

Here, Khalidi reveals the foolishness of comparing real-life violence with glorified, whitewashed, Hollywood movies. Unlike on the Death Star, there is no single, convenient self-destruct button that Hamas can hit to wipe out the Iron Dome. Unlike in the Hunger Games, assassinating one corrupt leader, such as Netanyahu, will do nothing to dismantle the Zionist project. There's no simplistic, one-shot military solution. For as long as Palestinians are under assault, Hamas—or some group like them—will continue to resist, because as Khalidi also explains in that interview, "Occupation breeds resistance—inevitably, necessarily, historically, always, everywhere." But Khalidi also cautions that due to the fact that Israel is now a settler-colony several generations old, where the people claim a profound, religious tie to the land, they will not give up Palestine as easily as French colonizers in Algeria or USian soldiers in Vietnam and Iraq did. Israelis will continue occupying Gaza "indefinitely," unless that massive turn in public opinion can end the killing. And every day this genocide grinds on, Palestinian families and children are suffering and dying in some of the most violent ways imaginable.

After the year we've had, some may doubt the power of public opinion, and, granted, due to the influence of corporate money, Western political leaders are increasingly divorced from concern with public opinion. But they're not *completely* divorced yet. If Israeli opinion continues to turn against this war, they may run out of soldiers to fight it. If it becomes so unpopular that all the tech bros leave Israel, their economy may collapse, and they'll no longer be able to fund it. And, if US public opinion turns overwhelmingly and bipartisanly against Israeli aggression, far more decisively than it is right now, we may actually be able to stop the flow of armaments and aid to Israel, which would render their apartheid state nonviable in a matter of months.

So I think the reporting of Ghazawi journalists like Bisan Owda, Hind Khoudary, Belal Khaled, Wael Dahdouh, Motaz Azaiza, Ahmed Khouta, and nine-year-old Lama Abu Jamous, to name just a few, has been far more effective at forwarding the cause of Palestinian liberation than Hamas's attack on October 7th was. But, then again, Bisan had spent years before October 7th trying to spread Palestinians' story on social media. Calling herself the *Hakawati*, or storyteller, she made beautiful, well-produced videos educating the world in English and Arabic about life under occupation in Gaza. But she did not gain an audience of millions until after October 7th. If Hamas had never carried out Operation Al-Aqsa Flood, and Israel had never commenced this mask-off genocide, would any of us in the West be listening to Palestinian journalists on a daily basis? Would I even know Bisan Owda's name?

Maybe, as Ghassan Kanafani insisted, it takes some combination of art and stories and education *and bullets* to overthrow a colonial occupation.

Maybe the fact that he represented all those strategies in one man was why Israel assassinated him in 1972, when Mossad* agents planted a bomb in his car in Beirut, Lebanon. They showed no concern that someone might be with him when the bomb went off—and there was. The explosion also killed his seventeen-year-old niece, Lamees. Similarly, in 2024, Mossad agents would plant bombs in the pagers used by thousands of people in Lebanon in order to target Hezbollah agents—without concern for how many children and doctors and nurses would be killed as collateral. I bring Israeli terrorism up, because in all this scrutiny on Hamas, we risk losing sight, once again, of who are far and away the most blood-soaked, genocidal, raping, torturing, massacring military force in occupied Palestine today. Let's not forget that in just the first five *months* of this genocide, Israel killed more children than were killed over the past four *years* in all armed conflicts worldwide.[123]

So while I'll condemn a war crime, I won't condemn armed resistance in the face of such brutal terrorism. And again, I think no one should give a shit what I think about Hamas, because I've never experienced anything like the suffering Israel has inflicted upon the people of Gaza.

But I fear I might someday. Aimé Césaire and Hannah Arendt, two scholars who studied imperialism, describe an "imperial boomerang," the idea that any repressive techniques an imperial power uses on its colonies will eventually be deployed domestically, on its own civilians.

We're going off the rails in the US. In this last election, as both political parties embraced genocide, xenophobia, and populist nationalism in their campaigns, it became clear that whatever pathetic wisps of leftism have been holding back full-throated fascism in the US are now gone. Corporate capture of US politics seems total and unassailable. Trump is retaking power, emboldened and unfettered by Congress or the Supreme Court. Politically, shit seems on track to get real bad from here on out. And this collapse of neoliberalism will coincide with catastrophic effects from climate change, as our planet hurtles rapidly past 1.5 degrees of warming.

A decade or so from now, will I find myself crouched in an abandoned building, hiding out from the killer drones that hunt me, just as "Metalhead"

....
* Mossad is the national intelligence agency for Israel.

predicted? Just as my friends in Gaza have already experienced? Will the imperial boomerang of the genocide of Gaza come smashing into the US's heartland?

Maybe.

So what do I think of Hamas and Yahya Sinwar?

I think war crimes are bad. And, I think, if it comes down to it, I hope I have the courage to throw a fucking stick.

7. "Won't Anyone Think of the Colonizers?"

Another derailing tactic, a cousin of "But Hamas," are comments to the effect of: "Won't anyone think of the colonizers?" These comments sound something like, "But what will happen to Israelis if we give Palestinians the right of return?" or "If Israel doesn't defend itself, the Jews will be wiped out!" or "How would you protect the rights of Mizrahi Jews in a Palestinian state?" These comments swap your focus on the safety of those who are currently experiencing genocide, and they ask you to focus instead on the safety of those doing the genociding. You were advocating for Palestinians one moment, and the next, you're asked to consider the well-being of their mass-murderers, given some imaginary future inversion of the region's actual, current power dynamics.

These commenters might also ask you for a political plan for post-apartheid Palestine, and no amount of detail will appease them. It's okay to ignore this demand! Just like you don't need to be a PhD student of Palestinian history to speak against genocide in the present; you do not need to write a constitution for Palestine's hypothetical post-Israeli future in order to condemn apartheid happening right now. And if you don't live in Palestine, you probably shouldn't be writing their constitution anyway!

When someone says, "Won't anyone think of the colonizers?" you might point out that this is the wrong question to ask during a time of genocide. You might tell the following story from US history to illustrate your point.

Prior to the US Civil War, abolition was considered a radical ideology among white people, even in the North. The centrist position among white

109

northerners was that slavery was wrong and abhorrent, sure, but also that it was a necessary evil in order to preserve the economy, their own peace, and their racial privilege. According to historian David Williams in *I Freed Myself: African American Emancipation in the Civil War Era*, "Neither rights for blacks nor emancipation for slaves were issues that most northern whites cared to touch."[124]

Northerners feared freed Black southerners moving north to take their jobs. And they also feared the violence that Black enslaved people might unleash if they were suddenly freed. Surely people who had been treated so violently would want to take violent revenge on their enslavers. These fears weren't entirely unfounded—there had been 250 slave uprisings involving ten or more enslaved people attacking their enslavers during the antebellum period.[125] There were countless more cases of individual enslaved people killing their enslaver and running off into the night. If all Black enslaved people were suddenly freed, what would keep them from coming to the North, mass-killing white people, and causing total mayhem?

Won't anyone think of the enslavers?

Lincoln himself was not an abolitionist. While he was opposed to slavery morally, he advocated ending slavery gradually, over the course of generations, "gently as the dews of heaven, not rending or wrecking anything."[126] At the start of the war, he reassured enslavers in both the Union and Confederacy that he would continue to uphold the Fugitive Slave Act, vowing to capture any enslaved people who escaped north and return them to their enslavers.[127] He often stated a goal of preserving *both* the union and slavery. Lincoln only changed his mind after Black southerners began freeing themselves en masse—abandoning and revolting against their enslavers, destroying cotton fields, claiming land for themselves, and crossing Union lines by the thousands.[128] Under such conditions, enforcing the Fugitive Slave Act became impossible and a costly use of northern resources. Meanwhile, massive casualties and dwindling enlistment were threatening the longevity of the Union army. So Lincoln passed the Emancipation Proclamation, but only when he believed it had become strategically necessary to allow Black people who had already emancipated themselves to become Union soldiers—three years after the outbreak of the Civil War.[129]

Williams explains that emancipation was deeply unpopular among white northerners. Outrage over the Proclamation fueled major electoral losses by the Republican Party (Lincoln's party) in the midterm elections, and thousands of white Union soldiers deserted. In response, Lincoln passed a draft act, which led to riots "fueled by white animosity toward being forced to fight in an abolition war."[130]

White northerners justified their opposition to emancipation with tales of "negro outrages," including the murder and rape of white people. But in fact, Black refugees from the South were the ones most at risk of violence. In July 1863, white New Yorkers went on a "week-long rampage" in which they "beat, burned, tortured, and killed as many blacks as they could lay their hands on" in the city.[131]

The tens of thousands of Black soldiers who enlisted in the Union Army following the Emancipation Proclamation proved essential to victory. Though they were paid less than and treated abominably by their fellow white soldiers, Black regiments were praised for their greater bravery, discipline, and steadfastness in combat.[132]

However, after the war was over, the fear of Black violence against their enslavers remained in the white imagination.

But it wasn't Black people who formed a paramilitary to terrorize another race—that was white folks creating the Ku Klux Klan.

It was not Black people who would kill thousands of people as a spectator sport—that was white folks forming lynch mobs.

The people who have been doing terrible violence all along are the people most likely to continue doing terrible violence. Violence is a habit.

Once again: every accusation is a confession.

So asking, "If we free Palestine, what will become of Israelis?" follows the same logic as northern liberals in the Civil War era asking, "If we free Black people, what will become of white people?"

It's the wrong question to ask.

History teaches us that, on the first day that Palestinian liberation is achieved, in a post-Israeli society, our top concern should *still* be, "How do we keep Palestinians safe from Israelis?" How will we keep Palestinians safe from the former Israeli police, and former IOF, and violent settlers who have been terrorizing them for generations?

We also know, from South African history, that you can end legal apartheid and not make a dent in economic apartheid.[133] Even if Israelis give back every acre of Palestinian land they have stolen over the last seventy-five years, economic apartheid would persist in Palestine. Because, historically, most Palestinians made their living through agriculture, and Israeli development and land mismanagement has devastated much of the region's arable land.[134]

So when asked, "Once Palestine is free, what happens to the colonizers?" remind whoever's asking that anticolonial history teaches us that a more urgent question is, "Once Palestine is free, what happens to *Palestinians*?"

Now, is it possible that people who have been violently oppressed will become violent oppressors in turn? Of course it is. Just look what's happening within the nation-state of Israel. Descendants of the victims of the Holocaust are carrying out a new holocaust in Gaza.

Such a reversal has only been possible, though, because the Jews who colonized Palestine never, in fact, freed themselves from white supremacy, or anti-Jewish hate, or imperialism—they just negotiated a different role for themselves within empire. European Jewish immigrants could never have colonized Palestine were they not gifted a shitload of guns and tanks and bombs from the UK and the US. The US and the UK gave them those weapons in order to sabotage the formation of a unified Arab kingdom and protect Western economic interests in the Middle East. And those tanks came with strings attached.

Israelis are not free. They are trapped within an ever-accelerating cycle of violence that they must perpetuate to keep their supremacy intact. All of their children are forced to serve in the IOF and become killers. Compulsory military service is not a hallmark of a *free* society. Israeli media is some of the most heavily censored on earth, to prevent any non-Zionist, liberatory ideas from getting through to its citizens. Even the most tepid criticism of the government within Israel is met with brutal violence, arrests, and suppression. It's Israelis who live trapped within the barbed-wire cages they erect to keep Palestinians out of their settlements in the West Bank.

So Israelis are not Jews who got *free* of empire. They're Jews who became the foot soldiers of empire.

Could Palestinians fall into the same pattern? Sure. Could another imperial power—one that wanted to fight a proxy war with the US—decide to give Palestinians the kind of military arsenal they would need to defeat Israel? Maybe. Setting aside that such a proxy war could go nuclear and destroy all life on earth, let's say Russia did that. And let's say, given such an arsenal, some Palestinians founded a Muslim-supremacist apartheid state and began ethnically cleansing Jews who had been born and raised in Israel. In that highly unlikely hypothetical scenario, Palestine would not be *free*, it would have become part of empire. Palestinians would be behaving just like the colonizers they despise, and I'm operating under the assumption that the Free Palestine movement is thoroughly anti-colonial.

No one I know personally, when chanting "From the river to the sea, Palestine will be free" has such an outcome in mind. Now, online, I have certainly encountered some hateful, revenge-minded people who entertain fantasies of reverse genocide, but they are few and far between, and some of them may even be Hasbara sock puppets, deliberately stoking Jewish fears of another Holocaust should the Zionist state fail. The vast majority of those hundreds of thousands of people worldwide who have campaigned and protested over the past year for Palestine did not do so because they are dreaming about violence against Jews—they're dreaming of an end to such violence!

So when someone asks you, "Won't anyone think of the colonizers?" You can go ahead and reassure them that it's, "Genocide bad. Always, for everyone. Even for colonizers in hypothetical futures!" But then you should direct their focus from future hypotheticals to the very real and very bloody present, saying, "But right now, we're going to keep thinking of the colonized, thank you very much."

8. "Criticizing Israel Is Antisemitic"

It doesn't matter how tepid, normalizing, and equivocating your opposition to genocide is—anything less than a total endorsement of any and all atrocities committed by Israel, and Zionists will charge you with being antisemitic. No exceptions for being Jewish.

If you don't want to get into the weeds here, when someone says, "Criticizing Israel is antisemitic," you can just say, "No it's not." You can state that Zionism is not Judaism, and go.

But by now, you've probably figured out that I *love* getting into the weeds. And for this one, I plan to go beyond the weeds, past the tree line, into the shadowy hills beyond, so that we can get thoroughly lost in the wilderness. I'm going to share a bit of my life story, and my personal experiences with anti-Jewish hate, in part because I like talking about myself, and in part because those experiences explain the nature of anti-Jewish hate in the US, and how I came to be an anti-antisemitism educator. Then we're going to bounce around the world and through the past few thousand years of Jewish history. We're going to talk about Jewish ghettos, pointy hats, and Venetian sex workers. We'll delve deeply into the etymology of the word "antisemitism" itself, so I can explain why I no longer use it. We're going to talk about pillars of anti-Jewish hate and go beyond labeling them as such, daring to explore *why* certain anti-Jewish tropes exist by applying systems-level thinking to history that Zionists don't want you knowing about. When we finally make it back to the familiar environs of our conversation about Palestine, you will see, with the fullness of the epigenetic rage and grief I carry, why nothing could be further from the truth than the idea that "criticizing Israel is antisemitic." In fact, you will realize that fighting anti-Jewish hate *necessitates* fighting Zionism.

So pull on your hiking boots, because we're about to wade through some shit.

The state of anti-Jewish hate in rural Illinois

Before I dive into my personal experiences of antisemitism, I want to put a disclaimer right up front that, while these moments affected me deeply and were at times scary or dehumanizing, they were like tiny, little nothing-burgers compared to the kind of hate Palestinians face every day at the hands of the Israeli occupation. All the prejudice I experienced was interpersonal, and I can't point to any times I faced structural or systemic oppression for being Jewish, the way Black, Indigenous, and undocumented populations in the United States do. As far as the state is concerned, white Jews in the US are pretty much included in white supremacy. However, I've learned that many white Christians in rural areas do *not* see us Jews as part of their little club.

So I'm going to commit a cardinal sin of deference politics here: I'm going to center my relatively privileged, Jewish feelings in this book about Palestine. I'm going to kvetch about middle school bullying in a book about frigging genocide.

But Jewish feelings are *in the room* any time you mention Palestine, so I feel like mine are worth addressing, especially since I am something of an expert in anti-Jewish hate, in a way that the majority of US Jews of my generation are not.

My earliest memory of identifying *myself* as Jewish is also my earliest memory of experiencing anti-Jewish hate. In my neighborhood in rural Illinois, one of the kids I played with was a girl we'll call Lauren Duchak, and my main memory of our brief friendship was that she was weirdly rough with her dolls. She would cut off their hair and limbs, and color them with permanent marker so that all her dolls looked like "Weird Barbie" from the Barbie movie. Her mom didn't let her around scissors or markers. I found the intensity of Lauren's way of playing both a little frightening and alluring. Looking back, I wonder if her mutilated dolls weren't symptomatic of... *something*. We weren't best friends, but I remember the inside of her house vividly, so I must have been over there a lot.

And then one day, when we were maybe seven or eight years old, I ran into her and a pack of kids in the woods behind my house. She was sitting atop the enormous fallen stump of a hundred-year-old burr oak tree—a natural monument for us kids to gather around. And perched there, swinging her legs, in front of maybe four or five other kids, Lauren told me that she wasn't allowed to play with me anymore, because I was "a dirty Jew."

She reported this to me in a "My parents are such a drag" kind of way, like she was telling me that she wasn't allowed to drink soda. There wasn't any actual *hate* in her—not yet. She was bummed about this new development. I didn't get angry at her either—not yet. She ran off with some other girls, leaving me behind with my next-door-neighbor Grant who, in true solidarity, said he didn't care if I was a dirty Jew, because he didn't even know what that meant. Also, Grant and I were often *literally* covered in mud. Our friendship was built on a mutual willingness to pick up any toads, salamanders, turtles, snakes, or daddy long-legs we could find, and no grown-up bullshit—like an ancient, ethno-religious hate—would ever come between us.

I felt stunned and rejected and a little sad that I couldn't play with Lauren that afternoon. But mostly I was confused. Because I had never thought of myself as a Jew before! I knew my *dad* was a Jew, and my Nana, and all his family out in Los Angeles, plus the cousins in Cleveland and Brooklyn. But my mom wasn't Jewish. Sometimes my dad teasingly called Mom a "shiksa," which I thought was a cute nickname for a non-Jewish wife. Only much later would I learn this term was considered by some to be a nasty slur, but he didn't use it like that. My dad would sometimes refer to himself as Jewish, tell Jewish jokes, sprinkle Yiddish in his conversational English—but I didn't think any of that Jewishness extended to my brother and me, because we were being raised without religion. At this point, I had never set foot inside a church or a synagogue. We weren't Christian or Jewish, we were just "Americans"—right?

My dad had Jewish friends in Chicago, the Bachmans, and we'd celebrate Passover at their house every year. Now they were some Jews! They knew Hebrew prayers, and believed in God, and the boys wore the little hats on their heads throughout the seder. They regularly vacationed in Israel, which was a whole country of Jews. We would attend their seders as guests, and participate as best we could, sure. But if I had called myself Jewish around the Bachman boys, they would've laughed!

117

So Lauren was delivering some news to me—that I was a Jew! It was also news to me that "dirty Jew" was a slur people still said in 1993. By this age, I knew that anti-Jewish hate was, like, a *thing*. I knew that my Jewish ancestors had fled persecution in the old country. I had some bare-bones idea about the Holocaust. But I had never dreamed that my neighbors had Nazi ideas. I had never dreamed that other kids would be forbidden from interacting with me just because my dad was Jewish!

And how the heck had Lauren's parents *known* in the first place? I had certainly never brought up the topic, because again, being Jewish just wasn't a way that I thought about myself back then. Even though I spent time at Lauren's house, I had barely ever interacted with her parents, and I was certain my dad didn't know them. We were rural, free-range '90s kids, busting in and out of each others' homes all summer long, without our parents having any idea where we were. Lauren's family lived way on the other side of the neighborhood, a mile-long bike ride away, so our parents had no reason to talk to each other.

So how had they known? Did I *look* Jewish? *Act* Jewish? Did I give off some secret Jewish pheromone? Did all my friends' parents know I was Jewish? Did the neighborhood gentiles* gossip about our family, warning each other to keep their kids away?

Maybe! A week or two earlier, our family had attended the neighborhood's annual picnic for the first time. While I could easily bond with neighborhood kids over a shared love of creepy-crawly wildlife or Barbie dramas, there was a wide political, educational, and cultural divide between their parents and mine. My friends' parents were all Republicans; mine were liberals. My friends' parents mostly hadn't gone to college; whereas my parents both had advanced degrees. My friends' parents were all Protestant Christians, and we were Jews.

I realize now, my dad wouldn't have had to *tell* any of our neighbors we were Jews for them to know it. I'll put it this way: even though he was born and raised in Los Angeles, our neighbors often remarked on his "New York accent." Once *Curb Your Enthusiasm* aired on TV, my dad started regularly

----

* Gentile means "not Jewish." It's not a slur. Some Christians want to make it out to be a slur, but these are the same people who think the words "cis," "white," and "straight" are slurs, because they can't stand to be identified as a beneficiary of privilege.

getting stopped out in public and asked if he was Larry David. I don't see the resemblance, but I guess to small-town WASPS, all bald, Jewish men look the same. So my dad might as well have shown up to that picnic wearing tefillin, for all he blended in with the Christians.

I can empathize with my dad at that picnic, now. I imagine him standing at one end of a long folding table piled with Jell-O molds, marshmallow casseroles, and cheese logs, fully dissociating as our neighbors chit-chatted about where they went hunting or which church they attended, their conversations peppered with casual racism and sexism. Dad was probably regretting every decision in his life that had led up to him moving to that small town. While I played with Lauren and Grant and all the other kids, my mom and dad were having an awkward, bad time. They didn't stay long, and never went to another neighborhood picnic.

But the news was out! That weird tomboy kid, Sim, belonged to the stuck-up Jews who lived at the end of Elk Street. And Lauren's parents, for one, thought there was some danger in her associating with me.

Luckily, there was no domino effect. None of the other kids in our neighborhood were forbidden from playing with me, and none of them brought up my Jewishness—not yet. So I figured Lauren's parents must just be secret KKK-member weirdos. I avoided her street, and we never spoke when we passed on our bikes. But I had learned something—that being Jewish was more than the religion of the Bachman family. In the minds of Lauren's bigot parents, Jewishness was something tainted that you carried in your blood. It was about who your parents were, and it followed a one-drop rule. It was racial. And to people like the Duchaks, I would always be a Jew first, whether I identified that way or not.

Until middle school, I didn't go to school with any of those neighborhood kids. My parents instead drove me two towns east, to a proper Chicago suburb, where I went to a Montessori school. Blessedly, the Montessori was far more racially diverse than my neighborhood. All of us were weirdos—many of my classmates wound up there because their neurodivergence hadn't meshed well with the local public schools. Their parents tended to be liberals, like mine were, and there was even another Jewish family!

The only anti-Jewish incident I remember from my Montessori years happened at a sleepover party in fourth grade. I made the mistake of falling asleep first, and as a prank, my friends drew all over my face in red lipstick. They gave me clown makeup, a goatee, and in the middle of my forehead, they drew a bright red swastika.

I was in the bathroom, crying and scrubbing frantically at my face with hand soap and a washcloth while they laughed—at least at first. When I screamed at them to cut it out, Kelly's mom came to see what the fuss was about. I showed her my forehead, sure she would, at least, scold my friends for what they'd done. But Kelly's mom also chuckled, rolled her eyes at me, and told me to calm down. It was just a harmless prank. Couldn't I take a joke?

None of them could fathom the intensity of my reaction. These girls were my best friends. I knew they'd meant to tease me, not send me into an emotional breakdown. I don't think the swastika even had anything to do with me being Jewish—again, that's not something I talked about with other kids back then. To them, a swastika was just something shocking and taboo. They could've written "fuck" or drawn a dick instead, and it would've been the same joke to them.

But for me? I was thinking about Lauren calling me a "dirty Jew." I was thinking about the *Schindler's List* movie my folks had made me watch. I was thinking about Michael Kern's stories of attending school in Stanislawa, Poland, how the teacher refused to use the names of Jewish students, how he forced them sit silently at the back of the classroom and only referred to them as "yid." I thought about my nana's family in Ukraine, their entire community erased by Nazis. Most of all, I was thinking that if my dad arrived to pick me up before I could scrub every trace of red off my forehead, he would never let me go to a sleepover again.

Most of my encounters with anti-Jewish hate in my early childhood were few and far between, and they were all like this. Though my peers may have caused me distress, they had done so from a place of ignorance. They had meant to shock me, sure, but not to terrorize me *because* I was Jewish. I might've grown up believing these microaggressions were just isolated misunderstandings, aftershocks of an outdated bigotry that was sure to fade with my generation.

But then I went to middle school.

I transferred to public school, with all the other kids from my Podunk neighborhood. A few years back, we'd stopped playing Barbies and exploring the woods together every summer. My ride-or-die neighbor, Grant, had moved to Iowa, and I'd gradually lost touch with all the rest of them. So I had no friends as I started at Wredling Middle School.

But I remembered Lauren Duchak, and she remembered me. We rode the same bus route, and she was now a tall volleyball girl with shiny blonde hair, captain of the team *and* a clique of mean girls. I was this hopelessly nerdy, Montessori-raised, neuro-spicy orchestra kid, obviously queer to everyone but me, sharing the bus seat with my violin case. In transferring to public school, my test scores were so high, the district had skipped me a grade. So I was younger than anyone else in my class, but still a know-it-all. Wredling was populated almost entirely by white Christians, except for one Chinese-American girl a grade below, and then me: the Jew. This school was so white, the Italian kids got called the N-word for being slightly darker-skinned. I was doomed.

As a twelve-year-old eighth-grader, I was desperate to fit in. I was even trying to perform "girlhood," my assigned gender, to the best of my ability. For the first time in years, I'd grown out my hair long, and I wore sparkly blue eye shadow and baby-doll tees with butterflies on them. I said I liked whatever music other kids liked, and I saved up my allowance to buy the clothes in the Delia's catalog.

For a while, I hung out with my orchestra stand partner and three girls who played trumpet. We were "orch dorks," brainy and not particularly funny or pretty. In the school's strict social hierarchy, my friends and I were nearly at the bottom of the social ladder, with only the goths who cut themselves in class beneath us. I never really bonded with my Wredling friends, not the way I had with the kids at Montessori. But they were people to sit with at lunch, and I did my best to blend in with them.

Try as I might, though, I was just *so different*. I couldn't hide the parts of me that were raised by my West Coast intellectual Jew of a father. I remember a popular girl telling me once, "You use words I've never even heard of before." And one time a boy I had a crush on said, "You raise your hand a lot for a girl." Neither of these were said as compliments—more like warnings.

For my birthday, I had my four orchestra friends over for a sleepover, where I confessed to them my secret—that I was only just now turning thirteen. That night, one of them noticed a piece of art on the wall that I had never paid much attention to. It was a framed, Victorian-era, black-and-white film strip depicting a woman, filmed from behind, standing up while holding a bucket of water. An antique! A very early indie movie! You had to press your nose to the glass to even see what the film strip was about, as the figure is only about a half inch tall. But the woman with the bucket is naked. If you squint, you can see her lentil-sized butt. My friends squealed and giggled over the scandalous film strip. And at school the next day, they told everyone that my family hung pornography on the walls of our house.

Around this same time, I was riding the bus home from school, and somehow Lauren and I got in an argument. Usually, she treated me like a cockroach beneath her notice, but for some reason, this day, we'd got to talking, and the topic got heated. I don't remember what we were arguing about, but I bet I rhetorically dunked on her, because she suddenly turned bright red and screamed, "Shut up, you dirty Jew!"

It was the same thing she'd said to me all those years ago, in the woods behind my house. But now, that seed of hate had metastasized within her. Now, she *meant* it. She'd been dying to say it. What a release it must have been for her to shout "dirty Jew" at me, at the top of her lungs.

What happened next was the only time in that entire, miserable year I can remember anybody sticking up for me. Jenna Pakorney, a big, masc punk girl—who wore a dog collar around her neck and had blonde-tipped liberty spikes—stood up, turned around, and roared at Lauren to shut the fuck up. Lauren did, and I experienced a bit of a queer awakening. I think it's no coincidence my first serious boyfriend would look a lot, and dress a lot, like Jenna did. The moment passed, and Lauren never messed with me on the bus again. But the story of our argument spread far beyond the kids on our route—and along with it, the common knowledge that I was Jewish.

At the same time, word also got out that I was actually a year younger than everyone else in the class. I don't know whether this info was something my little clique had let slip after my birthday, or if Lauren also remembered I was supposed to be a year younger than her, and told on me. Either way, I was accused of "lying" about my age and my Jewishness. Facts that were, in the eyes of my peers, shameful secrets about my identity.

My orchestra friends wrote, signed, and served me a letter saying they couldn't associate with a liar like me anymore, and I was not to sit with them in the cafeteria. That night I begged them in a group chat on AOL Instant

Messenger to take me back into their group. They responded by copy-pasting our conversation into Microsoft Word, deleting what I'd actually said, and making it look instead like I was describing explicit sexual fantasies with the boy I had a crush on. They printed out a hundred copies of this forged conversation and passed out the stapled packets at school the next day.

Suddenly, I had no friends. I tried sitting with the punks and goths at lunch, but I was socially radioactive, and they wouldn't talk to me. Not even Jenna—she might defend me on the bus, but she wasn't about to be my friend within the halls of the school. I'm not even sure if she stood up to Lauren because she was offended by Lauren's bigotry, or if she just wanted us to stop arguing, because we were giving her a headache. I started skipping lunch, hiding in the bathroom until the period was over. This behavior only fueled new rumors: that I had an eating disorder. That I was a lesbian, hiding in the bathroom so I could spy on girls while they peed.

In the midst of this shunning, I made the grave error of a bold outfit choice. I bought a new shirt that reflected the teen angst in my heart—a long-sleeve black T-shirt with flames running up the sleeves and a fiery star in the center of the chest. I thought it was so rock and roll. And maybe I was hoping Jenna would be my friend if I dressed a little more punk.

But I had no idea what that Hot Topic shirt would unleash. As I walked down the halls in my new outfit, I came face to face for the first time with the full extent of the anti-Jewish hate that permeated the community I'd grown up in. Turns out, Lauren wasn't the only little proto-Nazi.

Until that day, I hadn't even known about the medieval stereotypes of Jews as demon worshippers. I had no idea that Christians had spent centuries accusing my ancestors of summoning devils, practicing black magic, and eating babies. The first time someone asked me where my horns were, I had no clue what they were referring to. But over the course of that day, and in the months to come, my peers would give me an education! The flaming star on the front of my Hot Topic shirt wasn't a pentagram, but it looked close enough to one to unleash a flood of pent-up anti-Jewish hate that had always lurked behind the smiling faces of my neighbors. From that day until the end of year, I was asked on a daily basis if I worshipped the devil, if it was true that Jews ate babies, and where I was hiding my horns. Kids would run past me and ruffle my hair to try and find them.

That same spring, on the 110th anniversary of Adolf Hitler's birthday, two teenage boys wearing black trench coats snuck guns into Columbine High School and killed twelve of their classmates and a teacher. It was the first mass shooting at a high school in the United States. Clearly, from the killers' open admiration of Adolf Hitler, anti-Jewish hate had been at least a piece of their ideology.

There were also two black-trench coat-wearing skinhead boys in my eighth-grade class, and they happened to ride my bus route. They sat in the far backseat every day, and they called me a "kike," and they liked to tell me "jokes" about pizza ovens, Anne Frank, and showering in gas chambers. The day after Columbine, both of these boys were suspended for bringing knives to school. So that was scary. I spent the rest of that year scared that they were maybe going to kill me. If those boys had planned a school massacre, you wouldn't need three chances to guess who their number one target would be.

My parents tried calling the principal about what was happening to me, but I can't remember any kind of intervention from staff on my behalf. Whenever this bullying would break out during class, my teachers' reactions were similar to how Kelly's mom had responded to the lipstick swastika. When other kids called me freak, kike, dyke, or lesbo, teachers might ask them not to use such language, but they seemed more annoyed at *me* for being the cause of the distraction. The message I got from my teachers was that somehow I must have asked for all this—by being such a pathetic little geek. If they'd known any Yiddish, they'd have told me to "quit being such a nebbish!"

Incidentally, an oasis for me in this year of bullying was my continued friendship with Mondana, a girl from another town I'd gone to Montessori with. Her family was Persian, her parents first-generation immigrants from Iran. They were not religious, but they were the only people I'd ever known from a Muslim-majority country, and I felt more at home in their house than in the houses of any of my other friends. Mondana's parents seemed so much friendlier than my Christian friends' uptight, frosty WASP parents. They included me in their celebrations of Nowruz, and there was a funny, teasing, loving relaxedness to their interactions that reminded me of gatherings of my own Jewish family. I never encountered an iota of anti-Jewish hate from Mondana or her parents. And I mention our friendship here because I think it's part of why I never fully bought the Zionist lie that Muslim people are my enemy. "Antisemitism" is a Christian invention, and I had only ever experienced anti-Jewish hate from white Christians.

In the week I've been working on this chapter, a video was released of Israeli students bullying a lone Palestinian child in their midst. At a Zilberman school in the Israeli town of Be'er Sheva (the Palestinian town of Bi'r al-Sabe, which was occupied during the Nakba of 1948) a Palestinian girl expressed sympathy for "children suffering and dying from hunger in Gaza" and was mobbed by dozens of her peers who jumped up and down, cursing her, and singing, "Your village should burn."[135] The school administration's response was to suspend the girl who had been attacked for sympathizing with starving children.[136]

Zionists accuse Palestinians of "teaching their children to hate," but remember: every accusation is a confession. It's Israel that teaches Jewish children to hate Palestinians; as I'll discuss in Chapter 9, genocide is literally built into the curriculum. And it is beyond sickening to me to watch Jewish children who have been taught to hate engaging in this kind of fascist, mob behavior. I cannot imagine the distress that Palestinian girl must be feeling, and the terror she must face going to school with peers who openly cheer for the genocide of her people. The bullying I faced at Wredling was not anywhere near that scale of intensity, and yet it devastated my mental health.

After eighth grade, I was desperate to go to any other high school than my local one. I don't know if I would've survived four more years as those kids' punching bag, as I was already experiencing suicidal thoughts. Our schooling options way out in the sticks were limited, though, which was how I wound up begging my parents to send me to an all-girls Catholic school. Anything had to be better than another year riding the bus with Lauren and the neo-Nazis.

Claiming Jewishness

On the application for Rosary High School, you had to indicate your religion, if you weren't Catholic, and "atheist" wasn't an option. I decided for the first time in my life that I would openly identify as Jewish. For the past year, other people had imposed that label upon me and shamed me for it, and I was never going to let that happen again. I would be Jew-forward. I would claim the narrative. From then on, I would make sure people knew I was Jewish before I let them get the least little bit close to me, so I could watch and gauge their reaction. So I could make sure they were safe.

At Catholic school, I made friends easily. I had been bullied so badly at Wredling, despite my best attempts to conform, that I'd decided to be unapologetically myself moving forward, and I was not going to give a fuck what anyone else thought about it. This bad attitude is one I continue cultivating to this day!

I was never bullied for being Jewish at Rosary; I think, in part, because at a Catholic school, religion and authority get conflated. Me being not-Catholic made me inherently anti-authoritarian—and teenagers are always going to find that cool.

My classmates at Rosary were fascinated by my Jewishness, which was a problem, because they frequently asked me stuff about Jews that I didn't know the answer to. I now knew the racist stereotypes, and I knew being Jewish meant a tragic family history of persecution and genocide, but that was about it. So I was actually excited to take the required theology classes at Rosary, because we would be reading the Old Testament—the Torah! I would learn a little bit about this religion I claimed to be part of.

I started reading the Jewish Bible, hoping to experience a divine revelation, but I found all those stories of child-sacrifice, incest, genocide, slavery, and rape rather off-putting. On my own, I dipped into Talmudic writings—the copious volumes of rabbinical commentary on the Torah that are supposed to reveal its deeper, nonliteral meanings, but I found those texts impenetrable and tedious. I checked out books on kabbalah, hoping for a mystical awakening, but they seemed even more nonsensical to me. Eventually, I learned to shrug and explain that I was "culturally Jewish but not very religious" when one of my theology teachers would ask me to clarify some matter of Jewish theology.

Even after giving up on becoming religiously Jewish, I was eager to learn more about my Ashkenazi ethnicity. I started valuing more the time I got to spend with my nana, my only living Jewish grandparent, trying to learn whatever I could from her about our culture and family history. She and I started lighting Hanukkah candles together every year, singing the prayers while the rest of my atheist family rolled their eyes. I hoped to learn Jewish cooking from her, but the only dish she could remember how to make was matzoh brei, and our first attempt turned out inedible. I was doubtful whether soggy-matzoh-and-scrambled-eggs was a real recipe, or she was forgetting a few key steps. We would later find out she was in the early stages of Alzheimer's, and both things were true. Also, my dad confided that Nana, being a 1950s mom, had never cooked much of anything that didn't come out of a can.

Meanwhile, at Rosary, even though I wasn't bullied for being Jewish, people were *weird* about it. Jews are a big "get" for Christians. I think if they convert a Jew, they get, like, ten thousand heaven-points or something. Every once in a while, a teacher would hold me after class to give me a pamphlet on "Jews for Jesus" and suggest I "check out this really cool group." The devout among my classmates would occasionally testify to me, and ask me why I couldn't just "make a leap of faith" and "accept Jesus into my heart." After I declined to memorize a long Catholic prayer called *the Memorare* for theology class, Sister Francis made it clear to my parents that passing theology was a requirement of my continued attendance. As a result, I'm a Jew who knows way more Catholic prayers than Jewish ones, way more about the New Testament than the Talmud, and I've been to Mass probably fifty times, while I can count the times I've stepped in a synagogue on one hand.

Recently, I was at my dad's house, going through my old things in the basement, and I came across a big stack of notes my friends had written to me in high school. I was shocked to unfold the little paper footballs and see that note after note started out with, "Sup, Jew?" or "Hey, Jew! I'm in Ms. Durndel's class. Sooooo boring." I had totally forgotten that at Rosary, "Jew" had been my nickname. And that that had felt *normal* to me. I brought this up to my brother, and he told me that, at his all-boys Catholic school, he had also been nicknamed "Jew."

Again, we weren't being bullied. These girls were my good friends, and I know they liked me a lot. But calling me "Jew," in place of my name, sure does rhyme with my great-uncle Michael Kern's experience in Stanislawa, where his teacher would only call the Jewish kids "Yid." I can't believe I let my friends get away with it! But then again, this was during a time when the most uncool thing you could do was admit to being offended by anything. The early 2000s were the peak years of edgelord humor, a backlash to the "political correctness" of the 1990s, and before the pendulum would swing the other way in the 2010s, when Twitter and Facebook would become battlegrounds of so-called social justice warriors, spreading the gospel of deference politics.

I'm sure my brother and I weren't the only Jewish kids to be nicknamed "Jew" in the early 2000s, because *South Park* was enormously popular at this time, and on that show, Eric Cartman always called Kyle Broflowski "Jew." One of South Park's creators, Matt Stone, is Jewish, and I've always assumed that Cartman's relentless bullying of Kyle is autobiographical. Stone intended for viewers to look down on Cartman for his ignorant bigotry, whereas Kyle is the most moral and sympathetic character on the show. But teenagers aren't the best at critical thinking, and, rather than reflecting on their own prejudices, many of my peers wound up parroting Cartman's insults towards Jews—and Black people, queer people, trans people, disabled people, fat people, etc.— adopting new slurs with each week's episode. My experiences at Wredling show that South Park was a pretty accurate depiction of rural kid culture in the 90's, so maybe I would've been called "Jew" and asked about my horns, even if South Park had never aired. Still, I wonder if some of the kids who accused me of being a greedy, devil-worshipping baby cannibal learned that hate, not from their parents—like Lauren Duchak did—but from Cartman.

The only incident of anti-Jewish hate that truly freaked me out during my high school years was when our house got vandalized. We woke up in the morning to find our mailbox smashed, our trees decorated with a Costco- sized amount of toilet paper, and a gigantic shaving-cream swastika drawn in the middle of our driveway. This kind of vandalism was a common pastime of extremely bored rural teens, pre-social media. In fact, I'm embarrassed to say I went out smashing mailboxes with my brother's friends a couple times. Our targets were always random, never personally motivated, so it's totally possible our house was chosen because it was way at the end of a street, unlikely to be patrolled by a cop. The vandals may have drawn the swastika, again, just because it was "edgy." It might have had nothing to do with the fact that we were Jewish.

Or. Or that swastika could have been a little reminder from Lauren Duchak, or the trench coat Nazis who used to sit on the back seat of my bus. They couldn't bully me anymore, because I didn't go to their school. But maybe they wanted to remind me that they still lived just down the street, and they still hated me and my family—and all Jews!

Why though? Why? *Whyyyyyyy* did they hate us? The fuck had I ever done to them?!!?!?

This question would become a focal point of my life, leading me to becoming an "anti-antisemitism educator," which, in turn, led me to anti-Zionism.

The impression I had gotten, by the time I graduated high school, was that throughout history, wherever we'd gone, gentiles had just irrationally hated Jews. To my young mind, this persecution extended to Israel. Unlike temple-going kids, I had never raised money to plant invasive pine trees in the West Bank or even seriously contemplated a birthright trip. But the sight of Yasser Arafat in a keffiyeh, interminable discussion of the Oslo Accords, and the First and Second Intifadas, were part of the background noise of my childhood. From the bits of mainstream media coverage I overheard while my parents listened to NPR in the car or watched the nightly news, I believed that this "war" in the Middle East was motivated by the same irrational hatred of Jews that had motivated the Holocaust and explained the bullying I'd faced in eighth grade.

But where did the hate *come* from?

When I asked my family why gentiles hated us so much, I got unsatisfactory answers. My dad would say it was just the fault of religion. In his mind, all religions were pretty much equally backwards, misogynistic, disgusting, violent, and tribalistic, and the only way we'd ever know peace was when everyone stopped believing. Jews were a tinier religion than Christianity and Islam, so that's why we were always getting beaten up over it. I could understand his disgust with fundamentalism—reading the rape-y, bloodthirsty Bible at Rosary helped make his point every day—but for me, his desire to eradicate our religion felt a little too close for comfort to the aims of Nazis.

When I asked my nana and my wider Jewish family, "Why do they hate us?" I often got a Jewish supremacist story. "They hate us because we are so successful and smart." "They hate us because we love education, and we work so hard." These model minority myths make Jews feel good about themselves, but sweeping generalizations are extremely dangerous. They prevent us from seeing the harm we do, and from seeing how we've benefited from white supremacy in the US and Israel. I sniffed out the bullshit of the "Jewish supremacy" story, even as a teenager, because it felt as empty as when my mom told me the kids at Wredling picked on me because I was so pretty and smart. No, Mom. No, there was something else going on there.

I didn't have the opportunity to make many Jewish friends until college, which was when I realized just how unusual my experiences were. Most US Jews live in cities, among lots of other Jews, or in communities diverse enough that being Jewish doesn't make you a target. These urban Jews would listen to my stories of swastikas drawn on my driveway and forehead, mouths agape, sometimes with horror, sometimes with disbelief, and sometimes even with a little a bit of envy.

Victimhood is such a central facet of Judaism that Jews who have lived sheltered lives of extreme privilege sometimes develop a perverse desire for persecution. When you've been told all your life that everyone else wants to kill you, but have seen zero evidence for it, you start to jump at shadows. These are the hysterical Zionists who show up to Free Palestine protests and start screaming and crying about how they feel unsafe, even though no one is touching or even talking to them.

I speak from experience, because a little of that same persecution complex led me, in my senior year of high school, to write a prose poem about all my murdered Jewish ancestors, called "Proud of My Blood." Thank god Facebook didn't exist back then, or I imagine that poem would've done the rounds among Zionist baby boomer Facebook groups. It nauseates me now to remember what an effective piece of Hasbara it was, tracing a bullshit pseudohistory from my imagined ancestors in "ancient Israel" through forced migrations, into shtetls in the Pale of the Settlement, to Brooklyn, Chicago, and eventually to me. Hurrrrrk. Blecchhh. Just the title makes me want to barf. My dad though, for all his staunch atheism, read "Proud of My Blood" with tears in his eyes. He passed it on to all our Jewish relatives, who contacted me, equally tearfully, telling me what it meant to them, and what an incredible writer I was. On a whim, I included the poem as an optional supplemental essay in my application to Harvard University, and I'm pretty sure that's the only reason I got in. Confirm the Zionist narrative and doors of opportunity open! Criticize Israel, and they slam shut.

Even just a few months after writing "Proud of My Blood," I couldn't stand to be reminded of the poem, because I knew it was some hacky shit. Play the Holocaust card, tug at Jews' persecution complex, and you get a predictable result. There was nothing insightful, original, or *me* about what I'd written; it was just gefilte fish-flavored pabulum. Still, for years after that and until today, even after publishing four other books, family members continue to bring up the poem as if it's the greatest thing I ever wrote.

I was so embarrassed about "Proud of My Blood" that I didn't write anything else remotely Jewish while pursuing my creative writing degree at college, or even until I was in my mid-thirties—as a new parent trying to figure out how Jewishness would factor into the way I raised my daughter. I had left teaching to pursue a career as a writer, and for my first novella, I decided to seriously reinvestigate the question that had plagued me, ever since Lauren Duchak first informed me that I was a dirty Jew.

Why did they hate us?

Why they hate us

I started reading Jewish history. Pre-Holocaust stuff—because I knew anti-Jewish persecution did not start with the Nazis. What I learned was that for every anti-Jewish stereotype, there was a kernel of historical truth. I started to understand the systems that had manufactured anti-Jewish hate, and, as a result, I gained a clearer understanding of white supremacy, racial capitalism, and Western empire.

From Joshua Trachtenberg's excellent book *Jewish Magic and Superstition: A Study in Folk Religion*, I began to understand the association between Jews, magic, demons, and devil worship. Trachtenberg lays out just how much magical thinking dominated ideas of cause and effect in the medieval imagination. Did *anything* bad happen? You got sick, your goat died, or you lost money playing cards? All such misfortunes were likely the fault of a ghost, a demon, or a curse. Likewise, the only way humans knew how to prevent misfortune, or to heal someone who was sick, was to use amulets, spells, incantations, and the like. Trachtenberg stresses just how much everyone in Europe—Christians, Jews, Muslims, and pagans*—thought like this in the Middle Ages. Everybody's religious

---

* I'll be using *pagan* as Medieval Christians did, as a collective term for all Indigenous European faith-traditions. There was never one faith tradition that called itself "Pagan," rather, Roman Christians coined this term to describe the many religious *others* within the empire that weren't Christians, Jews, or Muslims.

leaders were wearing fancy outfits, chanting in ancient languages, burning incense, lighting candles, and using amulets to ward off evil. Christians just came up with a trick of calling this "Mass," when they did it, and "black magic" when anybody else did it. Christians concocted a story of a great cosmic battle between good and evil, which only they could win, and in which Jews, pagans, Christian heretics*, and Muslims were on the side of evil. This way, Christians could justify exploiting, killing, and stealing from any people who weren't already under their rule. Everyone in Europe was either an evil emissary of Satan *or* already a Christian, and thus, already tithing** to the church and supporting the expansion of Christian empire.

Even the most learned men of science—physicians educated at the renowned medical college in Padua—told people shit like, "Strap moss and a deer spleen to your leg" in order to cure a cold. The line between medicine and magic was nonexistent, thus, Jews' reputation for sorcery was one reason they were particularly sought-after as physicians in Northern Europe. As Trachtenberg explains, "Their wide knowledge of languages, the availability of Arabic-Greek medical works in Hebrew translation, their propensity for travel and study abroad, their freedom from the church-fostered superstition of miraculous cures, relics, and the like, these often conspired to make of them more effective practitioners than their non-Jewish competitors," at least in the minds of their non-Jewish clientele![137] Treating Christians was dangerous for a Jewish doctor, though, because "if his ministrations were successful, he was a magician and might expect to be treated as such, with fear and respect ... if he failed, he was a magician, and could expect to be called upon to pay promptly for his crime."[138] And in Medieval Christendom, the payment for failing to heal a Christian client might involve a slow and painful death.

Even before the advent of Christianity, Jews were particularly sought out in the ancient world for their powers of exorcism. In *Between Worlds: Dybbuks, Exorcists, and Early Modern Judaism,* J. H. Chajes explains that for centuries before the Roman Empire adopted Christianity, Jews had been widely seen

....

*   *Heretics* was the word Roman Christian leaders used to describe anyone trying to follow Christ's teachings outside their authority.

**   Donating one-tenth of one's income (or produce, crops, goods, etc.). Tithing to the Church was mandatory throughout Christendom in the Middle Ages.

as experts in solving problems related to spirit possession. And by the third century, in the words of the early Christian theologian Origen, "We learn from the Hebrews" when it comes to exorcisms. According to Chajes, "many Jewish elements ... found their way into both pagan and Christian exorcism rituals."[139] The reputation of Jews as experts in matters of spiritual protection also extended into the Muslim world and into the modern era. Chajes quotes an early-twentieth-century traveler reporting that "in Cairo, Baghdad, and Damascus, Jewish silversmiths carry on a large trade in Moslem amulets. In fact, an amulet is supposed to have special power if it has not only Arabic but Hebrew letters on it."[140] Trachtenberg outlines many ways that, in the early medieval period at least, working-class Jews, Christians, Muslims, and pagans respected, saw validity in, and took advantage of each others' distinct spiritual practices.

Chajes maintains that spirit possession is "ubiquitous" in human cultures, "from time immemorial."[141] Likewise, nearly all faith traditions have some method of dealing with the problem of a community-member suddenly acting weird. In my humble, atheist opinion, what my ancestors called "spirit possession" is probably what I would call "mental health struggles." Thus, early Jewish exorcists were performing a societal role similar to what I would call "a therapist." They weren't necessarily good therapists—as sometimes the "possessed" person died in the course of theses exorcisms.[142] Regardless, Jewish exorcists, who would be known as Ba'al Shems in the early modern period, were attempting to heal a community member with a troubled mind. Again, we see Jews using their "magic" to act as healers among non-Jewish neighbors, a practice which could be lucrative or deadly, depending on whether the treatment worked.

So how did Jews go from being some of the most relied-upon dispellers of demons in the ancient world to being accused by Christians of demonic worship? Well, Christian church leaders did not like members of their flock going to Jews, or anyone outside their authority, for help in spiritual matters. How could the church wield supreme cosmic authority if its parishioners were going to Jews for amulets and salves and exorcisms? It just wouldn't do. As "an expression of the church's quest for centralization of authority," the church codified the *Rituale Romanum*—a method of exorcism that, again, borrowed heavily from Jewish traditional practices but could now only be performed by a specially trained Catholic priest.[143] In 1614, the *Rituale Romanum* became only the latest installment in the Christian church's effort to malign Jewish "magic." Its smear campaign against Jewish traditional healing practices had begun more than a millennium earlier.

Historian Lily Climenhaga asserts that "'Magic' acted as a description for individuals or groups who did not subscribe to the perceived societal norms of the medieval Christian community" and that "these beliefs created the preliminary conditions necessary for the mass persecution and intolerance towards witches and became inherent to the idea of the witch as the diabolical Other within Medieval Christian thought."[144] To dissuade Christians from seeking out Jewish help with spiritual matters, the church claimed from about 400CE, not that Jewish magic *didn't* work (such a claim would've been dismissed as ridiculous), but rather that Jewish magic, and the magic of pagans and Christian heretics, all derived from a "Satanic Pact."[145] In the Christian imagination, witches and wizards were synonymous with Jews. As Trachtenberg puts it, it's not that Christians accused certain Jews here and there of sorcery, but rather sorcery was attributed "to the entire people, *en masse.*"[146]

For example, the fact that the Jewish sabbath started at nightfall led to the myth of a nighttime "witches' sabbath." The twelfth-century Christian writer Walter Map described these sabbaths as events where witches and heretics met in "diabolical *synagogues*," where they kissed the devil "under the tail" and on his "private parts."[147] Illicit sex, devil worship, black magic, heresy, and Judaism all became conflated in the Christian imagination. Early Christians invented the character of Satan to represent the god of Jews, pagans, and heretics. To me, it's interesting that Christians imagined Satan to have horns and made horns a symbol of evil, because horns are exclusively a *defensive* trait. Only plant-eating animals have horns, to defend themselves from predators.

If the god of all non-Christians is prey, then who's the predator? Just saying!

The most destructive charge that medieval Christians leveled against Jews was the myth of "blood libel"—the accusation that Jews engaged in ritual murder and cannibalism. This myth, which has no credible historical evidence to back it up, persists to this day in the form of the Q-Anon conspiracy theory that a global Jewish elite are harvesting "adrenochrome" from children to prolong their own lives.

I, who was taunted many times about being a "baby-killing Jew" at Wredling Middle School, was interested to learn that Jews were far from the only group accused of blood libel by medieval Christians. Rather, Climenhaga explains how any spiritual "other" in the medieval Christian world—including Christian heretics—were accused of ritual murder and cannibalism by Christian authorities, and at times got burned at the stake for it.

These accusations of cannibalism are ironic, when you consider that it was the Christian church that had established the principle of transubstantiation at the Fourth Council of the Lateran in 1215. Transubstantiation meant that, according to Christian dogma, every time a Christian took the Eucharist, they weren't just sipping wine and eating a cracker, they were *literally* drinking the *literal* blood of their *literal* savior and eating his *literal* flesh. Jews had no such beliefs or practices around eating people, even symbolically.

Accusations = confessions, etc., etc.

Now, I don't believe in transubstantiation, and I certainly don't think medieval Christians were drinking anything other than wine or eating anything other than crackers at their masses. However, I *do* think these Christians contemplated cannibalism so much that they started projecting their people-eating fetish onto Jews, who had nothing to do with that mess. Jews also aren't the ones chopping up the bodies of their saints and passing them around the world, preserving finger bones and scapulas for centuries in fancy gold boxes called reliquaries, so that congregants can pray to the dead bits of Saint So-and-so. That kind of necromancy would be a uniquely Catholic practice.

The aforementioned Fourth Council of the Lateran was basically a large gathering of extremely rich and powerful Christian church leaders, where they planned how to further strengthen and centralize their authority. And, just spit-balling here, but you could also describe a meeting like that as "a cabal of global elites, plotting to take over the world."

But wait—oh, right. I just remembered the word "cabal" is derived from kabbalah—Jewish mysticism—and has historically been used as a dog whistle to describe fictions about Jewish elites engaging in the kind of global imperialism that Christian elites have *actually* been doing, in the open, for centuries. At the Fourth Council of the Lateran, for example, that cabal of Christian elites decided on many laws to strengthen their power and oppress religious minorities in Europe. One law passed at that council mandated Jews throughout Christendom wear a "peaked cap" as an identifying badge. I touched on the history of the Jewish badge briefly in Chapter 3, but while we're out here in the wilderness, let's take a closer look.

In the Middle Ages, many Jews were expert assimilators—adopting the language and fashions of wherever they settled and mingling with the local gentile population. As you can imagine, the high control church did not like this. To make matters worse, in some places, wealthy Jews didn't assimilate, but rather brought with them fashionable styles from other regions. The Archbishop of Bremen-Hamburg described "Jewish clothing" as "radiant" and "dignified," and one reason given at the Fourth Council of the Lateran for regulating Jewish dress was that "Jews . . . wear clothes . . . such as give them an aristocratic appearance."[148] The church couldn't have Jews blending in with local Christians, let alone looking wealthier and more stylish than them! If Christians got cozy with Jews, or, even worse, looked up to them, then those peasants might start questioning the narrative the church had been carefully crafting about Jews for centuries. If we weren't devil-worshipping, demon-smooching, no-good, garlic-eating cannibals, then the church's "flock" of sheeple might stop giving the church all their money to wage a holy war against us.

So, the Fourth Council of the Lateran decreed that Jews and Saracens (Muslims) must wear distinctive dress throughout Christendom, because "a difference of dress distinguishes Jews or Saracens from Christians in some provinces, but in others a certain confusion has developed so that they are indistinguishable. Whence it sometimes happens that by mistake Christians join with Jewish or Saracen women, and Jews or Saracens with Christian women.[149]" To prevent this "damnable mixing" between Jews, Christians, and Muslims, for the rest of the thirteenth century, lawmakers across German-speaking regions demanded that Jews wear a "peaked hat," a *pileus cornutus,* and in some areas a "pointed hood" or *Gugel.*"[150]

Zionists in my comments often point to *dhimmi* laws in Muslim countries, which required Jews and Christians to wear badges identifying themselves as non-Muslim, as evidence that Muslims have always been uniquely hateful towards Jews. But in the Muslim world, *ahl al-dhimma* meant 'protected person,' and Muslims were required by sharia law to protect

Jews and Christians, who were exempted from military service. Jewish badges were also required throughout Christendom, but in Christian lands, Jewish badges like the pointed hats were designed to humiliate, not just identify, Jews. And Jews faced far more poverty, oppression, and religious violence in Christian Europe than they did in Muslim lands.

Because Jews were already associated with magic, and now the pointy *Judenhut* was mandated for Jews across Europe, pointy hats wound up becoming synonymous with magic. In "The Wandering Hat: Iterations of the Medieval Pointed Cap," Lubrich details the appearance of pointy hats throughout medieval art and this headgear's associations, first with Jews, then with witches, wizards, dwarves, elves, giants, gnomes, and all manner of mythical creatures.

Despite being a dragon-obsessed fantasy reader throughout my childhood, I was fully in my mid-thirties and diving deeply into Jewish medieval history before I learned of this association. Once you start seeing them, pointy hats are everywhere throughout Christian mythology, as are other covert references to Jews. Scratch a fairy tale, and you'll find anti-Jewish sentiment, because again, ideas of "magic," "otherness," and "Jewishness" were all synonymous in the medieval Christian imagination. And any fairy tales that aren't covertly referencing Jews are probably pulling from Muslim or pagan faith traditions.

Along with black magic, pointy hats also became associated with criminality. Lubrich cites a fourteenth-century law in Seligenstadt, Germany, that forced Christians who committed Jewish-y crimes (usury or sleeping with a Jew) to wear a pointed hat as punishment. She also uncovers a 1421 municipal law in Ofen, Hungary, that mandated anyone convicted of sorcery to wear "a pointed Jew's hat."[151] Given this association between Jews, pointy hats, and punishment, I don't think it's a stretch to assume that the dunce cap is a descendent of the Jewish hat. I assume the association holds true for the capirote as well—a tall, pointed hood worn by Catholic penitents, an exaggerated version of the *Gugel,* and which in turn inspired the Ku Klux Klan hood.

While few USian Jews of my generation know anything about the history of the pointed Jewish hat, this association was still alive and well in 1930s Germany, where a company called Guenther & Co. released a boardgame called Juden Raus! ("Jews Out!"). Players were tasked with collecting six pointy, conical "Jews hats" from around the board and delivering them to a "roundup location"[152] where, presumably, the Jews would be ethnically cleansed from the community. What fun!

Outside of the Holy Roman Empire, the Jewish badge took other forms beside a pointy hat: "blue stripes in Sicily, a red cape in Rome, the Tablets of the Law in England, a yellow wheel in France, a red badge in Hungary."[153] To prevent Jews from looking too wealthy and stunning, many Christian regions also passed sumptuary laws for Jews, restricting their ability to wear velvet, silk, and gold and silver embroidery,[154] so no longer would Jews go around looking radiant! Meanwhile, Muslims on the Iberian Peninsula "had to wear a strip or bandage made of yellow woolen fabric on the right sleeve near the shoulder so that it was visible."[155] Although, historian Irina Varyash clarifies that Muslim badges were much less common than Jewish ones throughout the rest of Christendom, "for the simple reason that there were significantly fewer of them in Europe than Jews."[156]

In *Dress Codes: How the Laws of Fashion Made History,* fashion historian Richard Thompson Ford details how, across Italy, Jews and sex workers in the early modern period were required to wear similar badges—a move designed to otherize and humiliate both groups, and serve as a "wearable ghetto" that would follow them outside the physical confines of walled Jewish ghettos and red light districts. Ford explains,

> In the fifteenth century, Roman Jewish women were required to wear a red overskirt that prostitutes also wore; Jewish women in other parts of Italy had to wear a yellow veil—a sign of the prostitute in Italian cities from the fourteenth through the sixteenth centuries. In 1397, Venetian law required Jews to wear a yellow badge, and a 1416 law required prostitutes and pimps to wear a yellow scarf. In Viterbo, any Jewish woman who dared appear on the streets without her yellow veil could be stripped naked by the first person to apprehend her—the same punishment prescribed in other cities for prostitutes who strayed from the districts where they were allowed to solicit customers.[157]

In my mind, this sexual humiliation of medieval Jewish women rhymes with the rash of social media posts by IOF soldiers over the past year, in which they have dressed up in the clothes and lingerie of Palestinian women. After murdering many of these women and destroying their homes, the soldiers filmed themselves digging around in their victims' underwear drawers, rubbing panties on their faces, and donning bras over their body armor in an attempt to humiliate Palestinian women.[158] The punishment for medieval women in Viterbo—of being stripped naked in the street—also echoes with the frequent practice by IOF soldiers over the past year of mass-arresting civilians in Gaza, stripping them to their underwear, blindfolding them and exposing them to the elements.[159] Ashkenazi Jews in the IOF have become practitioners of the kind of sexual humiliation once used against their ancestors in Christian Europe. And to better understand this kind of violence, we can examine why the Christian church sought to conflate and humiliate sex workers and Jews, during the sixteenth century *in particular.*

Church leaders were fighting back against the reputation of the Italian Peninsula as a place where both Jews and sex workers had previously experienced comparatively high levels of wealth and freedom. Prior to their ghettoization in the sixteenth century, Jews had owned vineyards and orchards across the Peninsula and others amassed wealth as textile traders. Meanwhile, historian Antoni Maczak details how "visitors from northern Europe" were "astounded" by the "freedom and wealth, charm and elegance" of the courtesans of Venice in the early modern period.[160] For Venetian nobles, only the eldest sons were allowed to marry, in order to prevent family wealth from being split among too many descendants. Thus, unofficial relationships between the younger sons of noble families and courtesans allowed these women to amass a wealth, independence, and status that was unheard of for women throughout European Christendom. Maczak explains that the high status of sex workers was not limited to Venice. Because of the high concentration of priests in Rome, who were forbidden to marry, there was an "amazingly low" population of women there. And of those women who did live in Rome, a high proportion were sex workers, whose clientele included all those priests who were forbidden to marry. Maczak reports that pious pilgrims traveling to Rome were scandalized "to see cardinals, bishops, and Spanish prelates sitting in the first row of the theatre stalls alongside Rome's celebrated Spanish courtesans on Easter Sunday."[161]

Requiring Jews and sex workers to wear the same identifying clothing was designed to humiliate both groups and position them, on first glance, as inferior to married, Christian women. But if the sexual hypocrisy of the church's highest-ranking clergy members had been an open secret throughout the Middle Ages, why the sudden crackdown on prostitution in the sixteenth century? And why did this crackdown on prostitution coincide with the ghettoization of Jews?

Because the sixteenth century marked the first time in a millennium that the Catholic church's domination of Northern and Western Europe was seriously threatened. In 1517, Martin Luther had nailed his ninety-five theses to the doors of a church, sparking off the Protestant Reformation. Over the century to come, more and more kingdoms would convert to Protestantism, allowing the nobles there to seize land and power that had previously belonged to the Catholic church. The Catholic church was hemorrhaging land and power to Protestants, and this existential threat sparked a surge of authoritarianism. Catholics across Europe attempted to make up for their losses by stealing Jewish lands. And Italian Catholics simultaneously consolidated power by going after the wealth of the two most independent groups of women in the sixteenth century—sex workers and nuns.

As historian Silvia Evangelisti explains in *Nuns: A History of Convent Life*, early Protestants compared convents to brothels, and "regarded monks and nuns as men and women who devoted themselves to idleness, gluttony, and dubious sexual morality."[162] According to medieval logic, if nuns were sluts, then Protestant nobles were justified in stealing their property and displacing them to Catholic lands.

Here we find the logic behind IOF soldiers dressing up in Palestinian women's lingerie. European history contains a long tradition of justifying land-grabs by portraying the women who live there as sluts. Blaming victims of violence for their own assault, on the basis of the victims' alleged promiscuity, is a hallmark of what feminist scholars term "rape culture"—a society where sexual assault is normalized and trivialized. Justifying the genocide of women based on the contents of their underwear drawers is an extreme conclusion of the same type of logic that asks, "What were you wearing?" when someone reports a sexual assault. Israel and other Western nations don't have a monopoly on rape culture, by any means, but Israel is particularly afflicted by rape culture. Israeli forces and settlers have weaponized rape against Palestinians since the formation of the state of Israel.[163] Jewish Israeli citizens are also endangered by rape culture—a third of female soldiers in the IOF report sexual harassment on the job; one in five Israeli women report having been raped in their lifetime; and nearly half of those reported assaults were committed against minors.[164]

Unfortunately for sixteenth-century medieval nuns, once they'd fled from Protestants, they faced yet another land grab from the male leaders of their own faith, and what amounted to mass incarceration at the hands of their spiritual brothers. At the Council of Trent, between 1545 and 1563, Catholic church leaders passed the Tridentine reforms. A response to the Protestant Reformation, these changes were ostensibly designed to stamp out the corruption, sin, and hypocrisy within Catholicism. Before Martin Luther, if the pope and cardinals wanted to parade their favorite prostitutes at Mass, and monks were sneaking into convents to sleep with their nun girlfriends, who was going to stop them? They were among the most powerful men on the continent. But after Martin Luther, these sexual adventures became a major liability for the church, and Catholic reformers called for a crackdown. Among these Tridentine reforms were strict laws of enclosure for Catholic nuns.

Before the Council of Trent, nuns were able to be a part of the surrounding community, move about the secular world, and participate in economic activity. Nuns owned land, farmed, and ran shops and businesses such as apothecaries and goat farms. But following the Tridentine reforms, male church leaders stole the nuns' land and imprisoned them for life within the walls of their convents. After enclosure, if the convent grounds contained a cemetery, a girl might enter a convent knowing she would never again emerge, even after death. Throughout the sixteenth century, male church reformers insisted the walls of convents be built higher and topped with spikes. They installed grills on all the windows and turned convents into Renaissance-era max security prisons in the name of "protecting the virtue" of the nuns.

Can you think of what rhymes with this history in 2024? Once you've stolen someone's land, what are you going to do with them? How will you control them? Put them behind a wall! Top the gates with spikes! Don't let them out at any cost!

Sounds like the siege of Gaza to me.

The Tridentine enclosure of nuns also mirrored the enclosure of Jews in Italian ghettos, taking place at the exact same time. Despite these striking similarities, I couldn't find any historians who've written about the shared experience of nuns and Jews in the sixteenth century! I only noticed the comparison by going down two separate rabbit holes in researching my novel. So if there's any history students out there, help yourself to the free dissertation topic. Apply a Marxist lens! Tridentine enclosure and the ghettoization of Jews were both about money, power, and land all along! And the propaganda the Catholic church employed against nuns and Jews in the sixteenth century, in order to justify this land grab, is like a blueprint for Hasbara seeking to justify the genocide and theft of Palestinian land today. Making their targets out to be sluts was one tactic. Forcing them into poverty and criminality was another.

The Jewish ghetto of Florence provides a case study into the real history behind the stereotype of the greedy, money-grubbing, gold-obsessed Jewish banker. This stereotype is alive and well, something I know firsthand because, throughout my school days, other kids frequently used the word "Jew" as a verb meaning either to cheat, steal, or be stingy with money. Kids especially would say, "Don't Jew me, Jew!" anytime I was, like, asking to borrow a pencil. The truth is, many Jews *were* bankers in medieval and early modern Europe, and many contemporary Jews continue in that profession today. But why were so many Jews bankers? In short: because Christians needed us to be, and they didn't give us other options.

In *Jews and Magic in Medici Florence: The Secret World of Benedetto Blanis*, biographer Edward Goldberg explains how so many Jews of Florence, including the subject of his biography, Benedetto Blanis, came to be moneylenders. The Catholic church forbade Christians from engaging in usury—charging interest for a loan—because their savior, Jesus, had been famously against finance. According to the Christian Bible, Jesus flipped the tables of moneylenders outside the temple in Jerusalem—the only time he demonstrated such riotous anger. And Christians, until very recent history, took Jesus's ban on usury pretty seriously.

But the Catholic church often needed quick cash to build cathedrals or finance violent, settler-colonial wars. So, the church would permit Jews to practice usury and take advantage of their moneylending services—as when, in 1512, the pope gave Moyse Blanis de Lerda, an ancestor of Benedetto

Blanis, a permit to lend money at interest.[165] Having Jewish bankers around benefitted the economy while preserving the moral purity of Christian elites, who in turn could condemn and scapegoat Jewish bankers for ripping off poor Christians.

Usury was such good money, though, that many Christians found loopholes in dogma and practiced lending money with interest, and without the stigma Jews faced for the same behaviors. One of the most glaring hypocrites here is the Medici family, who initially amassed their great fortune through international finance.[166] But once the Medicis had established their own political empire, they quit the banking game and suddenly became deeply concerned about the evils of Jewish moneylending. The Medicis used their newfound disdain for the business that had made them rich as a pretext to steal the land and wealth of all their former Jewish competitors. Grand Duke Cosimo de Medici I cited Jewish usury as the justification for imprisoning Jews in the Florentine ghetto.[167] Most Jews in Florence would flee after his edict, and those who remained were forcibly displaced into two crowded streets, where they were required to pay rent to their imprisoners—the Medici family.

This outrage—of Jews having to pay rent to the very people who stole their land and ghettoized them—echoes *resonantly* with the situation in Sheikh Jarrah, Jerusalem. In the 1950s, twenty-eight Palestinian families displaced by the Nakba settled in Sheikh Jarrah, where the Jordanian government (which then controlled the neighborhood) built them homes. But in 1967, after Israel wrested control of East Jerusalem and the rest of the West Bank from Jordan, the Israeli government gifted ownership of these homes to groups of Israeli settlers. Ever since, Palestinians in Sheikh Jarrah are forced to pay rent to the people who stole their homes twice over, or face eviction.[168]

Black Marxist interlude: Ghettos everywhere are rigged economies, designed to extract as much wealth as possible from a captive, impoverished non-white population to benefit the white ruling class that ghettoized them.

Back in the seventeenth-century Jewish ghetto of Florence, Benedetto Blanis was a Jewish man, forced to pay rent to the Medicis through the limited economic activities legally available to him. Even though it was Jewish trade networks that brought in the textiles that made the city of Florence so wealthy, Jews of the ghetto were forbidden from working with those textiles. Ten years after the creation of the Jewish ghetto, the Silk Guild of Florence required silk producers to live within 200 yards of the guild headquarters, an impossibility for Jews required to live in the ghetto.[169] The Linen Guild and Silk Guild passed numerous ordinances to freeze Jews out of the market, so that by 1620, "Ghetto merchants ... could no longer sell new silk cloth by measure or by the cut piece, a grave financial loss ... to Jewish families."[170] As a result, Jews were relegated to selling thread, buttons, second-hand clothing, and engaging in scrapwork—ingeniously making masquerade costumes out of the scraps discarded by Christian tailors. However, this second-hand work didn't always pay the bills, so enterprising Jews like Benedetto Blanis did a little of all of the above, plus moneylending.

Usury was still *technically* illegal in the virtue-signaling world of Medici Florence, but it was a fact of life that went on "very nearly in plain sight."[171] Goldberg explains that moneylenders would issue bogus "notes of credit" for goods that didn't exist. So, rather than say "Don Giovanni owes me 100 scudi" the note would say "Don Giovanni bought 7 bolts of linen." Then, "the interest on the loan would be factored into the deferred payment for the nonexistent linen."[172] Through this method, Jews could employ the law to enforce the notes of credit and have defaulters arrested and jailed. But, as Goldberg explains, "moneylending was a risky business, since it took time and depended on the tacit collusion of the authorities. The magistrates, like everyone else, knew the real deal regarding the Jewish notes of credit they were called on to enforce."[173] If that "tacit collusion" by authorities was suddenly revoked, the Jewish moneylender could be left twisting in the wind, having lost the amount they'd loaned with no way to get it back. Or, as was the case for Benedetto Blanis, they could find *themselves* arrested if they tried to collect a debt from an aristocrat who was a little too powerful. In this way, elite Christians could help themselves to the wealth of the Jewish ghetto when they needed quick cash, and they might not even have to pay it back.

In the early modern Polish-Lithuanian Commonwealth, a comparative "heaven for Jews," Jews were not ghettoized. However, they gained a reputation for being greedy and miserly for another trade that Christian elites simultaneously shamed Jews for while benefitting from their services. They employed Jews to be estate agents. Historian Daniel Stone estimates that "between 13 and 15 percent of Polish Jews worked as estate agents and innkeepers; thousands of them doubled as business agents for Polish nobles."[174]

As estate agents, Jews were the people who came around to collect rent for the nobility—they were the face of the tax man. Jews were well-suited to this job because most were at least trilingual, speaking Yiddish and Polish, and using written Hebrew to conduct business. Jewish boys sent to yeshiva* were taught to read and write, as opposed to the majority of Christian peasants, who were illiterate. Jews were taught the basic math skills they'd need to conduct business at yeshiva as well. And Jewish religious training is highly focused on studying religious law, which translates well to secular law—a useful skill as a business manager. Many Jews also mastered enough Latin to be able to assist nobles in navigating Christian legal matters, which were conducted in that language. While all these skills were surely assets in the role of Jews as estate managers, I have a hunch that it was the *otherness* of Jews that made Christian nobles seek them out as estate managers most of all.

Jews were tasked with collecting money from tenants, but then they handed that money right over to the nobility, in exchange for a modest salary. Still, it's easy to hate the face of the person who shows up at your door to take your wealth or evict you if you can't pay. It's easier to hate that face if it looks different from yours—particularly if you believe that such people are baby-eating devil worshippers. You might start hating that face so much that you think people with such faces are the enemy, and you forget all about the noble who's living a life of ease in the palace on the hill. The noble is the person *actually* oppressing you, a parasite siphoning the wealth off of hundreds of hard-working peasants without ever having to lift a finger in labor. But you don't ever see them, unless they're tossing pennies at your feet out of a carriage, and then you thank them for it. No, it's the Jewish estate manager you blame for your poverty.

This dynamic might explain why, during the Khmelnitsky Revolt of 1648, Christian peasants massacred entire Jewish communities throughout Ukraine. Estimates of the dead vary widely, but whether 20,000 or 100,000 Jews were killed, Khmelnitsky's uprising was the largest single genocide of Jews prior to the Holocaust.[175]

Marxists might call those early modern Jewish estate managers "class traitors"—low-down, dirty cousins to kapos. Jewish estate managers lent their faces to what was actually the Christian-on-Christian violence of early-stage

* A Jewish school

145

capitalism. These Jews enforced the evictions, land theft, and oppression of Christian peasants that served the interests of wealthy elites.

Sound familiar? Jews in Israel are still patsies for a richer, whiter, and more powerful Christian empire in the US of A. Only today, the pain Jews in the IOF inflict at the behest of white nobles—I mean, "weapons and petrochemical shareholders"—is more overtly violent than the pain Jewish estate managers inflicted on Ukrainian serfs in 1648.

Israel's victims in 2024—in Palestine, Lebanon, Syria and Yemen—are likewise much better armed and organized than seventeenth-century Ukrainian peasants. And these resistance forces are (understandably) fighting the Jewish soldiers sent to massacre them and steal their land, while the architects of their oppression live safely in far-off castles.

By studying the history of my people in Europe, I finally understood anti-Jewish hate. I understood why kids had tried to find my "horns," and why I'd been asked if my family ate babies, and why stealing someone's French fry was called "Jewing them." And the more I learned, the more I realized that there was nothing particularly special or mysterious about anti-Jewish hate. The "anti-Jewish" part didn't even really matter. Hate is hate. Hate allows you to kill someone and take their stuff. Elites manufacture hate so they can enslave, exploit, and steal.

The Roman Empire adopted Christianity and used religion as a tool for dehumanizing others in order to justify killing people and taking their shit. And they didn't only target Jews! Christian elites meted out the same persecution onto countless Indigenous European cultures lumped under the moniker of "pagans." When Romanies arrived in Europe, they faced extreme violence and oppression at the hands of Christians. Muslims were repeatedly targeted by Christians for genocide in the Crusades. Even Christian "heretics," those who tried to follow the teachings of Jesus outside the gilt-clad dictates of the Roman Empire, were accused of being devil worshippers and massacred accordingly.

All that hate, for anyone who didn't bend a knee to the pope, was manufactured to justify killing people and taking their stuff. Same as it ever was.

Why I stopped using the term "antisemitism"

Throughout the course of learning this history, I became something of an anti-antisemitism educator on social media. As I learned each piece of what

I've shared above, I made TikToks about these topics, and people found them fascinating. In the US, so little of this history is well-known, because white supremacy covers its tracks! And nearly all the Jewish history I've shared above is contained behind the paywalls of book prices or academic journal subscriptions. By 2023, I had amassed enough of a following for my historical videos, that I was even getting paid to appear on "combatting antisemitism" panels and podcasts, put on by Jewish institutions.

But in the months after October 7th, I became increasingly sickened by the very word "antisemitism." The media and Western politicians were continually weaponizing the term to silence anti-genocide protesters and manufacture hate towards Palestinians. I was also getting comments from Palestinians, asking, "Aren't I also Semitic?" They claimed the term antisemitism, being used to refer only to Jews, amounted to Arab erasure. Other anti-Zionist Jews I trusted insisted the term had been originally coined to describe anti-Jewish hate, so it was fine to keep using it to mean that specifically. I decided to dig into this history myself, which thoroughly convinced me to drop the word from my vocabulary.

The term "antisemitism" was first popularized in the 1860s by Wilhelm Marr—a Victorian version of today's red-pilled, alt-right racist bros. In his youth, he was a communist who fought for minority rights. But after life kicked him in the teeth a bit—a failed revolution, a failed business in Costa Rica, two divorces (one from a Jewish woman, and another Jewish wife who died in childbirth)—his politics took a 180-degree turn and he decided his *whole thing* was going to be hating Jews.[176] (Have a field day with that, Freudians.) Obviously, hatred of Jews was already a well-established phenomenon in 1860s Germany, and it was literally called "Jew hate," *Judenhass*. What Wilhelm Marr did was turn this hate into a shiny, new political movement.[177]

In 1871, Jews were legally emancipated in the new Second German Empire and given rights equal to those of their Christian neighbors. Just eight years later, in 1879, Wilhelm Marr established the League of Antisemites, whose stated goal was reversing Jewish emancipation. There's always a backlash to anti-racist progress, isn't there? Like neo-Nazis rebranding themselves as "alt right" following the Obama presidency and electing Trump on an openly racist platform, Marr coined a new term for a very old hate, and he turned that hate into the political framework that would eventually become the Nazi Party.

The "semite" part of antisemitism comes from linguistics, which divides languages with Aryan roots, such as German, from those with Semitic roots, such as Hebrew and Arabic. According to eighteenth-century, galaxy-brained race scientists, this linguistic difference offered proof that Jews and Christian Germans were different *races* of people.

Now I have learned the hard way, from posting this content to social media, that most of my fellow USians are unaware that there is *zero* biological basis to race. So let's take a quick detour through the history of the science of racism. But I'll start with the end of the story—because that's the most important part.

By 1950, genetic science had revealed that there was no biological basis to race whatsoever, and UNESCO released a statement called "The Race Question" in which the group concluded, "For all practical social purposes 'race' is not so much a biological phenomenon as a social myth."[178] Since then, developments in genetics and anthropology have only confirmed that there is no scientific basis to racial categories. Unfortunately, seventy-five years after UNESCO's pronouncement, a whole lot of people have not gotten the memo.

So allow me to clarify: these categories we put people in of Black, White, Asian, etc., don't actually tell us how related people are genetically. There's more genetic diversity *within* races than *between* races. Svante Pääbo, a biologist and director of the Max Planck Institute for Evolutionary Anthropology, explains, "What the study of complete genomes from different parts of the world has shown is that even between Africa and Europe, for example, there is not a single absolute genetic difference, meaning no single variant where all Africans have one variant and all Europeans another one, even when recent migration is disregarded."[179]

A dark-skinned person from North Africa may have far more in common genetically with a lily-white Frenchman than with a dark-skinned person from South Africa. But we look at those two dark-skinned people and say "Black." But "Black" is not a meaningful category, scientifically speaking. Similarly, a person from Western China might have more DNA in common with a blonde-haired, blue-eyed lady from Moscow than with someone from Vietnam. But we have been socially conditioned to focus on epicanthal eye-folds and go, "Asian!" But "Asian" is not a meaningful category, scientifically speaking.

Still, many people think there's something natural about the way we are socially conditioned to see race. Like, even if there's no scientific basis, isn't it kind of obvious that there's Black people, Asian people, and White people, etc.? But in fact, these divisions are socially constructed and only about 250 years old. And the racial divisions that appear on US census forms—Black, White, Asian, and Native American—weren't the first or only attempt at categorizing human beings into races.

That first attempt was made by Francois Bernier in 1684. He lumped all Europeans, North Africans, Middle Easterners, Indians, Southeast Asians, and Native Americans into one race. All those people got to be "white" in Bernier's taxonomy. His second race was sub-Saharan Africans. His third race was East Asians, and his fourth race was the Samí people—the Indigenous people of northern Scandinavia. Based on seeing exactly two Samí people in his lifetime, Bernier concluded they were an entirely separate race unto themselves, and he was extremely hateful towards them, saying they were "ugly animals" with "faces like a bear's."[180]

In 1785, Johann Christoph Gatterer would publish a competing racial taxonomy—including the first use of "Semite" as a racial category—at the birthplace of scientific racism, the University of Göttingen in Germany. Gatterer had the type of brilliant scientific mind that just, like, *decided* that the time span from creation to the birth of Christ was 4,181 years.[181] Which is close! He was only off by about 13.7 billion!

Because the Bible said that Noah's sons, Shem, Ham, and Japheth, settled in Canaan, the Mediterranean, and Egypt respectively, Johann decided that this meant there were three races of human beings originating from each of those areas. Semites, descended from Shem, were Middle Easterners. Hamites were North Africans, and Japhetites were Europeans.[182] He also decided Japhetites were the superior race. Because ... he said so, and he wrote it down, and in the eighteenth century that was enough to make any old idea that popped into your noggin a fact.*

....
*   Not much has changed, if we consider the existence of flat-earthers, anti-vaxxers and UFO-truthers uncritically accepting the testimony of random YouTubers as evidence for their unscientific views.

Probably thanks to Wilhelm Marr's resurrection of it in the 1860s, "Semite" as a racial category has stuck around, but few people refer to Hamites or Japhetites anymore. Those categories have been forgotten in favor of the racial taxonomy of Carl Linnaeus, who in 1767 put forth the Black/White/Yellow/Red, Crayola-colors racial taxonomy that is still in vogue today. However, here are two ridiculous things about Linnaeus's taxonomy you probably didn't know.

First, those "colors" that are associated with the races—black, white, yellow, red? They're not describing skin colors. They're referring to humorism, an ancient Greek medical theory that claims the human body is made up of four fluids—blood (red), phlegm (white), and two types of bile—yellow and black. According to humorism, illnesses and even peoples' personalities, behaviors, and flaws are caused by imbalances in these humors.[183] Just to be clear (because hard experience has taught me there is no end to scientific ignorance floating around on the internet), there is no medical truth to humorism.

Before the nineteenth century, no one referred to East Asians as having "yellow" skin. That "yellow" comes from Linnaeus's hunch that East Asians had an excess of yellow bile. So if your brain goes, "*Yellow!*" when you look at an Asian person, and "*Red!*" when you look at an Indigenous American person, that is because of social conditioning stemming from this preposterous, made-up eighteenth-century "race science," which in turn is based on ancient Greek ideas of medicine from the fifth century BCE.

The second ludicrous thing about Linnaeus's ideas is that he didn't just create four categories of races. He had a fifth category of—get ready for it—MONSTERS.

That's right, the *Homo Sapiens Monstrosus*, including wolf-boys, giants, and the "dwarfs of the Alps."[184]

So if you see the world primarily in terms of black, white, yellow, and red, know that the idea of those races as meaningful categories of people was invented by a dude who believed in werewolves.

In the 1830s, Samuel Morton developed "craniometry," the practice of measuring skulls, to give these racial categories the veneer of being based in evidence. Morton believed in polygenesis—the belief that different races of humans had been created separately by God—rather than monogenesis, the belief that all humanity came from one common ancestry. Morton's data on skulls revealed that white people had the biggest skulls and Black people had the smallest—evidence, according to him, that white people had superior intelligence and therefore slavery was justified. However, according to historian Steven Jay Gould, Morton got these findings by selectively reporting data, manipulating samples, and mismeasuring skulls, allowing his bias, either consciously or unconsciously, to skew his results.[185]

Along comes Darwin, who would revolutionize our understanding of evolutionary biology. But as we saw with Linnaeus (whose taxonomies for categorizing plants and animals have proved foundational for biologists) mapping observations of the natural world onto human society is a dangerous business.

Some Darwinian historians claim that he wasn't racist, because he was a staunch abolitionist. But Darwin, like many white Europeans of his time, also believed in racial hierarchy, and he wrote, "the civilised races of man will almost certainly exterminate and replace throughout the world the savage races."[186] Fucking *yikes*.

Regardless of what Darwin himself thought, his theory of natural selection was eagerly adopted by nineteenth-century race scientists and weaponized against non-white peoples worldwide. These race scientists pointed to the fact that Europeans had colonized the entire planet as evidence of European racial superiority. Darwin had argued that "survival of the fittest" was a law of nature, so, as these followers of his alleged, didn't that make the people in charge the "fittest?"

Darwin's ideas also influenced a wave of late-nineteenth- and early-twentieth-century scientists who embraced eugenics—the idea that humanity should be improved through selective breeding. Ever since, eugenics has been used to justify genocide all over the world. Notably, Nazis were eugenicists who believed in improving the human race by mass-murdering Jews. Because, remember, Nazis believed that Jews were of a different race—a race of Semites, "sons of Shem," because way back in 1785, Johann Christoph Gatterer said so. Then, in the 1860s, Wilhelm Marr made Antisemitism a political platform. Manufacturing hate to kill people and take their stuff? It was the old, medieval Judenhass, but with new, pseudo-scientific trappings.

The bogus race science of Gatterer, Linnaeus, Morton, and Marr continues to this day in the racist apartheid state of Israel, where only Jews have a right to settle and enjoy full civil and legal protections under the law.[187] Because I have a Jewish grandmother, I could claim "birthright" and move to the West Bank and steal a Palestinian's home at gunpoint, and the Israeli military and courts would back up my right to do so. According to Zionists, my "Jewish race" (not a real thing) gives me this right, even though that Palestinian family may have lived on that land for tens of generations, while my ancestors all came from Eastern Europe.

In this apartheid state, Palestinians are not included in the Jewish race, and can therefore be treated as subhuman. Even Palestinian Israeli citizens do not have equal civil rights under the law. And, at the moment, Palestinians in Gaza do not even have the most basic of human rights, as Israel is restricting their access to food and water, destroying anything that might shelter them, and is actively mass-murdering them.

Since Zionism was first articulated, anti-Zionist Jews have called out the fact that Zionism *is* Antisemistism—and I'm using the capital-A term Antisemitism here, in the historical sense, as in, the political ideology of Wilhelm Marr and other proto-Nazis.

You'll recall that regular-degular Judenhassers, since the Middle Ages, had hated us Jews because they thought we were wizards who worshipped the devil and drank blood. If we'd just cut it out and convert to Christianity, we'd be fine in their books. But Marr and his self-titled Antisemites were modern, secular men who hated us because we were a different race, according to "science." If Jews were a different race, this meant no matter what Jews did— no matter how much we assimilated to German culture, secularized, gave up our languages and cultural distinctions, and even converted—Jews would still be a threat to Germany, because our "badness," according to Antisemites, was racial, was in our blood.

In "Towards a History of the Term Antisemitism," historian David Feldman explains that in the early twentieth century, this distinction felt so novel that Jewish writers such as Lucien Wolf were careful to distinguish between this new Antisemitism thing taking hold in Germany, and the old-fashioned Judenhass of Russia. The latter, Wolf assumed, was just that old medieval superstition that was sure to die out in a modernizing world.[188]

Lucien Wolf was also a fiercely anti-Zionist Jew because he saw Zionists agreeing with Antisemites' worst fantasies. Antisemites claimed Jews could never be truly German, and Zionists were saying the same exact thing. Wolf said, "To claim a Jewish nationality now … would be to shipwreck all the rights we have gained in Western countries, and so far from helping our persecuted brethren in [Eastern Europe], we should involve the whole of Jewry in one great outburst of justified anti-Semitism."[189] Now I don't love the word "justified" in that quote, that is some stanky, victim-blaming respectability politics. But Wolf's prediction was not wrong.

Early Zionists were the original self-hating Jews, expressing an open dislike of their fellow European Jews that mirrored the rhetoric of Antisemites. Vladimir (Ze'ev) Jabotinsky, one of the founders of the Zionist movement, described his fantasy of transforming the Jews of Europe, whom he saw as nebbishy and despicable, into a new, macho, tough-guy kind of Jew. "Because the Yid is ugly, sickly, and lacks decorum, we shall endow the ideal image of the Hebrew with masculine beauty. The Yid is trodden upon and easily frightened and, therefore, the Hebrew ought to be proud and independent. The Yid is despised by all and, therefore, the Hebrew ought to charm all. The Yid has accepted submission and, therefore, the Hebrew ought to learn how to command. The Yid wants to conceal his identity from strangers and, therefore, the Hebrew should look the world straight in the eye and declare: "I am a Hebrew!"[190] Talk about toxic masculinity—Jabotinsky was the Andrew Tate of the early twentieth century.

Zionists in Jabotinsky's time, and to this day, insist Jews must all come to Israel, because we will never truly be safe or at home anywhere else in the world. When I heard this sort of rhetoric as a child—one who had never had any particular interest in Israel—I found the idea weird and presumptuous. If I was going to claim a spiritual homeland anywhere, it would've been Japan—the home of Nintendo and Final Fantasy and my beloved Sailor Moon and Studio Ghibli cartoons. Only now do I realize just how Antisemitic it is to claim that I "belong" in Israel, because of my Jewish race. Guess who else agreed that Jews did not belong in Europe and must be expelled? Adolf Hitler and Wilhelm Marr!

Joe Biden has also echoed this rhetoric throughout 2024, repeatedly claiming things like, "Were there no Israel, there's not a Jew in the world who will be safe."[191] What the hell are you talking about, Joe? Is that a threat? Sounds like capital-A Antisemitism to me.

In the early twentieth century, anti-Zionists like Lucien Wolf wanted to see equal rights for Jews, wherever they might live. Wolf fought for minority rights at the Paris Peace Conference after World War I and secured the "minority treaties" from the League of Nations, which were supposed to protect ethnic and religious minorities across Europe. Given that the Holocaust would take place a few decades later, this treaty obviously did not pan out, because the League of Nations was even more toothless and ineffective than today's UN. As Wolf said, "scarcely had the ink of the signatures become dry before various provisions of the Treaties were violated in Poland, Romania, Hungary, Lithuania, and Greece."[192]

Following World War I, half of Europe was desperately impoverished, and desperately impoverished people are easy to manipulate. Antisemitic politicians were getting elected by whipping up hate towards Jews, and Eastern and Central Europe saw an explosion in anti-Jewish violence. By the 1930s, Wolf and other Jewish writers dropped the distinction between the old, superstitious Judenhass and the new, political Antisemitism.[193] They started using the terms synonymously, because hate is hate. You can give it a shiny new coat of paint, but it's the same old shit. After World War II, lowercase "antisemitism" emerged as the dominant English term for anti-Jewish hate, whether it was coming from self-described Antisemitic politicians or not. Scholars even began to use the word to describe events that took place long before Wilhelm Marr had popularized it in the 1860s.

David Feldman argues that the meaning of the word "antisemitism" changed once again, with the founding of the state of Israel in 1948. Shortly thereafter, Zionists began making the bullshit claim that serves as the title of this chapter: "Criticizing Israel Is Antisemitism." Bullshit, because Zionists, as Lucien Wolf correctly identified in the 1920s, have always *been* Antisemites! Zionists did not *like* Jews, as we were, and they agreed with Antisemites that Jews did not belong in Europe.

Early Zionists actively collaborated with Antisemites to displace Jews to their colony in Palestine. Theodor Herzl, known as the Father of Zionism, wrote in his diaries that "the anti-Semites will become our most dependable friends, the anti-Semitic countries our allies."[194] Herzl courted Arthur Balfour, an Antisemitic British politician and Christian Zionist who had sponsored the Aliens Act, which prevented Jewish immigration to England. Herzl and Balfour's partnership led to the Balfour Declaration in 1917. In that fateful decree, Balfour stated Britain's intent to support a Jewish "national home" in Palestine. This Jewish home would serve two purposes. First, it would extend British influence in Greater Syria and Iraq, while outsourcing the cost of maintaining that influence onto Jews. And secondly, a Jewish home in Palestine would attract Jewish immigration—emptying Europe of all those no-good, dirty, money-grubbing Jews.

Zionists were also on strikingly good terms with the Nazi Party throughout the 1930s. Historian Joseph Massad details the extent of their collaboration: "In 1935, the German Zionist branch was the only political force that supported the Nazi Nuremberg Laws in the country, and was the only party still allowed to publish its own newspaper the *Rundschau* until after Kristallnacht in 1938. Nazi officials would visit Palestine as guests of the Zionists in 1934 and in 1937."[195]

In 1933, Zionists struck a deal with Nazi Germany called the Haavara Agreement. The Nazi Party at this time was facing a global Jewish-led boycott of its goods—one that had cut German exports to the US by over 70 percent and was a significant concern for Nazi party leadership.[196] The Haavara Agreement broke this boycott, allowing German Jews seeking to flee the Nazi regime to move to Palestine, provided that they first purchased essential goods manufactured in Germany and had them shipped to Palestine in advance of their departure. By 1939, 105 million marks worth of German goods were imported to Palestine under this program. In today's US dollars, that's close to $800 million of Jewish wealth that was transferred into the Nazi-controlled German economy by the Haavara Agreement.[197]

Nowadays, Zionists justify Haavara, and the breaking of the Jewish boycott, as a necessary evil, motivated purely by a desire to help German Jews escape Hitler's clutches. But, as Massad points out, the idea that Zionists were so concerned with the fate of German Jews "does not square with the facts that during Nazi rule, Jews from Britain and the United States were given priority by the Zionists over German Jews for immigration to Palestine. Indeed, two-thirds of German Jewish applicants to immigrate to Palestine were turned down by the Zionists."[198] Granted, Zionists in Palestine could not have accepted everyone, even if they wanted to, as Palestine was still under the British Mandate. Britain set quotas for immigration that became severely limited after 1936, when Britain sought to quell tensions between the influx of recently-arrived Jewish European immigrants and Palestinians. However, throughout the 1930s, Zionists gave thousands of these limited slots away to applicants from the US and the UK.[199] These Western Jews were not in immediate danger of antisemitic violence the way Jews in Nazi Germany were, but they better met the Zionists' criteria of young, able-bodied, Hebrew-speaking, and independently wealthy applicants.[200]

Do many nation-states, to this day, employ classist, eugenicist, and white supremacist immigration requirements? Of course. In 2018, Trump notoriously questioned why the US should accept immigrants from "shithole countries" in Africa, as he pursued policies of closing US borders to anyone from the Global South—immigration policies that Democrats under Joe Biden continued. So it's not *surprising* that early Zionists had racist, classist, eugenicist priorities when it came to immigration as well. But these features prove that they were more motivated by those concerns than by a desire to save all their Jewish brethren from the threat of Nazism.

Zionists did not only direct European Jews towards Palestine. In "Sephardim in Israel: Zionism from the Standpoint of its Jewish Victims," Israeli historian Ella Shohat explores how Zionists also directly and indirectly instigated the mass displacement of Arab Jews to Israel, where they met with structural racism at the hands of an elite Ashkenazi minority.

Arab Jews, prior to the establishment of Israel, lived "comfortably" within Muslim-majority countries, where "the situation of these Jews over fifteen centuries was undeniably better than in the Christian countries."[201] Yes, both Jews and Christians in these countries held *dhimmi* legal status as "tolerated and protected minorities," but this inequality was "not the product of a pathological European-style anti-Semitism."[202] These Sephardic Jews, Shohat states, "were simply not eager to settle in Palestine and had to be 'lured' to Zion."[203] In many cases, Arab Jews were not easily lured, and Shohat charts the history of early twentieth-century anti-Zionist resistance from Jewish communities in Palestine, Iraq, Syria, and North Africa.

Unfortunately, that resistance proved short-lived. Aggressive Zionist colonization in Palestine—well underway decades before the official establishment of Israel—raised tensions between Muslim Arabs and their Jewish Arab neighbors, whether those Jews were Zionists or not. "Zionism, then, brought a painful binarism into the formerly peaceful relationship between the two communities... For the first time in Sephardi history, Arabness and Jewishness were posed as antonyms."[204] Arab Jewish communities that had existed for centuries were increasingly forced to choose between their Arabness and their Jewishness, and most would choose their Judaism.

Still, despite rising tensions and a few, isolated acts of mob violence towards Jews in Arab countries, by 1950 "most Arab Jews were not Zionist and remained reluctant to emigrate."[205] Shohat explains how the Iraqi government, under pressure from international Zionists, worked together with Israeli Zionists to inspire Jews to leave the country. When luring the Jews of Baghdad to Israel with financial incentives failed, "a Jewish underground cell, commanded by secret agents sent from Israel, planted bombs in Jewish centers so as to create hysteria among Iraqi Jews and thus catalyze a mass exodus to Israel."[206] To this day, Zionists and the Israeli government deny that Israel had anything to do with the bombings. But in his 2023 book, *Three Worlds: Memoirs of an Arab-Jew*, Avi Shlaim, whose family fled Baghdad in the wake of the bombings, concluded after extensive research that at least three of the bombings were carried out by Israeli agents.[207] In the wake of the bombing, 110,000 Iraqi Jews immigrated to Israel.

The Ashkenazi Zionist elites who orchestrated the mass migration of Jews from Baghdad, as well as from Yemen, Algeria, Morocco, and other Arab countries, espoused openly racist attitudes towards these Arab Jews, viewing them as uneducated, superstitious, and even subhuman. Former Prime Minister David Ben-Gurion described Arab Jews as people, "without a trace of Jewish or human education."[208] Still, Ashkenazi Zionists desired Arab Jewish workers to serve as a captive pool of manual labor, though they were concerned about too-large of an Arab Jewish population "tainting" their society. As a result, only select "young and healthy" people were chosen for immigration, a "quasi-eugenic selection," "repeated during the fifties in Morocco, where young men were chosen for aliya* on the basis of physical and gymnastic tests."[209]

....
* Jewish immigration to Israel

Only after the Holocaust, when the majority of European Jews chose to immigrate anywhere other than Israel, did "the Zionist establishment [decide]to bring Sephardi immigrants en masse."[210] Zionists needed the large populations of Jews throughout the Arab world to accomplish their settler-colonial aims.

Because settler colonizers aren't supposed to do manual labor, you guys!!! That's hard work!!! That's for Indigenous and Black and Brown people!!! Related fun fact, residential construction in Israel fell by 95 percent in the last months of 2023, because after October 7th, Israel suspended work permits to the Palestinians from Gaza and the West Bank who perform the manual labor that is the bedrock of the Israeli economy.[211] For the summer of 2024, Israel imported Indian people to do its agricultural labor—a move those farmworkers would quickly regret, as they have been subjected to widespread labor violations, wage theft, and subhuman living conditions since arriving in Israel.[212]

Back in the 1950s, Ashkenazi Zionists wanted Arab Jews to do all that sweaty, outdoorsy labor for them. Israel colluded with Arab governments in Yemen, Algeria, Morocco, and Iraq to convince Arab Jews to move to Israel through a combination of lofty promises, financial coercion, and anti-Jewish rhetoric. Shohat details how as soon as these Arab Jews came under the power of Zionists, they were dehumanized and exploited, in many of the same ways that Indian farmworkers in Israel have been dehumanized and exploited this past year, and as Palestinian workers were dehumanized and exploited before them.

After the creation of the state of Israel in 1948, when 10,000 Yemeni Jews had been convinced to move to Israel by Zionist propaganda, they found themselves forced into hard agricultural labor, abused, and crowded into cellars or forced to live in the fields they worked, where "unsanitary conditions and malnutrition caused widespread disease and death, especially of infants."[213] Once again, Nazi-esque, eugenicist ideas justified such treatment. When similarly "inhuman conditions" on the migration route between Yemen and Israel resulted in "hunger, disease, and massive death," Itzhak Refael of Israel's Nationalist Religious Party reassured Zionist investors that "there is no need to fear the arrival of a large number of chronically ill, as they have to walk by foot for about two weeks. The gravely ill will not be able to walk."[214] Some 850 Yemeni Jews died in trying to reach Israel. Seeing as these Yemeni Jews were intended for exploitative hard labor, Refael saw their deaths as a feature, not a bug.

As rumors of the inhuman treatment of Yemeni Jews in Israel reached North Africa, immigration declined. Algerian Jews were staying in transit camps in crowded, makeshift tin structures (sounding much like the types of housing accommodations now afforded to Indian laborers in Israel). When a group of these Algerians tried to go back home, they were taken onto the ships "by force."[215] Once they arrived in Israel, Zionists separated Arab families and communities against their will, replaced their given names with more "Jewish" ones, and moved them largely to rural territories where Palestinians had been most recently displaced. In these border towns, Arab Jews faced discrimination in "infrastructural needs, educational and cultural advantages and political self-representation" compared to Ashkenazi communities.[216]

The Zionist desire to destroy Arab Jewish communities was most horrifyingly expressed in the human trafficking of some 600 Yemenite babies in the 1950s. Israeli medical personnel stole babies from their biological parents, who were told their children had died in childbirth, and gave the infants to Ashkenazi families.[217] During this time, perhaps 2,000 babies of Yemeni and North African Jewish immigrants were either kidnapped and trafficked or died in medical care, and their bodies were never returned to their families. In 2021, the Israeli government declined to apologize, but rather expressed its "regret" for the stolen children and offered financial compensation to 1,050 of these families, whose cases had been previously vetted. Families could only claim this compensation (equivalent to between $46,000-$61,000) if they agreed to waive the right to any future legal action against the Israeli government.[218]

European Zionist Jews had fled the ghettoes of Europe, only to ensnare their Arab Jewish cousins in a similar system of structural racism, poverty, and disenfranchisement. European Zionist Jews had fled the genocidal, eugenicist violence of the Nazi regime, only to enact genocide on Palestinians and eugenics on Arab Jews. As Lucien Wolf predicted way back in the 1920s, by actively relocating Jewish communities around the globe to Israel, European Zionist Jews fulfilled the ambitions of Antisemites like Wilhelm Marr and Adolf Hitler.

Whether you call it Antisemitism, anti-Semitism, antisemitism, Judenhass, racism, anti-Arab hate, or Islamophobia—hate is hate. All these terms stand for different flavors of white supremacy, and all that's changed from Nazi Germany to modern-day Israel is who gets to define whiteness.

So when the Anti-Defamation League,* a university board of trustees, major Western media outlets, or the US Congress say, "anti-Zionism is antisemitism," that's like saying a thing is its opposite. It's as absurd as saying, "anti-racism is racism." *Zionism* is Antisemitism—Lucien Wolf correctly identified that truth a century ago, and thousands of anti-Zionist Jews like me are still shouting it today. Our antisemitism historian, David Feldman, sums up the absurdity of Israel's redefinition, writing, "The creation of the state of Israel transformed the relationship of Jews to state power ... it fundamentally changed the relationship of Jews to the question of minorities." In terms of the persecutions they faced, and their material reality, my Jewish European ancestors had way more in common with today's Palestinians than they do with today's Israeli Jews.

Lately, whenever I hear someone use the word "antisemitism," I tune out, assuming whatever comes next will be Zionist bullshit. And even though capital-A Antisemitism was coined to mean Jew-hate, and has always been used to mean Jew-hate, Palestinians and Arabs generally feel erased by the term, and I take that seriously. I don't see the point in continuing to use a term that is confusing, that Zionists have twisted to mean its opposite, that was coined by Hitler's idol, and is based in eighteenth-century race science.

So I've gone back to using the OG term *Judenhass*, or, in English, "anti-Jewish hate." That's actually one syllable shorter than "antisemitism," a meaningful time-saver for a content creator like me. With the term "anti-Jewish hate," you can swap out the "anti-Jewish" part for "anti-queer," "anti-disability," or "anti-Black," making clearer the commonality between anti-Jewish hate and all other hates. Seeing that commonality is crucial if we ever want to end hate, end genocide, and achieve collective liberation.

....
* The ADL is a non-governmental organization that claims to "combat antisemitism, bigotry, and discrimination," but its true purpose is to silence criticism of Zionism and Israel.

How Israel legitimizes anti-Jewish hate

Israel doesn't just do the work of Antisemites by depopulating diaspora communities. Israel, by conflating itself with Judaism, and then behaving evilly, confirms hateful stereotypes about Jews. It's like the state of Israel keeps looking at the worst things Christians have ever imagined about us, and saying, "Hold my beer."

Take the story of blood libel, which you'll recall is the lie that Jews kill gentiles and eat them or drink their blood.[219] By the medieval period, the accusation that Jews kidnapped and used the blood of Christian babies, specifically, to make matzoh for the Passover seder was used to justify massacres of Jews and the theft of their property.[220] Quick recap: there is zero credible historical evidence that any Jews ever did such a thing. The medieval Christian church made up stories like this to manufacture hate towards Jews, Romanies, Christian heretics, and Indigenous European faiths alike as a divide-and-conquer tactic. This story effectively distracted peasants from realizing that church leaders were the ones who were stealing all their wealth and keeping them in poverty, so the pope could build giant, gold cathedrals. This divide-and-conquer ruling strategy still works great for gold-loving property developers today—see: Donald Trump.

Accusing the people you intend to genocide of baby-killing is also still effective propaganda—hence, the bullshit "Hamas beheaded 40 babies" story, which both Israeli heads of state and the US president repeated in October 2023, but which the Israeli government press office has since admitted was a lie.[221]

Anti-antisemitism educators, like I used to be, spend a lot of time online endlessly repeating that, no, Jews don't and never did kidnap babies and kill them for use in religious rituals. The hateful allegation of blood libel is something our community has been fighting for over a thousand years.

But then along came the State of Israel, and they slapped a Star of David on their flag and claimed to speak for all Jews everywhere. They have made themselves synonymous with Judaism as far as Western governments and media are concerned—and you know what else they've done?

They've routinely kidnapped, tortured, and massacred children through every year of their existence.

An estimated 10,000 Palestinian children have been kidnapped from their families and held as political prisoners by the Israeli military over the past twenty years, held without sentence and prosecuted by military courts.[222] Since October 7th, 2023, children released from Israeli prisons report beatings and torture, medical neglect, and starvation within Israeli detention.[223] But the routine abuse of children did not begin on October 7th. Ten years ago, a social justice group found that 40 percent of children detained in Jerusalem were sexually abused by Israeli police.[224] And since October 2023, the genocide in Gaza has physically and psychologically tortured over a million children. Tens of thousands of children have been violently killed by the Israeli state in every manner imaginable—bombed, sniped, suffocated, burned alive, beheaded, vaporized, gassed, and crushed to death by buildings and tanks. One six-year-old girl, Hind Rajab, was trapped in a car for hours with the dead bodies of six of her relatives, as she waited for rescue from paramedics. When the ambulance arrived, Israeli forces destroyed it with an anti-tank round. The bodies of the paramedics and Hind Rajab were not able to be recovered until two weeks later. The car containing Hind, her cousins, and her aunt and uncle had been shot 355 times.[225]

Israel's total siege of the Gaza Strip has killed tens of thousands more Palestinian children by starvation, dehydration, and medical neglect. Babies and toddlers, like Manal Mattar whom this book is dedicated to, are dying from heart attacks, because of the intensity of their fear and trauma. Some children have even contracted polio, and at the time of writing, at least one was paralyzed by this nearly extinct disease. Twenty-one thousand children in Gaza are reported missing; 17,000 are reported orphaned.[226] All have lost loved ones. All have seen horrific violence that no child should have to witness. All have been tormented by preventable disease, starvation, exposure to the Eastern Mediterranean winter and summer, and psychological torture from the constant threat of violence and omnipresence of deafeningly loud drones overhead. All are now at a greatly increased risk of cancer due to ingesting polluted water and inhaling clouds of particulate matter, including asbestos, from demolished buildings. Almost all have been forcibly displaced multiple times, all have witnessed the near-total destruction of their community, and all have experienced a level of trauma even most hardened combat veterans can scarcely imagine. If the genocide ends tomorrow, the physical and psychological aftereffects of so much trauma will reverberate for generations.

All these horrific acts towards children have been committed under the blue-and-white Star of David. So that even I, a Jew, can't look at this symbol of my people's faith anymore without feeling sick to my stomach. Some anti-Zionist Jews want to fight to reclaim the Magen David from Zionists, and more power to them. But for me, this symbol has become irreparably associated with hatred. I flinch at the sight of it, the same way I flinch at a swastika or the Confederate flag. I've packed away in the attic all our Judaica decorated with the Star of David, because I can't stand to look at it anymore. I got myself a new menorah carved from a lovely piece of cherrywood.

I'm not giving anyone carte blanche here to shower hatred on Jews who choose to still wear or display the Star of David——that symbol is much older than the state of Israel. I'm just being real about how it makes me feel, and I'm Jewish! I'm sure many others who are not Jewish, and who have closely paid attention to this genocide, also feel strong, negative feelings when they see the Magen David.

Thanks for that, Israel.

Israel's crimes against humanity have been filmed and broadcast to millions of people around the world, along with the desperate pleas of children for aid, the screams of people burning alive in tents, and the wails of those trapped under rubble who cannot be reached. Meanwhile, Israeli IOF soldiers have been doing cutesy TikTok dances on the ruins of families' homes and posting videos of themselves playing mockingly with the toys of the children they've massacred.[227] Not only do Israeli Jews mass-murder children, they do so with *glee*.

Anyone who dares to publicly criticize this massacre of children gets accused of antisemitism by Zionists. And not just by Israeli Zionists, but by Western media, politicians, and celebrities marching in genocidal apologia lockstep. No one is immune to charges of antisemitism, including Jewish politicians, like Jill Stein or Bernie belatedly-calling-for-a-ceasefire Sanders, Jewish film directors, like Jonathan Glazer and Sarah Friedman, and even rabbis and Holocaust survivors who organize with Jewish Voice for Peace.

Anti-Zionist Jews like me can shout ourselves hoarse that Israel does not speak for all Jews, but all the most powerful voices of Western empire keep contradicting us, relentlessly pushing the narrative that Israel = Jews.

Now, bear with me, the transitive law of mathematics states that if a=b, and b=c, then a=c. So, if Jews = Israel (as Zionists insist) and Israel = baby-killers (which I have demonstrated is a fact) that means Jews = baby-killers. So we're right back to blood libel! All those years I spent trying to convince the internet that Jews don't kill babies, flushed down the toilet by tens of thousands of videos of the Israeli army massacring children.

And Israel isn't just enacting blood libel. Israel outperforms all kinds of harmful stereotypes about Jews! Have you heard that we're greedy? Wait till you learn how, during the Nakba, Israel stole not just Palestinian land, homes, and possessions, but everything in their bank accounts too.[228] A crime it repeated this year, stealing $54 million from Gaza banks.[229]

Have you heard the one about a global cabal of wealthy Jews controlling Western governments, media, and education? Wait till you learn about AIPAC* spending over $100 million to influence the US election this year alone![230] Or how the CEOs of major news networks have admitted to taking direct marching orders from Israeli government officials about how to report on the region, and even who they should fire for being too sympathetic to Palestinians.[231] Wait till you hear how Columbia University was pressured by Congress, which is bought out by AIPAC, to remove due process for students who participated in anti-genocide protests this past spring.[232]

That stereotype, the one about Jews plotting to take over the world, originally derives from one of the most enduring and damaging pieces of anti-Jewish hate in history: *The Protocols of the Elders of Zion*. This fraudulent book, most likely written by Russian secret police, claims to report the meeting minutes of a group of Zionists who are plotting to take over the world. *The Protocols* may have originated as satire, an in-group joke among Jew-hating Russians mocking early Zionists' ambitions. But it was later published under the guise of a serious, leaked document, and the years after its publication saw a surge in violence towards Jewish communities. In 1921, the British newspaper *The Times* provided conclusive evidence that it was a forgery, with portions of the text copied from an earlier work of French political propaganda, Maurice Joly's "Dialogues in Hell Between Machiavelli and Montesquieu."[233] The writers of *The Protocols* had simply swapped in Jews for Napoleon III.

....
*   American Israel Public Affairs Committee, a pro-Israel lobbying group

Keep in mind, the "Protocols" were published at a time when Jews were some of the most vulnerable and impoverished people in Russian territory. The Russian imperial army had violently forced tens of thousands of Jews from their homelands into a strip of land the Western Russian empire called the Pale of Settlement. The Pale covered parts of current-day Ukraine, Belarus, Poland, and the Baltic States, so it was much larger than other territorial ghettos like, say, the Gaza Strip or the West Bank. But like Palestinians, many of the Jews in the Pale had been forced there by violence, and within the Pale, their movement, civil rights, and economic activity were tightly constrained by a racist imperial army. Jews of the Pale, like Palestinians of the West Bank, faced frequent pogroms—outbursts of mob violence from their non-Jewish neighbors.

Many people are unaware, even today, that the *Protocols* is a forgery. As a Jew who talks about anti-Jewish hate, I have gotten many comments over the years mentioning the *Protocols* as something "everyone should read to know the truth about Jews." Sometimes these comments clearly come from openly white-supremacist neo-Nazi accounts. Sometimes they come from well-meaning folks whose compassionate support for Palestinians has led them down a rabbit hole of misinformation. Regardless, both these types of comments used to trigger the ol' epigenetic trauma for me, and I would immediately delete those comments and block whoever posted them.

But, god help me, there's nuance here that needs to be unpacked. If we're going to talk with clarity about anti-Jewish hate, we need to look with clear eyes at what is frequently cited as the single most influential document driving anti-Jewish hate.

So I decided to actually read the *Protocols of the Elders of Zion*. And I have to admit: folks who have paid close attention to the actions and speech of the Israeli government over the past year may be forgiven for thinking this document might be legit. (Again, it's not!). But what I found most striking is how Israel has rendered the *Protocols* totally obsolete. Because on a weekly basis, Israeli government officials say and do shit that's at least as genocidal and megalomaniacal as anything contained in that document.

Nothing in the falsified *Protocols* is as shocking as the fact that Israel is mass-torturing and mass-raping Palestinian civilians, including children and medical workers who have been indiscriminately arrested in Gaza, in a network of torture camps. At these camps, of which the notorious Sde Teiman is only one, Israeli guards have raped their victims with fire extinguishers,[234] hot metal sticks, cattle prods,[235] and trained dogs.[236] Why would you turn to the comparatively tame *Protocols* to stoke hatred of Jews, when instead you could just point at the Israeli Jews who rioted in support of the IOF's *right to rape people*, after a few soldiers at Sde Teiman were detained for such practices?[237] Why use the words of Victorian Zionists, when you could play a clip of a member of the Israeli Knesset in 2024, who, when asked if it was legitimate to rape someone with a stick, responded "Yes! If he is a Nukhba,* everything is legitimate to do! Everything!"[238]

There's just no reason to point to a debunked, century-old forgery to whip up hatred of Jews. Just look at what Israel is up to! It's almost like the Knesset has taken the *Protocols of the Elders of Zion* as a guidebook.

Take the opening claim of the *Protocols*: that "might makes right." What could be a greater expression of this ideology than a country that claims to have "the most moral army in the world" while bombing hospitals, schools, bakeries, places of worship, and densely populated refugee camps?

Take Protocol 7, in which the elders plot to "create ferments, discords, and hostility" throughout other continents, in order to "keep in check all countries, for they well know that we have the power whenever we like to create disorders or to restore order."[239] Since its inception, Israel has destabilized other sovereign nations. Across Latin America, Israel has funded, trained, armed, and even fought alongside brutal right-wing dictatorships and militias.[240] In Sudan right now, Israel is exerting influence on *both* sides of the regional civil war, because Israeli leadership is split on who to support, with the Israeli Foreign Ministry working with General al-Burhan of the Sudanese Armed Forces, and the Mossad wanting to back Hemedti, head of the opposing Rapid Support Forces. Israel's indecisive involvement, along with the US, Saudi Arabia, and the UAE's meddling, "has significantly hindered efforts to resolve the ongoing conflict" in Sudan, according to the Arab Center Washington DC.[241] Volumes of books can, and have, been written about Israeli efforts to destabilize the Arab nations it shares borders with—Egypt, Lebanon, Syria, Jordan, and, of course, Palestine.

....
* Al-Nukhba is the special forces unit of Hamas's military wing.

AIPAC, the ADL, and the Israeli government's extreme influence over USian politics, media, and universities come to mind when you read Protocol 9: "We have got our hands into the administration of the law, into the conduct of elections, into the press, into liberty of the person, but principally into education and training."[242] Who can doubt it, when lawmakers across the globe have criminalized criticism of Israel and Zionism over the past year? When countless students have been disciplined, arrested, stripped of their diplomas, and in some cases expelled for peacefully protesting against Israel's genocide?

I could go on and on and on, drawing comparisons between practically each sentence of the *Protocols* and the actions of Zionists. But again—we know *conclusively* that this book was a forgery! So what's up with that similarity? How does a 120-year-old book describe the actions of the modern-day nation-state of Israel so well?

Easy. Because *The Protocols of the Elders of Zion* describes the behavior of empire.

Any empire!

Remember that saying I keep coming back to—"every accusation is a confession"? That adage seems to be true of most imperialists throughout history, not just of Zionists. The *Protocols of the Elders of Zion* doesn't capture how *Jews* think and behave, it captures how imperialists think and behave—and that includes Napoleon III, who was the target of the original ripped-off book the *Protocols* was based on. The early twentieth-century Russians who created the forgery were imperialists, and so are present-day Israeli Zionists. The *Protocols* also does a pretty accurate job describing US empire. Destabilizing other countries? Of course we do! Might makes right? Sure seems like that that's our doctrine, when the US promotes itself as some moral authority, despite waging perma-wars in other countries, imposing sanctions that starve millions, incarcerating more people per capita than any country on earth, and being founded on genocide and slavery!

So in the *Protocols*, the Russian secret police were telling on themselves. At the time, Russia was seeking imperial domination, conquering vast swaths of the European continent, and trying to exterminate undesirable ethnic and religious groups within its colonies. For the Russians, perhaps the joke (because remember, the book may have begun as satire), was that these impoverished, stateless Jews could ever hope to achieve the kind of authoritarian empire that they currently enjoyed. "Shlomo ben Yid-face thinks he's gonna win over the masses by controlling the media, like we do? What a laugh!"

The colonizer's paranoia likely also motivated the writing of the *Protocols*. As I shared in the section "Won't anyone think of the colonizers?", enslavers fear being enslaved in turn. Genociders fear being genocided. When Palestinians call for *freedom* "from the river to the sea," Zionists hear them calling for genocide—even while Israelis are the ones *actually carrying out genocide*! In the *Protocols*, Russian imperialists accused Jews of plotting to oppress gentiles, while the Russians were the ones *currently oppressing Jews*.

Another kernel of truth here is that early Zionists really did want to imitate empires like Russia. Zionists—who represented a tiny minority of Jews at the time of the writing of the *Protocols*—wanted to overcome their oppression by becoming oppressors in turn. Early Zionists like Theodor Herzl and Vladimir (Ze'ev) Jabotinsky spoke openly of Zionism as a colonial project.

Jabotinsky, in his 1923 "Iron Wall" essay, said of Palestinians, "Every native population in the world resists colonists as long as it has the slightest hope of being able to rid itself of the danger of being colonized. That is what the Arabs in Palestine are doing, and what they will persist in doing as long as there remains a solitary spark of hope that they will be able to prevent the transformation of 'Palestine' into the 'Land of Israel.'"[243] Thus, Jabotinsky explains that an "Iron Wall" must separate Palestinians from the Jews—accurately predicting the apartheid walls that today separate Gaza and Palestinian areas of the West Bank from Israeli settlers.

Where had Jabotinsky and his ancestors seen such walls, dividing one captive, undesirable ethno-religious group from the ruling majority?

From the walls around Jewish ghettos in Europe, of course.

So from the very beginning, Zionism didn't seek to put an end to anti-Jewish hate, but to make Jews into the kind of people who would wield such hate against others. I suspect the *Protocols* began as a hyperbolic satire of the first Zionist Congress of 1897, and Zionists at that congress really were eager to make Jews into the kind of imperialists who had oppressed them for centuries. But those early Zionists were just focused on establishing a nation-state in Palestine, not on global domination. And Herzl and Jabotinsky still showed some humanitarian restraint. They wrote of buying out Palestinians, economic colonization, and erecting iron walls. They did not call for the mass-murder of gentiles, as Netanyahu does when he calls Palestinians "Amalek"—referencing a biblical story in which God called for Israelites to completely and totally destroy the Amalekites, down to their last possessions.

What the Russian secret police found both comical and terrifying about the first Zionist Congress was the idea that Jews—those nebbishy weirdos whom they'd been killing for sport for the last few centuries—might someday behave in exactly the same way their own empire did. And so, the *Protocols* exaggerated the scope of those early Zionists' ambitions. Being first-generation imperialists, early Zionists just didn't have the bloodthirsty, world-hungry imagination of long-practiced imperialists like the Russians who were spoofing them.

But by 2023, my God, Zionists have arrived as warlords.

Israel is living up to—if not exceeding—many of the predictions of those Russian secret police from the 1900s. But in the big scheme of things, Israel is still a bit player in a much larger Western empire. Empires destroy civilizations, commit genocide, and lie. That's the game—regardless of which religion or ethnicity is playing—and the mechanisms of that game just aren't that hard to predict.

So if you're horrified by the contents of the *Protocols*, you shouldn't hate Jews. You should hate empire, racial capitalism, authoritarianism, and colonization, wherever those forces exist. Which, unfortunately for us, is all over the world.

This book is focusing on Israel, though, not because of antisemitism, not because the world hates Jews in particular, but because Israel is currently enacting a genocide. Based on the findings of the Lancet, Israel has likely killed over 200,000 people in the past year at the time of writing this chapter.

And do I need to tap the cover again?

GENOCIDE BAD!!!

GENOCIDE VERY FUCKING BAD!!!!!

Anti-Zionist Jews like me may have spent the past year shouting ourselves hoarse in solidarity with Palestine, but the gutting truth is that the majority of Jews in the US, even throughout the diaspora, are likely still Zionists. We're gaining ground with young Jews, but a poll released in April of this year found that, despite watching months of Israel's genocide, 72 percent of US Jews still said "Israel makes them proud" and only 28 percent supported an "immediate ceasefire."[244] The latter number had risen since November, but only by 8 percent.[245] When most Jews are "proud" of the raping, torturing, genocidal Jewish nation-state, when thousands of other Jews in my comments have called me "not a real Jew" or a "self-hating Jew" for criticizing Israel, well then, you know what? I can stretch my imagination a little and understand where animosity towards Jews *as a whole* might be coming from.

But I'll remind you that the schism between Zionist and anti-Zionist Jews is as old as Zionism itself. Zionism emerged from a population of people who had faced dehumanizing racism, ghettoization, exile, and genocide for many centuries. After being on the receiving end of hate for over a millennium, Zionist Jews said, "We'll be the haters now!"

At first, most other Jews, including Lucien Wolf, responded like that *Veep* meme with, "What the fuck?" and "How about we just try to stop hate, altogether?!" Zionism in its first decades was an unpopular, fringe movement.

By the mid-twentieth century, however, Zionists were winning the ideological war. Partly because hurt people hurt people. Some who are abused as children will grow up to stop the cycle of violence, but many will perpetuate abuse onto their own kids. That kind of generational trauma can, clearly, also direct the behavior of entire ethnicities and religions.

But, to give us some credit, I suspect an even greater reason that Zionism became so successful is that empire prefers Jewish fascists to Jewish leftists.

Zionists made powerful allies among the Antisemitic nations of Europe, as Theodor Herzl had predicted. Zionists were enjoying the friendship of Arthur Balfour and the Nazi Party, while the anti-Zionist, socialist Jewish Labour Bund was being violently suppressed throughout Eastern Europe.[246] Zionists have continued to find ways to cozy up to white supremacist imperialists, making themselves useful to empire, whereas anti-Zionist lefty Jews seek to disrupt empire. US politicians don't deploy cops to violently suppress anti-Zionist Jewish speech because they genuinely think we're antisemitic, and they give a shit about anti-Jewish hate. They silence us because they think we're all commies! Nothing is more intolerable to US empire than socialist ideals like, IDK, "We should take care of one another."

So, Zionists have been rich, while anti-Zionists have been poor. Zionists have been defended by the most dangerous militaries on earth, while anti-Zionists have been beaten in the streets by the police of those nations.

Zionists' voices have been amplified by Western media, while anti-Zionist voices have been systematically shut out of publishing, academia, and the political sphere. Given all that, is it any wonder that Zionists have won most Jews over to their side, despite being morally bankrupt?

Only social media, and the inability of elites to fully control and censor it, has allowed anti-Zionist Jews to make serious headway in disrupting the Zionist narrative within the Jewish community over the course of the past year. We have truth and morality on our side, and through clever manipulation of social media algorithms, we've managed to broadcast that truth and moral clarity to a wider audience than ever before. I'm immensely proud of whatever part I may have played in that effort. And I hope that I'll see the end of a Zionist majority among US Jews in my lifetime. But we have a long way to go before that's the case, and all along, we'll be fighting some of the most powerful and wealthy interests on the planet.

I've explained how the word "antisemitism" comes from capital-A Antisemites, a German political party that was a forerunner of the Nazis. I've explained how Zionists share key ideas with those Antisemites—including the scientifically bogus idea that Jews are a distinct "race," and the idea that anyone who belongs to this Jewish race will never be at home in a non-Jewish nation. I've explained how Zionists accomplished the goals of Antisemites by working throughout their history to depopulate Jewish communities across the globe, even using violence to compel Jews to leave their homes and settle in Palestine. And I've demonstrated how, by continually doing evil shit, while claiming to be one and the same with Jewishness, the state of Israel spreads anti-Jewish hate all over the world.

To stand against anti-Jewish hate, therefore, *necessitates* criticizing Zionism.

But as a former anti-antisemitism educator, can I just say, I don't actually care much about "the anti-Jewish" part anymore. I want to stand against *hate*. I want to see an end to ALL the hates. Anti-Black, anti-queer, anti-Arab, anti-disability, etc., etc. Fuck all those hates.

And so, what's far more important to me than the fact that Zionism spreads anti-Jewish hate in these indirect ways is the fact that Zionism overtly spreads anti-Palestinian, anti-Muslim, and anti-Arab hate, in order to justify the genocide of these people.

Hate is manufactured by elites to dehumanize people, so you can kill them and steal their shit. That's what medieval Christians did to European Jews (and Muslims and pagans and Romani and Christian heretics and prostitutes and nuns). That's what the Nazis did to us as well. And that's what Zionist Jews do to Palestinians today.

Stars of David in Trump Country

If you're Palestinian, or you love a Palestinian person, or if you're Arab, or you love an Arab person, or even if you just see Arab people as people—then you have plenty of just cause to despise the State of Israel. And because of the conflation of Israel with Jewish people generally, I can understand why such people might have negative feelings towards Jews generally. In fact, it's sort of shocking that there isn't more anti-Jewish hate within the Free Palestine movement—but truly, in years of organizing, I have never encountered any.

During the student encampment protests of spring 2023, Western media was combing through the actions of thousands of student groups at hundreds of colleges for evidence of antisemitism, but all they found were a few singular instances of lone protesters calling aggressively Zionist students "Nazis." Big flipping deal—I've been called a Nazi by thousands of Zionists online—and you don't see me clutching my pearls to the *New York Times*.

All the Palestinian organizers I've worked with are crystal-clear that their beef is with Zionism, not Judaism. As I shared in Chapter 6, even Hamas is crystal clear that their beef is with Zionism, not Judaism!

Remember, the only people I've met who *actually* hated Jews were not Arab people; they were all rural, white, Republican Christians.

Nowadays, I live in Texas, where we have plenty of those. So imagine the mind-fuck when I started seeing the Star of David proliferating in Trump country this year. One day, I saw a rolling-coal Ford F-450 dually truck flying a full-size Israeli flag and a full-size Trump 2024 flag from the back two corners of its truck bed, and my brain almost broke. They're disappearing again now, but in those first few months after October 7th, any time I left central Houston, I'd see "Stand with Israel" bumper stickers next to "Thin Blue Line" stickers, and Israeli flags flying side by side with US flags outside of people's homes.

At this point, I would not be surprised to learn that Lauren Duchak, who once called me a "dirty Jew," had an Israeli flag emoji in her Instagram bio.

It's not that these Trumpers suddenly stopped hating Jews. It's that they hate Arabs way more. And white supremacists recognize other white supremacists. Fascists stick together.

If I were going to middle school in rural Texas in 2024, I might still get a little bit of shit for being Jewish, but if there were any Arab students in the school, I bet whatever bullying they'd face would be way, way worse. After October 7th, the Lauren Duchaks of my school might have let me cozy up to them, as long as I joined them in punching down on an even-more-despised minority. When I remember how lonely and desperate for acceptance I was in eighth grade, I have to admit—given the opportunity, I might have become the very kind of bully that bullied me.

On a national scale, and with unimaginably devastating consequences, that's what the nation of Israel and the ideology of Zionism have done.

In 1898, Viennese Jewish writer Karl Kraus lampooned Zionists in his essay "A Crown for Zion," in which he describes hearing the Antisemites cry "Out with you Jews!" And "Zionism replying with the echo, 'yes out with us Jews,' which apart from the more solemn tone doesn't exhibit the slightest difference."[247]

Zionism *is* antisemitism. Israel is an Antisemitic nation. And criticizing Israel is essential for fighting both anti-Jewish and anti-Arab, anti-Muslim, and anti-Palestinian hate.

9. "Jews Are Entitled to Palestine"

Zionists claim Jews have a right to Palestine. Actually, not just Palestine, many far-right Zionists insist that Jews have a right to what they call "Greater Israel," or *Eretz Yisrael,* which also would include the entirety of Lebanon and Jordan, plus parts of Egypt, Syria, Iraq, Saudi Arabia, and Kuwait. Perhaps the drive to establish Eretz Yisrael explains part of the IOF's motivation for launching a ground invasion of Lebanon—something that has just begun on October 2, 2024, the morning I am drafting this chapter.

So far, eight Israeli soldiers have been killed in the attempted invasion, and Western media is making several meals of these *specific* casualties. Cry me a river, though, because over the past week, Israel has killed over 500 civilians from their indiscriminate bombings in Lebanon.

Depending on how far-right and militaristic they are, Zionists disagree whether the nation-state of Israel should be expanded to contain most of the Middle East—as in the aspirational *Eretz Yisrael*—or just the Gaza Strip, the West Bank, and Golan Heights, or whether it should be limited to those borders established in 1967 at the end of the Six-Day War. But at the very least, all Zionists agree that Jews are entitled to a homeland outlined by the borders that Israel claimed by force in 1948.

What provides the basis of this entitlement?

Many Zionists treat the Bible as either a property deed or a history book. Some Jewish Zionists claim that their God promised them the land, and they find that rationale satisfactory for enacting genocide on the region's non-Jewish inhabitants. Even secular Zionists will still point to the Bible as if it is a reliable history book, saying the Torah provides proof that the Jews' "homeland" is where the modern-day nation-state of Israel is. (It doesn't.)

Other Zionists point to imperial legal documents to prove the validity of their nation-state. The Balfour Declaration, UN General Assembly Resolution 181 and Security Council Resolution 242, the Basic Laws of Israel, and a mountain of Israeli laws, property deeds, court cases, and military documents are the magical pieces of paper with ink on them that justify a century of massacring Palestinians and seizing their land.

When the African decolonization struggles of the 1960s and '70s engendered worldwide sympathy, Zionists rebranded themselves from "colonizers" to "Indigenous" people. They coopted the terminology of these struggles, claiming that Greek, Roman, and Arab colonizers expelled them from Palestine in the first place, so by returning to establish a Jewish nation-state they were just righting that ancient historical wrong. Since the 2010s, Zionists have compared their settler colonialism to the #LandBack movement of Indigenous people in Australia and the United States.

Finally, even if we reject all the above justifications, there's the matter of Israelis who were born and lived their entire lives on the soil of occupied Palestine. They didn't ask to be born there. Regardless of their parents' motivations or crimes—doesn't one have the right to continue living where they were born? And don't they have a right to self-determination—to decide how they will be governed? And to keep themselves safe?

"Jews are entitled to Palestine because the Bible says so"

Actually, it doesn't. And more importantly, who cares? Religious texts written thousands of years ago cannot provide the basis of how we organize ourselves in the twenty-first century as a pluralistic society of human beings with different and contradictory faith ancestries.

But even if, *even fucking if,* the Torah had any bearing on modern-day property disputes, what's actually *in* the Bible doesn't help the Zionist case all that much, as Israeli historian Shlomo Sand points out in *The Invention of the Land of Israel: From Holy Land to Homeland.* Because "neither Abraham, the Father of the nation, nor Moses, its first great prophet … were born in the land; instead, they migrated there from elsewhere."[248]

Abraham was a Babylonian, born in modern-day Iraq and living in Haran, in modern-day Turkey, when God told him, "Get thee out of thy country ... unto a land that I will show thee."[249] Abraham stays in Canaan—modern-day Palestine—for all of four verses of the Bible before moving on to Egypt because there was a famine in Canaan.[250] Meanwhile Moses, famously, was born and raised in Egypt, not Palestine.

Can we pause here for a quick reality check? There is no archaeological or historical evidence that Jews were ever enslaved in Egypt.[251] The falsehood of the Exodus story is an excellent reason to treat the Bible as nothing more than a work of ancient fiction, riddled with plot holes and contradictions, and one that encourages incest, child abuse, spousal abuse, child abandonment, human sacrifice, slavery, rape, murder, and genocide. And that's just in Genesis!

Shlomo Sand also charts the repeated insistence throughout the Bible that Jews not only weren't *from* Canaan, they also did not intermarry with the local Indigenous population. Isaac "imported the attractive Rebecca from abroad" and later, at Rebecca's urging, forbade his son Jacob from marrying a Canaanite woman.[252] Jacob, then, left Canaan, married his cousins Leah and Rachel, who were not Canaanites, and sired twelve sons and a daughter, "eleven of whom ... constituted the eponymous fathers of the tribes of Israel [and] were all born in a different land."[253] In Deuteronomy, Moses would again issue instructions to the Hebrews not to intermarry with any of the locals in Canaan.[254] The authors of Genesis went way out of their way to make clear that the Israelites are strangers in their own "promised land."

The character of God promises this land to Moses on Mount Sinai, while the Jews are wandering in the desert between Egypt and Canaan for forty years—in an area that can be crossed on foot in a matter of weeks. God promises Moses the land between "the Red Sea even unto the sea of the Philistines, and from the desert unto the river." This promised land, that roughly maps to modern-day Palestine, would be granted, conditional upon Moses keeping a series of commandments. But the commandments outlined in Exodus are literally impossible to keep, because even within that same book, many contradict each other. For example, this God character says, "Thou shalt not kill," but then proceeds to command the killing of children who hit their parents (Exodus 21.15), children who curse their parents (21.17), enslavers (21.16), the negligent owners of oxen who gore people (21.28–32), witches, (22.18), people who commit bestiality (22.19), and people who make sacrifices to other gods (22.20).[255] God is similarly self-contradictory in this book alone on whether or not slavery is forbidden or mandatory in certain circumstances. He also forbids the making of "graven images" but then instructs the building of gold, graven images on the fancy ark he commissions from the Hebrews.

The god of Exodus is patently unreliable, impossible to satisfy, and one who would murder children for cursing at their parents. When my kid was in her toddler years and got mad at me, she used to say, "No dinner for you for one hundred days!" I don't know where she got this idea from—we never deprived her of food as punishment, in fact, in a strict departure from the Old Testament God's approach, we don't punish her at all! Regardless, when she used to get so mad at me and yell "No dinner for you!" I thought it was funny—a furious lil' chubby-cheeked three-year-old issuing draconian punishments—and I would laugh it off, then offer her a hug, and she'd calm down about one minute later. The god of Exodus, on the other hand, would've had me *LITERALLY MURDER HER* for cursing her parents.

In my humble opinion, this god of Exodus is a bad dude, and his "promise" should have zero bearing on property disputes in the twenty-first century. It certainly does not justify ethnic cleansing and genocide. And remember, if we're accepting the Bible as permissible evidence of land-ownership (which we shouldn't), its authors are very clear—Jews are not *from* Canaan!

Why did biblical authors stress Abraham's Babylonian origin and Moses's Egyptian upbringing? Sand argues they may have wanted to claim a Jewish association with these powerful empires, because early Jewish communities were, frankly, pretty rinky-dink. "Archaeological findings show that historical Jerusalem was no more than a large village that gradually evolved into a small campus."[256] Biblical Jews were *never* a powerful imperial force on par with Babylonians or Egyptians, but associating their origins with these more powerful cultural centers gave the early Jews a certain cultural clout. It also posits Jews to look down upon the Indigenous people of Canaan. The authors of the early books of the Bible set out to manufacture a hatred of Canaanites that should sound very familiar to those who've read the last chapter. As Sand explains, "Most authors of the biblical texts loathed the local ... tribes, who were tillers of the soil and idol worshippers; step by step, they lay the ideological foundation for the tribes' eradication."[257]

Sure enough, after delivering contradictory orders to Moses, the God character promises to give Moses and his followers the land of Canaan by ethnically cleansing the locals. "I will send my fear before thee, and will destroy all the people to whom thou shalt come."[258] But, God cautions, he's going to ethnically cleanse the land gradually "lest the land become desolate, and the beast of the field multiply against thee."[259] There aren't enough Jews to manage all of Canaan yet, so God will send hornets to drive out the Hivites, the Canaanites, and the Hittites, little by little, year by year, until Moses and his followers have made enough Jews to farm the land. God's hornet plan sounds to me like how you might ret-con the establishment of a "large village that gradually evolved into a small campus" into some sort of epic, God-gifted foundational myth.

After the death of Moses, God ramps up his violent ambitions. He tells his "chosen people" to cross the Jordan River—leaving the boundaries of the land he had promised on Mount Sinai—to go into modern-day Jordan and commit genocide. The Book of Joshua details this mass murder that "completely destroyed every man and woman, both young and old, and every ox, sheep, and donkey" and "did not leave any who breathed."[260] After murdering a bunch of kids, Joshua and his army burn the city to the ground, saving only "the silver and the gold, and the vessels of brass and of iron."[261] Killing people and stealing their shit—a tale as old as time. But reality check: this genocide also never happened—as "fieldwork has provided increasingly decisive evidence that ... the land of Canaan was not suddenly conquered during the period identified in the Bible."[262]

Ahistorical and morally horrific as it is, the Book of Joshua, Sand asserts, was a "favored text" of Zionists, including David Ben-Gurion, until recently. "The accounts of the colonization and the return of the people of Israel to their promised land lent power and fervor to the founders of the State of Israel, and they pounced upon the inspiring similarity between the Biblical past and the nationalist present."[263] Disturbingly, Sand explains that the Israeli Ministry of Education mandates the teaching of the Bible as a historic text and "under no circumstances is it permissible to skip over the book of Joshua" and "exclude from the curriculum these shameful accounts of extermination."[264]

Talmudic scholars who attend yeshiva in Orthodox Jewish communities have always understood that the Bible is not to be read literally, but that is how it's being taught in Israeli public schools. And through the Book of Joshua, Israeli children are taught to hate the Indigenous people of Canaan, and that it is their God-given right to genocide them. Israeli children are also not taught, as yeshiva students were for thousands of years before them, that God's promise was always conditional—and the Bible is very clear that the first Israelites failed those conditions. "The promised land is neither a one-time grant nor an irrevocable gift" and "Like a zealously possessive husband, [God] would not forgive someone who betrayed him, and when his believers sinned, sanctions were activated immediately. At the end of the story, the recurrent themes of destruction and exile are actualized,"[265] and God evicts the Hebrews from their holy land as punishment!

Even if you believe in the literal truth of the Bible, even if you can somehow compartmentalize its many, many thousands of self-contradictions, and even if you are not disturbed by the moral horrors it extols, the Bible gives you no evidence whatsoever that biblical Israelites are *from* Canaan. What the Torah does provide is a blueprint for violent settler colonization by foreign invaders. But the even greater irony here is that archaeological evidence is conclusive that the Hebrew colonization of Canaan described in Exodus and Joshua *did not happen.*

Only over the past hundred years have people who believe themselves to be the great-great-great-etc. grandchildren of these fictional biblical colonizers attempted to carry out the type of civilization-ending destruction that the Bible's authors fantasized about.

The Book of Joshua is morally repulsive to me. Many of the commandments God gives to Moses are morally repulsive to me. The God of the Torah's genocidal plans are morally repulsive to me. And Abraham, the first Jew, is morally repulsive to me—in handing his wife over to the pharaoh to be raped, in raping his own slave, Hagar, in order to conceive a child in his eighties (or 130s, depending on the verse), in encouraging his jealous wife to beat Hagar for conceiving a child, in later banishing Hagar and their son Ishmael in the wilderness, in nearly murdering his other son Isaac because the voices in his head told him to ... until they didn't—Abraham was a piece of shit by any measure of a man.

I could go on and on and on about stories in the Bible that are just evil and contradictory to everything I believe to be true and good in this life.

And look, I know principled, anti-Zionist Jews who find a deep well of meaning in our religion, who wrestle with the contradictions and outrages of the Torah through a nuanced lens, informed by thousands of years' worth of rabbinical philosophy. But I think you might have to grow up with religion to want to pursue that kind of study. For my part, I'm too horrified by the foundational text of Judaism, on its face, to want to spend my one precious life grappling with its hidden meanings. Not when there are so many other books to read!

As I've made quite clear over the course of this book, I'm also horrified by the nation-state of Israel, which claims to speak for all Jews everywhere as it enacts genocide on Palestinians. And I'm horrified by a majority of my fellow Jews, who have at best been silent in the face of a genocide enacted in our names, but far more often are vocally supportive of Israel's existence as a racist, apartheid state that has been ethnically cleansing Palestinians from their land for more than a hundred years.

So I can understand completely why our Israeli historian of this chapter, Shlomo Sand, announced in 2014, "I wish to resign and cease considering myself a Jew."[266] Disgusted by living in Israel, one of "the most racist societies in the Western world," Sand announced in his book *How I Stopped Being a Jew* that he was "determined no longer to be a small minority in an exclusive club that others have neither the possibility nor the qualifications to join."

There have been many times over the past year when I have felt a similar impulse. What is keeping me tied to Jewishness when I am not religious, and when I do not share a common belief system—or even the most essential of my moral instincts—with a majority of the world's Jews? As I shared in the last chapter, my earliest associations with Jewishness came in the form of experiencing anti-Jewish hate from Christians. Ethnically, I have Ashkenazi ancestry—that fact can't be changed—but why continue calling myself a Jew? Because I like the pretty lights and fried potatoes of Hanukkah? Because I like to pepper my vocabulary with a little Yiddish, for spice?

If it would do Palestinians any good for me to renounce my Jewishness, as Shlomo Sand has done, and cease referring to myself as a Jew, I would do so in a heartbeat. But that principled rejection of apartheid privilege, coming from an Israeli citizen, would be a cop-out coming from me, as a diaspora Jew. It would be a relief, at this point, to walk away from whatever still ties me to Jewishness. To not have to continue associating myself with a people that seem hell-bent on making themselves synonymous with genocide. But it is precisely because of the way Jewish identity and history and grief is weaponized against Palestinians that I am *obligated* to continue being Jewish, even when Zionism makes being Jewish infinitely more dangerous and difficult and humiliating.

I used to feel at home among other Jews. There was an instant connection, a vibe, a shared sense of humor and conversational patterns. We were all part of one big family—a global mishpocha! I would seek out doctors with Jewish last names, feeling cozy in their care. I would get a thrill when discovering a new acquaintance was also Jewish.

Over the past year, however, that association has curdled into fear. I switched ob-gyns for my most recent pregnancy, in part because my former doctor was Jewish, and I did not know her politics. I needed a C-section and was too scared to go under the knife of a potential Zionist after I'd received thousands of death wishes from Zionist Jews. Recently, I was out walking my dog along the bayou when I came upon a family I'd never seen in the neighborhood before, the men wearing kippahs, traveling the same direction as I was. It was Friday night and presumably they were out for a walk after Shabbat dinner. I followed behind them, monitoring my heart rate as it spiked with every step they took closer to my own house, so that I was in a panic by the time they turned into the house across the street from mine—the one that had just sold the week before to new owners. I couldn't sleep that night for fear of the Jews living across the street, terrified they would find me on social media, discover I was such a known anti-Zionist, and enact retribution on my children.

Even as I recognize this fear of Jews as a kind of anti-Jewish hate, my experiences over the past year make this flinch a reasonable reaction. Zionism has taught me to fear my fellow Jews, until proven anti-Zionist. And for however much fear I feel towards Jews of unknown genocidal sympathies, I cannot imagine how much fear Palestinians feel towards my "people."

Instead of walking away from my discomfort with Judaism, I am choosing to lean into it. I am purposefully building an anti-Zionist Jewish community through the Houston chapter of Jewish Voice for Peace. I have no interest in deepening my relationship to the Jewish religion—I think I've made my feelings about the Torah quite clear. But I am embracing Jewish holidays and traditions that I find meaningful or heartening. I am continuing to research Jewish history so that I can better dispel Zionist misinformation and propaganda. And I will continue to claim Jewishness—always in the same breath as I claim anti-Zionism—in hopes that someday the majority of Jews will stop being so racist and join me on the side of understanding: ALL genocide bad.

Jews are entitled to Palestine because international law says so.

Should Israel exist because Arthur Balfour said so in 1917?

Fuck Arthur Balfour, a British Antisemite who only supported the establishment of a Jewish national home in Palestine because he didn't want more Jews coming to Britain.

Should Israel exist because the UN said so in 1948's UN General Assembly Resolution 181?

Why should a bunch of white Western bureaucrats at the UN, without a Palestinian representative, have been able to decide the fate of land that Palestinians had lived on for generations?

The UN exists to launder the reputations of violent, racist imperialist nations, providing a façade that these, in fact, bloodthirsty, genocidal, planet-destroying regimes are actually concerned with lofty concepts like "international cooperation," "self-determination," and "peace." I don't give the UN much credence. But if you do, then at least be consistent about it!

Yes, the UN called for the establishment of Israel in 1948, but the same resolution called for the establishment of a Palestinian state, a commitment Israel has violently prevented from coming to pass for seventy-six years and counting. If you're going to grant the UN legitimacy to impose settler-colonial nations on land where Indigenous people have lived for millennia, you don't also get to ignore the findings of UN courts: that Israeli settlements on Palestinian land are in violation of international law,[267] that Israel's building of a separation wall through the West Bank is illegal,[268] that Israel is guilty of enacting racial apartheid,[269] or that Israel is plausibly committing genocide.[270] Not even when the International Criminal Court issues arrest warrants for Benjamin Netanyahu and Yoav Gallant for war crimes.[271]

At the very least, to abide by so-called international law, Israel would need to immediately recognize a Palestinian state, withdraw all Israeli settlers from the West Bank, demolish the apartheid wall, lift the siege of Gaza, allow the right of return for Palestinians in the diaspora, and extend full, equal civil, legal, and political rights to all citizens, regardless of ethnicity or religion. Oh yeah—and send Netanyahu and Gallant to the Hague.

Such radical changes would not be sufficient to say Palestine was "free," but they would be a few large steps towards justice and equity. Most Zionists I've encountered dismiss the notion of abiding by such basic tenets of international law as absurdly radical and unworkable. They carry this attitude, despite the fact that they may appeal to the same international law as a legitimate basis for the founding of their nation-state.

Truly, I can't understand how Zionists live with such dizzying mental gymnastics. How are they not constantly puking, tripping, rolling on the floor, howling at the discomfort of living inside a mind that is so contradictory?

Jews are entitled to Palestine because Jews are Indigenous to Palestine

As I've already shown, according to the Bible, Jews aren't even from Palestine.

I can't stress enough, though, how much the Bible shouldn't be treated as a history book. Did a monotheistic people calling themselves Hebrews live in Canaan at least as early as the Hellenistic period? Yes. Do historians and archaeologists know how long these Hebrews were living in the region prior to the fourth century BCE? No they don't—from what I glean there's a ton of debate, mostly grounded in speculation, on that topic. Were the Hebrews *from* Canaan, or did they migrate from elsewhere—maybe Babylonia, as the Bible suggests of Abraham? And in which century BCE did this monotheistic religion either arise spontaneously between the Jordan River and the Red Sea, or get imported there from elsewhere, possibly Persia? And who even were the many different human authors who wrote, re-wrote, edited and eventually compiled the often-contradictory texts that became the Torah? What evidence or authority did they possess to document the events they wrote about? We can't know, and besides, the answer would have no bearing on the matter of whether or not Jews are Indigenous to Palestine.

"Indigeneity*" is commonly misdefined as referring simply to the people who are "from" some bit of land. But set the clock back far enough, and no one is "from" six of the Earth's continents. Human beings (or at least our closest ancestor, *Homo erectus)* evolved in Africa two million years ago, so every person living outside Africa has ancestors who migrated there at some point.[272]

Zionists want to stop the clock for determining Indigeneity at a very precise moment in Biblical myth—after the Babylonian Abraham and Egyptian Moses came to Canaan and colonized it (events that did not happen), but before the destruction of the Second Temple and mass expulsion of Jews (an event that also did not happen). They want to pause at the Kingdom of David (Remember? That wooden village of Jerusalem that eventually grew to a "small campus"?) and use that as proof that Jews are "from" Palestine. Based on this threadbare, selective biblical evidence, they attempt to justify taking over Palestine by force from its actual inhabitants.

Let's pretend for a moment the biblical story is a valid claim, and that all Jews in fact do trace ancestry to Canaan (they don't; stick a pin in that). Imagine what chaos we would unleash upon the world if we started honoring millennia-old property claims! Many Arab people trace ancestry to Spain and Portugal, so they could say, "We once had a thriving civilization on the Iberian Peninsula," and—with far more extensive historical documentation to justify their claims than Israel has to Palestine—violently establish an Arab caliphate that stretched from Lisbon to Barcelona. I, who have Norwegian ancestry on my mom's side, could go to Norway with an AR-15, pick out a house I liked, force out the family living there at gunpoint, and go inside and change the locks. Now imagine that the Norwegian family had a problem with that, and went to the authorities, only to find out that the entire police, military, and political apparatus sided with my right to steal their home. That story sounds absurd and obviously immoral and unjust, and yet it's a pretty good characterization of how Israel has stolen over 95 percent of Palestinian land over the past seventy-six years.[273]

....
* My copy editor here suggested that I should only capitalize "Indigenous" when being used as an identity label, and not when speaking generally or discussing the word's origins and etymology. But I found the difference in caps confusing and distracting, so I'm just gonna capitalize it everywhere. Sorry, grammar wonks!

But back to that pin we need to unstick—Jews *don't* all trace ancestry to Palestine. Jewish converts may come from any ethnic background. But according to the State of Israel, they have the right to settle Palestinian land because of their *religion*, even though many of these converts can't even make the fatuous claim of being ethnically Jewish and therefore "from" Palestine.

Before the establishment of Israel, yes, there were Palestinian Jewish communities who had been living in Palestine for untold generations. But these were a tiny fraction of global Jewry, and their numbers quickly became overwhelmed by Ashkenazi settlers, and later, Jews from other Arab countries, as Zionists began the colonization of Palestine.

I had always accepted it as a given that Ashkenazi Jews were exiled from Palestine at some point, before making their way to Europe. I included this ethno-mythology in that god-awful poem I wrote in my senior year of high school, "Proud of my Blood," and I enshrined it again in my first book, *Depart, Depart*. During the emotional climax of that book, the Jewish protagonist greets the spirits of all his ancestors, a crowd of specters "filling the road that stretches back into the village—way back, past the borders of Vilna and a hundred other shtetls, little villages strung along dirt roads winding all the way down the spine of the continent, all the way back to antiquity, to Israel, and further still—to the dawn of his people in the world."

Pretty words, but these days, they give me the ick. Because I've learned from Shlomo that this idea that I grew up believing—that I came from Palestine, that there was some mass exile of Jews from Canaan into Europe—is as bogus as the Exodus story.

If there had been a massive migration of Jews from Palestine to Europe in the first century, that would show up in the historical record—in coins and pottery and textiles and historical texts, but the evidence just isn't there. Sand explains that many of his critics insist on "defining historical Jewry as a people ... one unique, exceptional, and immune to comparison. Such a view could be maintained only by providing ... a mythological image of the exile of a people that ostensibly took place in the first century BCE, despite the fact that the scholarly elite was well aware that such an exile never really occurred during the entire period in question. For this reason, not even one research-based book has thus been written on the forced uprooting of the "Jewish people.""[274] Sand accuses his critics of obfuscating the truth that Judaism from the second century BCE to the eighth century CE was a proselytizing religion, and that Judaism mostly likely spread throughout Europe, North Africa, and Southwest Asia through conversion. So Jews today are not all one, ethnic "people," or *race*—as Antisemites and Zionists jointly assert. We're a bunch of different ethnic groups who share a religion, or, more often, we have ancestors who once did.

Sand's work has been denounced by some Israeli geneticists, who claim to have established definitively that Ashkenazi Jews as a whole can trace their origins to Palestine. But another Israeli geneticist, Eran Elhaik, has accused those researchers of manipulating data to fit a preferred narrative.[275] Elhaik's findings, along with research by others, shows, "at least 90% of Ashkenazic maternal ancestry is Indigenous to Europe and likely originated through conversion of local populations with the remaining ancestries having East Asian or unidentified origins. These finding are supported by ancient DNA evidence showing 0–3% Levantine ancestry and a dominant Iranian ancestry (88%) in modern-day Ashkenazi Jews."[276]

When I went to actually read those genetic studies to see what I thought, I quickly realized that I lack the scientific knowledge to make heads or tails of them. But what I do know is that genetics is a very young scientific field, and that its application in this arena bears many similarities to the efforts of eighteenth-century "racial scientists" discussed in Chapter 8. All scientific disciplines, but particularly very new ones that few people understand, are subject to political pressures. Zionism exerts political pressure on any geneticist, historian, or scholar who can strengthen their supposed ties to Palestine and will dismiss the work and smear the reputations of any courageous scientists or intellectuals who question its narrative.

Ultimately, whether 0% or 3% or 100% of my DNA is found to be similar to the DNA of ancient humans unearthed in Palestine is irrelevant to the question of the colonization of Palestine. No percentage would give me the right to violently dispossess people currently living on their land.

Let's return to the word "Indigenous," which, as I said at the beginning, does not even mean this popularly held idea of having ancestors who, at some conveniently chosen point in time, lived in a place.

Words come from somewhere, and their origins can teach us a lot. So let's dive into the etymology of the word "Indigenous," just as we examined the history of "antisemitism," and see how Zionists have similarly co-opted it and stripped it of all meaning.

The word "Indigenous" was created by colonizers. From the Latin *indu* (in, within) and *gignere* (to beget, produce).[277] The first recorded use was in 1588, when an English diplomat used it to describe the Samoyed people of Siberia as "Indigenæ, or people bred upon that very soyle."[278] He probably *literally* meant "sprung from the soil," because in the sixteenth century, some scholarly Europeans believed in polygenesis—the idea that different races had originated in different places on earth, independently of one another.

The term "Indigenous" begins to appear in more European writings in the 1640s, the height of the colonial era, to describe the people, flora, and fauna that were living in the places that colonizers were colonizing.[279] So the word "Indigenous" has always existed within a binary, a Western framework of colonizer and Indigenous person. One does not exist without the other. And according to this framework, an Indigenous person cannot be a colonizer and vice versa.

In 2024, many Western liberals hold a great deal of token reverence for Indigenous people. And because deference politics asks us to defer uncritically to the most marginalized person in the room, Zionist claims of Indigeneity to Palestine have a way of shutting down criticism of Israel. Non-Jewish liberal white people, frightened of being accused of anti-Indigeneity, are particularly susceptible to this silencing tactic. Their critical mind shuts down, and they forget that when people walk like colonizers, talk like colonizers, commit ethnic cleansing and devastate the land like colonizers, they *are* colonizers. And colonizers *cannot* be Indigenous.

I'm not the only person to think that colonizers and Indigenous people are mutually exclusive categories. In "When does a native become a settler?" Mizrahi Jewish sociologist Yuval Evri and political theorist Hagar Kotev argue that, in the early twentieth century, there *were* Palestinian Jews who were Indigenous to Palestine. These Palestinian Jews were subject to Ottoman and British colonizers. But when Jewish Zionists took power in the region, most Palestinian Jews assimilated into Ashkenazi society. In doing so, they gave up their Indigeneity to become settlers.[280]

Evri and Kotev report that in 1900, Palestinian Jews welcomed Jewish immigration, but "most of them viewed Zionism's European character as an interruption, if not a destruction, of the fabric of life in Palestine, and were critical of its separatist approach."[281]

Evri and Kotev reject the label "immigrant" for the Ashkenazi Zionists who came to Palestine in the early twentieth century. Instead, these Zionist Jews rolled up to Palestine as *settlers*. "Unlike immigrants, settlers do not seek to integrate into existing structures to become part of the place to which they move or to protect their identities within their own enclaves in that place, but rather to transform the place so it takes their own image, to eliminate the natives, and so to become the new law of the place."[282]

Ashkenazi Zionists charged into Palestine to become the new law of the land. They did not want to learn the language that was spoken there by Christians, Jews, and Muslims alike—which was Arabic. They did not want to learn about Indigenous agricultural practices that were sustainable there, instead importing European agriculture that has led to the desertification of Palestine.[283] They were not curious about Palestinian culture, because they were bringing with them European white supremacy.

One Palestinian Jewish journalist pointed out the hypocrisy of the early Zionists, saying, "You come to France and learn French, go to Germany and learn German ... why is it ... when you want to enter Palestine you will not learn Arabic—the language of the people of the land with whom you live every day?"[284] Immigrants come to a new land and learn the language spoken there. Only colonizers arrive in a new land and insist on making their imported language the language of business, law, maps, and street signs—which is exactly how Ashkenazi Zionists imposed Hebrew onto Palestine.

Prior to 1880, Hebrew was not quite a dead language, but it was not fully alive either. Nowhere were Jews speaking it in their daily lives. Hebrew was a liturgical, religious language, similar to how Latin was used at the time in the Catholic church. Most poor Jews and Jewish women would never learn Hebrew beyond some familiar prayers and songs.

Yiddish—which is just the German word for "Jewish"—was the dialect of German used as the conversational, daily language of Ashkenazi Jews in Central and Eastern Europe. Other diasporic Jewish groups spoke in distinctly Jewish dialects of whatever was the dominant language of the land they were living in. Many Sephardic Jews continued speaking Ladino—or Judeo-Spanish—even after their violent expulsion from the Iberian Peninsula in 1492, during the Spanish Inquisition.[285] Jews in the Arab world spoke distinct Arabic dialects, depending on where they lived currently and where they'd lived before that. Yemeni Jews developed a Judeo-Yemeni Arabic that was distinct from Baghdadi Jews' *haki mal yihud*, or "Jewish speech." Prior to Zionism, Sephardic Jews living in Palestine might have spoken Ladino, while Palestinian Jews of Ashkenazi origin might have spoken Palestinian Yiddish or Ashkenazic Arabic, or both.[286] Meanwhile Arab Palestinian Jewish communities spoke Judeo-Arabic.[287]

So much linguistic diversity was intolerable to Zionist colonizers. Early Zionists decided to reject all these varied languages, erasing history and cultural distinctions, and instead revive Hebrew as a common lingua franca to be the official language of their colonizing project. As I've described in Chapter 8, Zionists systematically and intentionally sought to erase the cultural distinctiveness of Arab Jews from different regions. Since the term "Arab" might foster solidarity between Arab Jews and Arab Muslims, Zionists instead referred to Arab Jews as *bnei edot hamizrah* or "descendants of the oriental ethnicities." In the 1990s, progressive Israelis shortened this identity label to "Mizrahim."[288] Based on comments I've gotten from Zionist Mizrahi Jews, many are deeply offended if you refer to them as Arab Jews (despite the fact that their ancestors self-identified as Arab). Instead, they embrace the term Mizrahi, which means "Oriental" or easterner, an inherently Eurocentric term, as it describes a spatial relationship to Central Europe.

Today, although 50 percent of Israeli Jews have Arab ancestry, only 10 percent of them still speak Arabic.[289] In the late nineteenth century, organizations like the Jewish Colonization Association and the Jewish National Fund were buying up huge swaths of Palestinian land, and as early as the 1880s, Eliezer Ben-Yehuda spearheaded a revival of the Hebrew language to unify newly-arrived Zionist Jews settling those lands.[290] In 1948, the newly-established Israeli state would change the names of Palestinian towns and streets to Hebrew versions[291] and erect a bureaucracy conducted in Hebrew that would exclude anyone who was not a Hebrew speaker. Zionists turned Hebrew into a weapon, a tool of colonization, a cudgel of assimilation—something that should offend religious Jews, who are supposed to hold the *loshn kodesh** sacred. Today, the

---

* In Hebrew, "holy language"

official language of the nation-state of Israel is this artificially resuscitated language, modern Hebrew. English is secondary. In 2018, Arabic was removed from the list of official languages—the culmination of seventy years of linguistic erasure.[292]

Back to Evri and Kotev—our authors explain how, in the early twentieth century, Palestinian Jews predicted and resisted Ashkenazi erasure, and they hoped to find common cause with other Arabic-speaking Jews settling in Palestine. But when Britain wrested control of Palestine from Ottoman rule, Arabic-speaking Jews suddenly lost influence in Palestine. British officials preferred to work with the newly arrived, often English-speaking Ashkenazi Jews, who had more in common with them as fellow Europeans. These European Jews quickly became, and remain to this day, the ethnic elite within the region. Even though they were treated as second-class citizens by Ashkenazi elites, many Arab Jews chose Zionism over their Arab roots, giving up their unique cultures and languages in order to cozy up to white supremacy. When they did this, Evri and Kotev contend, they gave up Indigeneity and became settlers themselves.

To this day, there remains a small community of Palestinian Jews who object to Zionism. For example, in 1996, when armed settlers took over an area in Hebron, a group of thirty-seven descendants of the original Palestinian Jews of Hebron took out a full-page advertisement in *Haaretz* saying these settlers are "alien to the way of life of the Hebron Jews, who created over the generations a culture of peace and understanding between peoples and faiths in the city." These Palestinian Jews, continuing to resist Zionist aggression, might still have some claim to Indigeneity. But those who embrace the *Mizrahi* identity gleefully serve in the IOF, and violently oppress and mass-murder Indigenous Palestinians in order to steal their land—they have become colonizers. And a colonizer is not Indigenous.

Connection to land is another aspect of Indigeneity. Remember the word means "sprung from the land." Regardless of the word's racist, unscientific origins, this association with land stewardship remains a crucial component of how we understand and use the term to this day. Indigenous leadership is recognized to be essential to the climate movement because, in places where Indigenous people are stewards of the land, there are lower rates of deforestation, higher rates of biodiversity, and greater overall environmental health.[293]

By the metric of land stewardship, Israelis have proven they cannot possibly be Indigenous. The impact Israel has had on the ecology of Palestine over the last seventy-six years has been nothing short of catastrophic. Israel has replaced native agricultural crops like carob, hawthorns, oaks, olives, figs, and almonds with four million trees of non-native European species.[294] These artificial forests, often planted to hide the evidence of Palestinian villages that were ethnically cleansed during the Nakba, contribute more to global warming than cooling, have destroyed endangered native ecosystems, and are susceptible to extreme wildfires.[295]

Olive trees grow sustainably in Palestine, and for centuries, olives and olive oil were Palestinians' main export. To break this economic backbone, Israeli forces have uprooted and destroyed over one million olive trees since 1948,[296] including centuries-old, and even millennia-old trees. Indigenous people wouldn't do that, wouldn't cut down thousand-year-old trees. Indigenous people would not have drained the Kabbara marshlands, causing the extinction of Palestinian crocodiles.[297] Indigenous people do not pour concrete into drinking water sources to spite the people living there.[298] Indigenous people also wouldn't have broken up the West Bank into 227 distinct Palestinian enclaves, surrounded by Jewish settlements—settlements which they create by leveling the tops of Palestine's lovely rolling hills, and building shitty three-story townhomes there, surrounded by barbed wire fencing. These settlers then dump their trash, untreated sewage, and wastewater into the valleys to pollute Palestinians' land and water sources.[299] Indigenous people wouldn't connect all those settlements with a system of walled highways that have devastated the habitat ranges of the natural flora and fauna, pushing many species native to Palestine to the brink of extinction.[300]

Some Israelis have tried to claim that, because they see themselves as Indigenous, their settlement of Palestine is part of the global #LandBack movement. But for the past fifty years, Indigenous communities in the Americas have rejected this premise, accusing Israel of committing the same type of settler colonialism that robbed them of their own lands and allying instead with Palestinians.[301]

In another world, perhaps Ashkenazi Jews, fleeing persecution in Europe, could have come to Palestine as immigrants. They could have learned the languages spoken there and learned how to live sustainably on the land from local populations. Perhaps, after many generations of humility and basic decency and neighborliness, these Jews might plausibly have been able to claim they were "Indigenous" in Palestine.

Or, in another-other world, Palestinian Jews might have banded together in solidarity with Palestinian Muslims, Christians, and Arab Jews from other states. Together, this multifaith Arab alliance could have resisted Ashkenazi Zionist erasure and provided a counternarrative to Jewish antagonism of Palestinian Muslims. A Jewish-Muslim-Arab coalition might have prevented Zionists from collaborating with Antisemites in Arab governments to facilitate the mass migration of Arab Jews to Palestine. To this day, there might be thriving, Indigenous Jewish communities in many Arab countries, as there were before the 1880s.

But that's not what happened. Ashkenazi and Mizrahi Zionists alike chose to be colonizers in Palestine, and so they have no standing to claim they are Indigenous to the land.

Jews are entitled to Palestine because they were born there.

We've established that Israeli Jews are not Indigenous to Palestine, because they are colonizers, and you can't be both. But aren't the kids of colonizers entitled to keep living where they were born? If the plan is to decolonize Palestine, what are you going to do with the nearly 80 percent of Israeli Jews who were born in Israel?[302]

Here, Zionists will suddenly abandon the claim to Indigeneity, and instead compare themselves with white people in the United States. In my comments, they say things like, "We'll give back our homes in Palestine when you give your house to a Native American."

But there's a bit of nuance here. Family lore holds that I do have at least once ancestor, on my mother's side, who bought and settled stolen Native American land from the federal government in Wisconsin, over a hundred fifty years ago. But, if true, that act of settler colonialism occurred at least four or five generations ago. My mom visited the farm as a child, but the land was inherited by male cousins of hers, who divided and sold it off, and she didn't see a dime from the sale. Granted, my mother benefited indirectly from the wealth generated by this farm which sustained her own mother in childhood. But she inherited no wealth from it. And I will inherit nothing from her, as she has completely cut me out of her life and out of her will, because she calls me an "antifa terrorist," in part because of my support for Palestinian liberation. Even if she hadn't cut me off, my mother has been unemployed for over ten years and lives modestly on my dad's alimony payments, so I don't think there's any wealth there to inherit. Meanwhile, my husband and I have paid off eleven years of a thirty-year debt on a quarter-acre plot of land in Houston, Texas. In common parlance, that means we "own" our modest little house, but we live paycheck to paycheck, paying down that mortgage to the bank.

I support #LandBack, and the reparations to Indigenous communities in the form of the return of federal lands. I recognize that white privilege has made it easier for me to navigate the racist society of the United States of America, in terms of making a living, obtaining medical care, and avoiding police brutality. My parents' and grandparents' white privilege generated enough wealth for them to send me to private schools, where I got the kind of education that enables me to write a book like this.

But for me, and millions of descendants of white settlers of the United States, there's no simple way to make right the sins of our distant ancestors. I cannot give back that farm in Brothertown, Wisconsin, because I am separated from ownership of it by multiple generations. Blackrock probably owns it now, just as Blackrock truly owns the debt on the little house we "bought" and are trying to pay off before either we die or it's destroyed in a catastrophic hurricane.

The situation in Palestine is markedly different.

By the time of this book's publication, Israel will have existed for a mere seventy-seven years. Meanwhile, Israeli settlers have been stealing land from Palestinians as recently as *yesterday*.[303] Many Israeli settlers live in fully furnished homes stolen from Palestinians at gunpoint, where they settle their asses on the furniture of the original inhabitants, sheltered by stone walls that were built *by hand* by the ancestors of living Palestinians. Many Palestinian Nakba survivors, and their descendants, still carry the front door keys to homes that were stolen in 1948 or 1967. Israeli settlers have colonized Palestine incredibly rapidly in the past seventy-six years, like a deranged, neighborhood kid who charges into your house and starts licking all your toys, saying "mine," "mine," "mine." But just because you lick something—or take it by sticking a gun in someone's face—doesn't make you its legitimate owner.

So are Israelis born in Palestine entitled to keep living there? Somewhere there, sure. But at the very least, Israeli settlers, and, yes—their children— need to give back the homes they stole within living memory. At the very least, all the settlements in the West Bank, built since 1967 in violation of international law, must be abandoned by Israeli Jews and the land returned to Palestinians.

Having to give back a stolen house is not ethnic cleansing. No one is calling for the ethnic cleansing of Jews from Palestine. Well, okay, not *no one*. As Paolo Freire cautioned us, "When education is not liberating, the dream of the oppressed is to become the oppressor." As I shared in Chapter 7, there are some individuals who dream of doing to Zionists what Zionists continue to do to Palestinians. That's an understandable reaction, given what victims of Zionism have suffered—which, let's recall, includes theft, torture, rape, dismemberment, the mass murder of family, friends, and loved ones, the destruction of civilization, and the attempted extermination of an entire people. But the vast majority of Free Palestine organizers and supporters that I'm in community with are calling for an *end* to genocide, not a flipping of the script of who gets to genocide whom.

When the oppressed call for "liberation," colonizers hear "genocide," because that's all they know—they can only conceive of violent, oppressive relations between enslaver and enslaved. But decolonization is not genocide. Postcolonial scholar Priyamvada Gopal examines the history of decolonial struggles and determines, "The historical record shows that the end of colonization was achieved by a variety of means in different places but there is no context in which genocide was inflicted upon ruling peoples or racial groups. Anticolonial methods certainly involved both violence and non-violence, from uprisings and riots to guerilla struggles, armed warfare (the Algerian War of Independence being a particularly bloodied example), destruction of property, strikes, mutinies, boycotts, civil disobedience, non-cooperation, and political negotiations. In no case was there a planned physical extermination of entire communities or races, though there was certainly a push to recover land, property, wealth, and political institutions."[304] The decolonization of Palestine will not be bloodless—Israel has assured that by violently suppressing every nonviolent attempt made by Palestinians to assert their rights, such as the First Intifada or the March of Return. But the decolonization of Palestine will not entail the genocide of Israeli Jews. They just have to give back the stuff they stole—again—in *living memory.*

Is it possible that Palestinians regain control of their ancestral lands and enact apartheid and genocide upon Jews born there? Sure, it's *possible,* although as we explored in Chapter 7 and as Gopal's research reveals above, that outcome is highly unlikely. We know, from the example of Zionist Ashkenazi Jews, that those who have suffered under genocide are fully capable of conducting genocide in turn. But if that happens, Palestine won't have decolonized, it will just have shifted colonial leadership.

Genocide, apartheid, border walls, and ethnic cleansing—these are colonial machinery. A genocide of Israelis could only be accomplished with vast weapons arsenals supplied to Palestinians by another imperial country. Palestinians would become the attack dogs of this other, more powerful regime, in the same way Israelis are attack dogs of the US. The Palestinians would be pawns in an imperial proxy war in Palestine that's really all about oil and generating a forever war that keeps weapons manufacturers gaining ever-more obscene wealth. In such a scenario, Palestinians would become as deranged, divorced from their humanity, and ensnared by the chains they wield as Israeli Zionists are today.

In that case, Palestine would not be "free." Anyone dreaming of such a future does not understand the meaning of "freedom." And, as Freire taught us, those folks—whether they call themselves Zionists or anti-Zionists—need some liberatory education.

Recently, a fellow content creator and scholar I admire, Hasanain Jaffer, posted a video titled "Free the Zionists," in which he shares a bit of this liberatory education and explains why Israelis should welcome decolonization. He describes "a teaching of the prophet [Mohammed], where he tells his companions to help both the oppressed and the oppressor. And when asked how, the prophet says, 'By stopping them from oppressing.'" Jaffer draws comparisons with more modern liberatory thinkers. "Franz Fanon talks about how the black man is enslaved by his inferiority and the white man is enslaved by his superiority … Martin Luther King, Jr repeatedly pointed out that race thinking has a capacity to make its beneficiaries inhuman, even as it deprives its victims of their humanity." And he concludes, "True liberation in Palestine and Sudan and Congo, it doesn't just free the oppressed from their chains, it frees the oppressor from the need to wield those chains … freeing Zionists from the weight of that hatred and fear."[305]

Wouldn't it be nice, Zionists, to put down the fear and hate? To not have to serve in the IOF and mass-murder children? Wouldn't it be nice to tear down the border walls and barbed wire and checkpoints that blot the horizon? To give up the constant surveillance and violence required to keep millions of people dispossessed, captive, and suffering? Wouldn't it be nice to free yourselves of the weighty cognitive dissonance required to convince yourself that genocide is justified?

What are Israeli Jews entitled to? They're entitled to human and civil rights, regardless of their religion or ethnicity. Same as Palestinians. But they are not entitled to keep living on land, and in houses, that they or their parents stole from Palestinians within the last century. And they are not entitled to an apartheid ethnostate.

We live in a diverse, heterogeneous world, and human beings have been moving all over its surface for many tens of thousands of years. We cannot untangle our lineages and try to plug people back into homelands that *some* of their ancestors may or may not have inhabited thousands of years ago. Why would we even want to do that? So we can all enjoy our own ethnically and religiously homogenous territories? What a hateful little fantasy that is. And it ignores the existence of multiracial, multiethnic people!

What are Jews entitled to? Well, if you believe in principles like equality and justice, then you must believe we're entitled to exactly the same things as anyone else on earth. And that means, that no, we're not entitled to a "homeland," an ethnostate just for Jews, where everyone else is a second-class citizen.

If you're committed to principles like equality and justice, then nobody gets an ethnostate!

197

Part III.
Towards Collective Liberation—
What Does "Free Palestine" even mean?

There are millions of people in the Free Palestine movement, each with their own vision of what those two momentous words really mean. It's important for us to take time to share those visions, to make sure we're stretching our imaginations to dream of true liberation and not, as Freire cautions, just "dreaming of becoming the oppressor."

I'm not claiming to speak for Palestinians here, nor claiming authority to decide what is the correct definition of "Free Palestine." But I am going to share what those two words mean to *me* when I say them, as your friendly, local, anti-Zionist Jewish anarchist.

Imagining a world beyond imperialism and capitalism is hard. In my experience, the average USian can't do it at all. Mass media constrains our imaginations to stories of individual heroism and vengeance as justice, never collective liberation. Batman "saves" Gotham from a never-ending series of criminals. He locks up "bad guys" in little boxes in Arkham Asylum, but he never redistributes his exorbitant wealth to alleviate the poverty that created the conditions for crime in the first place. Bruce Wayne, criminally hoarding the wealth of the people of Gotham, creating the artificial scarcity that drives them to steal, is never identified as the true enemy of the people.

The visions of the future we are offered by Hollywood and our most celebrated novelists are invariably bleak, depressing dystopias. Capitalism, imperialism, and individualism persist in even more brutal extremes in the worlds of *Mad Max*, *Black Mirror*, *The Road*, and space westerns like *Star*

Wars and *Firefly*. We can call to mind countless visions of scorched, trashed, uninhabitable or barely habitable Earths—even in our children's media, like *Wall-E, City of Ember*, and *The Lorax*. But there are no major movies that paint a clear vision of how humans might reverse course on planetary destruction.

The *Star Trek* universe offers a rare post-capitalist exception to dystopian futures. But even the United Federation of Planets is a colonial, neoliberal utopia—one where the end of human-on-human violence was achieved not through cooperation but through the invention of "replicators"—an impossible technology that magically solved the problem of scarcity, without the wealthy ever having to give up their unfair hoards.

When we are given such bleak fodder for our imaginations, it's unsurprising that many of us, in trying to envision freedom, can only picture a slightly more comfortable cage.

If you want to improve your capacity to imagine what deep freedom would look like—freedom from white supremacist patriarchal imperial colonial capitalism in all its forms—then you're going to have to consume some media from off the beaten track. I've found it helps to read both fiction and nonfiction—and these are largely books you're going to have to seek out from indie presses like this one.

By reading radical leftist scholars, publishing through leftist presses like Haymarket or Verso (or Interlink!), you can get ideas for how we might organize human society outside of racial capitalism. You can read decolonial history published by academic presses, examining the successes, failures, and pitfalls of previous liberation movements. And what's been most powerful of all for me is reading utopian fiction written by authors who have undertaken this kind of political education for themselves. In the genres of solarpunk, Black futurism, and Indigenous futurism, authors use story to transmit their visions of a better world.

I've been seriously applying myself to this work of writing utopia for five or six years now—so I am still quite new to the practice! But in that short time, I've been able to expand my understanding of liberation so vastly that I sometimes struggle to communicate what I mean to progressive liberals, who see the world much as I did before I ever read *The Dispossessed*.

Utopian Fiction That Will Stretch Your Political Imagination

- *The Dispossessed* by Ursula K. LeGuin
- *A Country of Ghosts* by Margaret Killjoy
- *Inara: Light of Utopia*, edited by Yaffa As
- *A Half-Built Garden* by Ruthanna Emrys
- *Multispecies Cities: Solarpunk Urban Futures*, edited by Christoph Rupprecht, et al.
- *Love After the End: An Anthology of Two Spirit and Indigiqueer Speculative Fiction*, edited by Joshua Whitehead
- *Sunvault: Stories of Solarpunk and Eco-Speculation*, edited by A.C. Wise, et al.
- *A Psalm for the Wild Built* by Becky Chambers
- *Real Sugar is Hard to Find: Stories* by Sim Kern

When I say "Free Palestine," these people want to know—"What kind of nation-state do you have in mind for after Israeli apartheid is toppled?"

But I don't dream of nation-states. Because I'm an anarchist!

When most folks hear "anarchy," they think "chaos," every person for themself. But that's not what anarchism is. Anarchism calls for the abolition of hierarchies, of haves and have-nots when it comes to the power of self-determination. Anarchism stands opposed to violent coercion—whether that's the coercion of threats of violence and arrest or the coercion of contrived hunger and homelessness compelling you to labor and conform. Anarchism demands not isolation and individualism, but a far more cooperative, interconnected, and complex society.

If a voice in your head is shouting, "Impossible! Humans can't create that kind of world! We suck too much!" please consider that you have been socially conditioned to dismiss—or not even be aware of the existence of—anarchist ideas, thanks to a tightly controlled, right-wing media landscape. Consider that the CIA infiltrated creative writing programs and literary magazines across the globe in the 1950s to ensure the suppression of leftist literature that might help you envision such a world,[306] and to stop the publication of books like those titles I've listed above.

And so, just this once, tell the little Joseph McCarthy in your head to hush-em-up, and allow yourself to dream with me.

Dream of Israel's apartheid wall and the wall at the US-Mexico border torn down. Dream of a world where humans and animals have freedom to migrate across the imaginary lines colonial racists drew on a map to divide us. Dream of a world where citizenship is irrelevant, because wherever you live, there you are, and you are deserving of equal rights. Dream of a world where no bank, landlord, or colonizer can steal your home, or hoard more land than they need. Dream of a world where no one sleeps on the streets in cities where thousands of luxury condos stand empty.

Dream of an end to forever wars and fossil fuel consumption. Dream of oil rigs, fracking wells, petrochemical refineries, and weapons factories disassembled, their parts repurposed for sustainable energy generation. Dream of cars and guns and warheads melted down to build rails for solar-powered trains. Dream of construction equipment used to dig up hundreds of millions of miles of asphalt roads and parking lots, all made irrelevant by purposeful public transit infrastructure! Dream of the settler freeways in the West Bank and the US Interstate Highway System re-wilded with native plants to heal the scars in the land.

Dream of crocodiles returning to the Jordan River and of buffalo returning to roam the Great Plains, from the Arctic to the Gulf of Mexico.

Let's *not* dream, though, of ecological restoration accomplished through genocidal fantasies of killing off most of the human population. Let's not give in to eugenicist, survival-of-the-fittest fantasies where humans have reverted to Stone Age technologies, sustaining life for just a few able-bodied hunter-gatherers to enjoy.

Dream instead of a world where people gather together in sustainably reengineered cities, or tend to the land in rural areas, according to their want. Dream of communities designed around accessibility for children, disabled, and elderly people, rather than for cars. Dream of the death of suburbia—of transforming that sprawl of parking lots and monoculture lawns into permaculture food forests and wildlife corridors. Dream of a world where you don't feel so compelled to travel to remote, pristine landscapes because the landscape where you live has been restored to its natural beauty. Dream of a world where the air you breathe is clean, and the river in your town is safe enough to drink from.

Dream of an end to the artificial scarcity of hunger—a world where we quit wasting 1.3 billion tons of food each year, to rot methane into our atmosphere, and instead we just feed everyone. Dream of eating food grown locally and sustainably, in season, rather than loaded with preservatives and shipped halfway around the world. Dream of an end to fast fashion, polyester, and plastic packaging. Dream of sacrificing conveniences and consumerism in exchange for a guarantee that all your needs will be met, and that you will leave a habitable earth to future generations.

I do not dream of representative democracy. I do not dream of voting for some elite candidate, chosen by elite interests, who will somehow magically grow a conscience and enact these changes. Even I can't imagine a world where that would happen! Instead, I dream of the abolition of political elites. I dream of direct democracy—a system where you can vote on any and every issue that impacts you, locally or globally.

Such a system might be possible if we used the incredible power of the Internet, not to enrich a tiny group of Silicon Valley elites, but to facilitate such a democracy. Imagine if social media was designed, not to manufacture consumerist want, and spread misinformation and hate, but to facilitate the kind of education and debate necessary for healthy, direct democracy.

In this world, the hoarding of wealth and power would be despised as much as we despise poverty today. Such hoarding would be impossible—not because we would punish those who attempted to seize power with violence, but because "wealth" and "power" are imaginary constructs. People must believe in "wealth" and "power" in order for them to exist, and in this world, we would inoculate the masses, through liberatory education, against believing in the wealth and power of anyone who would hoard them for individualistic gain.

Dream of a world where you are judged by the education you have amassed or the services you render your community, not the wealth you have hoarded.

Dream of labor. Chosen and engaged in freely, according to one's interests, and in service of one's fellow people. Dream of doctors, free to treat whoever is hurt or ill, without the intervention of violent for-profit bureaucracies. Dream of chefs, free to cook for their communities without the violent coercion of the profit motive. Dream of teachers, free to teach in schools that are modeled not on prisons or factories but as spaces to maximize creativity and inquiry. Dream of scientists studying topics to enrich our collective knowledge, and of engineers inventing technologies to improve our lives sustainably, free from the necessity to generate corporate profits.

Dream of the labors it will take to heal the damage we have done to our climate and ecosystems over many generations—long tasks of excavating landfills and repurposing their contents, of weeding invasive species, pulling plastic from the ocean, harvesting sustainable crops, and tending to nuclear waste. Dream of a world where billions of humans all work towards healing the Earth and taking care of each other, rather than enriching the already rich at the expense of everyone else.

Dream of clearing the rubble of Gaza, rebuilding homes, and planting olive trees.

Dream of a world where you choose to work because it feels good to help your community—a community that extends to encompass the entire living world. Dream of a world where you set your own hours, and no one forces you to labor in order to survive. Dream of a world where peace is maintained, and boundaries respected, not through the threat of violent retribution but from a shared recognition of our interdependence.

That's the kind of freedom I imagine when I say, "Free Palestine."

When I say, "Free Palestine," I am also saying, "Free the United States," and "Free the World," because I recognize that Palestine is a uniquely important crux of global empire. The United States has demonstrated over the past year that it will double down again and again in support of its colony of Israel, because the loss of that colony is an existential threat to the West's global domination.

If we can free Palestine from empire—and I mean *all* empire, not just swapping out one imperial power for another—then we can free anyone, anywhere. Then we can free the whole ding-dang world.

Call me an idealist, naïve, insane for dreaming such a dream, I don't care. I won't let fascists constrain my imagination to their right-wing, planet-eating, death-cult-approved dystopias. I will not restrict my demands for equality to the incremental window-dressings of neoliberalism. And, though I adore and respect many communists, I also won't restrict my liberatory imagination to the self-defeating pragmatism of Marxism, which asks me to bend the knee for someone who, they promise, will be a kinder, more equitable ruler, and who, they promise, will someday give my freedom back to me.

I believe the first step to freeing Palestine, and thus, the world, is freeing your own mind from individualism, supremacy, and violence. If you can do that, you can start freeing your interpersonal relationships from coercion. If you can do that, you can free your family, your friends, comrades, and communities. And if enough of us undertake this work, eventually all these liberated communities will start to connect, borders will blur, we will reach a tipping point, and we will free the whole world.

I truly do believe humans are capable of cooperation. In fact, I believe we're hardwired for it, whereas capitalism requires constant propaganda and violent coercion to enforce. Still, I don't know if we can accomplish liberation before our society crashes into planetary limits that will result in an uninhabitable earth. The US-Israeli genocide in Gaza foreshadows a looming genocide of far-greater magnitude: the death of billions of people through famine, drought, heat-related deaths, and disaster fueled by climate change.

Or maybe Israel will launch its nuclear arsenal at Russia or Iran, and we'll all be wiped out even sooner.

The same elites profiting off Israel's war in Gaza—petrochemical and weapons manufacturing shareholders and their paid foot soldiers in imperial governments—are equally responsible for the coming collapse of all life on earth. Across the globe, elites protect themselves with armies of ever-more-militarized police and ever-more-sophisticated surveillance technology. They wield enormous influence over academic institutions, journalism, and the entertainment industry to prevent liberatory education from reaching the masses—to keep most people *believing* in their wealth and power. As the imaginary "wealth" of billionaires' balloons, as the gap between the ultra-wealthy and the rest of us stretches to incomprehensibly vast chasms, it can feel like the power of elites is more unassailable than at any time in human history.

Except. Except despite all their power, they're losing control of the narrative.

And here's why the past year brings me hope. Despite all the horrors we've witnessed, despite having come face to-face (at least through my phone screen) with the unfathomable violence and destruction and rot at the heart of our civilization. Despite all the grief and rage and despair I have felt watching this genocide unfold, watching as a global protest movement of millions has, as of yet, proven incapable of stopping it. Despite all that, I cling to the hope I see in the movement for a free Palestine.

Because in the past year, more people across the globe than ever before have expressed empathy and solidarity with Palestinians than at any moment in the past seventy-six years. Because liberatory education is spreading on social media faster than corporate censorship can stop it—a development so threatening to elites that the US government is seeking to ban TikTok. I have hope because people all across the US are making connections between genocides in Palestine, Congo, and Sudan, and the climate change ravaging their communities in the form of hurricanes Beryl and Helene and Milton, and the abandonment of their government, the crumbling of infrastructure, and the tyranny of the police state. I have hope because never have the lies, hypocrisy, and fascism of all the liberal "democracies" of the world been so blatantly exposed. And I have hope because millions of voices have spent a year sharing truth, exposing bullshit, and challenging the power of an empire.

Many millions are now standing in truth, but not most. And we need most—we need an overwhelming majority of people to overturn global empire. Here in the imperial core of the West, 99 percent of polled voters are about to cast their vote for either of two openly fascist, genocide-supporting, cop-loving, fossil-fuel-bootlicking, duopoly candidates. A mere 1 percent nationally are considering a third-party, anti-genocide pick. For the vast majority of my fellow USians, their political imaginations remain trapped in red or blue cages. People on both sides congratulate themselves on being "champions of freedom" for submitting their ballots—with which they co-sign their oppression, and the mass murder of Palestinians, and the impending doom of life on earth.

And so, liberatory education is spreading, but can we spread it fast enough to save us? To save Palestine? Many people get overwhelmed by the seeming impossibility of the task and give up. As for me, my lifetime of activism has taught me that you just gotta keep on keeping on, divorced from an expectation that in your lifespan—or even the lifespan of humanity—that you will "win." You keep on keeping on because your cause is righteous, and because you are standing in truth. Because the pain of confronting oppression is less severe than the pain of selling your soul or lying to yourself. Because the comrades you make will become the best friends you've ever had. Keep working towards collective liberation, because what else are you doing with your brief, miraculous life?

Do it for your kids, and everyone else's kids, and for all the cute lil baby animals, and even the creepy-crawly bugs and those deep-sea fishes with the headlamps and giant pointy teeth. Keep fighting because you love all the funny little creatures that have evolved on this miraculous green-and-blue planet, creatures that eat and shit and fuck and *live,* and you want them to go on living their funny little lives. Do it because you love people, most of all, with their giggles and jokes and poetry and farts and music and dancing and languages and cake. Do it because genocide bad!!!

Keep on fighting for liberation because, even though it seems highly unlikely we will live to see a *truly* free Palestine, or a deeply free world, we can, at the very least, free our own minds. At the very least, when alone with ourselves, we can take a break from all the bloodthirsty violence and selfishness and suffering of the physical world. There's one corner of Earth cops will never be able to police—and that's the space between your ears. Try it! Try imagining your way out of empire and capitalism, and watch how the relationships in your life heal and deepen and become more peaceful and joyful. Discover what an enormous relief it is, to allow yourself to envision a better world, and speak that vision aloud.

That's what I'm doing when I say "Free Palestine."

Your vision might just be catching. You might just free your neighbor—or even a Zionist relative, whose mind was trapped in a web of lies and racial supremacy. It's difficult, but if we keep repeating truth and logic and basic moral teachings over and over and over and over, we can actually free each other. It's slow going, but countless people who've reached out to me over the past year, sharing that my videos helped them see their way out of Zionism, have convinced me that it's possible.

Finally, if all else fails—if you are truly in the pit of despair and see no reason to hope that anything, ever, is going to get any better, so there's no point in resisting empire—remember that when hope is depleted, there's always spite! I have found within myself that spite is perhaps the deepest and most reliable well I can draw from.

Empire would like nothing more than for good people of conscience to give up. Elites would desperately like you to shut your mouth and obey.

Fuck 'em. Keep being a pain in the ass of your overlords, even though it's hard and there's no guarantee we will win.

I could care less how pure your intentions are. I can't know and don't care whether you're motivated by guilt or rage or the noblest of ideals.

Call for a Free Palestine because it's cool. Wear a keffiyeh because you look great in one. Dunk on Zionists because you don't want to be associated with them, because they're the biggest dorks and losers on the planet. Say "Free Palestine" because Macklemore and Kehlani said so. Shout "Genocide bad!" over and over and over again—for clout, for followers, for fame, or for deep moral conviction—it's all the same to me. Act out of sacred self-interest. Organize against empire because you *yourself* want to be free, and you recognize that your freedom is bound up with the freedom of Palestinians, and all people, and all life on earth.

Find whatever reason you can to keep showing up.

You won't be alone. If you have one comrade left, it's me. If you have zero comrades, I'm dead. But in fact, you have hundreds of millions of comrades, and if we can convert a few hundred million more, maybe, just maybe—just a fool's hope in hell *maybe*—we can Free Palestine, fuck empire, topple all tyrants, and save life on earth.

Notes from the families of babies born during the Genocide of Gaza

In February of 2024, I gave birth via C-section in a clean, state-of-the-art hospital that was not being bombed or besieged by a genocidal army.

I was acutely aware that the same was not true for those giving birth in Gaza.

I felt no pain during this major surgery, as I was on an epidural, and my pain was minimized throughout my ensuing recovery with powerful drugs.

Meanwhile, pregnant people in Gaza were undergoing C-sections in tents and field hospitals, without any pain relief whatsoever.

I had hot showers, clean sheets, a warm bed, and a roof over my head as I recovered.

Post-partum mothers in Gaza were sleeping on rubble, in the streets, beneath tarps, or in tents pitched on wet sand.

I had a bassinet, diapers, wipes, warm running water, a swing, changing table, nursing pillow, and a dozen cute outfits with which to welcome my baby into the world with softness and bright colors.

Parents in Gaza had rubble and screaming mortars and the whine of armed drones.

I knew these parents loved their babies every bit as much as I loved mine. Their babies were every bit as deserving of gentleness, safety, warmth and care. Their babies also beheld the wonder of the cosmos when they first opened their eyes, and they could light up the coldest heart with their smiles.

I wanted more than anything to help these babies, so two weeks after my kid was born, I started fundraising for pregnant and post-partum women in

Gaza. I used a random number generator to select a family to support off a spreadsheet of such fundraisers.

Each of these families was trying to raise the tens of thousands of dollars in bribes that they would need to give to Egyptian officials in order to evacuate Gaza through the Rafah Crossing. My followers, my incredible misphocha, raised over $500,000 for these families, but only one family was able to evacuate in time. Thanks to their generous donations, baby Farah was born in a hospital in Egypt. But for the rest, Israel closed the Rafah Crossing before they could evacuate.

I have been able to stay in touch with some of the families I fundraised for. The money we raised for them has allowed them to buy tents, food, diapers, and other necessities from markets in Gaza—because, yes, capitalism endures even amid genocide. But I cannot make Israel open the borders to allow in humanitarian aid. I can't help them buy the medicine and food and supplies that don't get through.

So, for this book, I wanted to hand the mic over to some of these parents and close out by letting them speak directly to you, my English-speaking audience. I hope their words will ground you, fuel you, and deepen your commitment to ending genocide.

Elena

Elena was born on June 8, 2024, in Gaza, to parents Nevin and Waseem. The following was written by her father, Waseem Mahmoud Hmeid.

When any war starts, our children become the weakest point affected by hostilities, falling within the sights of countless dangers, and deprived of the most beautiful years of childhood. Therefore, the protection of children is important, without a doubt. Our children are the present and the future, they must enjoy a decent life like your children, they have been deprived of everything, it is enough that their lives have been robbed. So all we wish is that we as parents and the whole world can help our children get out into a safe life and a bright future soon, and away from any wars.

Please save us before it's too late.

Manal

Manal Mattar was born in Al-Aqsa Hospital in July 2024 to mother Manar and father Mohamed. Tragically, Manal did not survive her first night of life. Israeli forces heavily bombed the area near the Mattar family's tent, and baby Manal's heart could not take the terrifying sounds of the explosions. She died of a heart attack, not one day old.

Manal's aunt Nour wrote this message for you:

We were living a safe life in Gaza in our beautiful home. My children were living their innocent childhood, until this brutal aggression came to reverse all the scales.

Our home was bombed, our lives were displaced, and our childhood was killed. Life has become impossible. We have lost even the glimmer of hope in the new generation.

What is the fault of these children in this displacement? What is the fault of Manar who endured all the hardships of pregnancy in these circumstances, and then did not survive with her baby? What is the fault of the baby Manal, who was killed before she saw the light?

I want to address my speech to the whole world: Stop the aggression against Gaza. We have the right to live like all people. Leave us to continue our dreams.

Heba

I already introduced you to Heba's family in Chapter 6. Heba was born to mom Shahd and dad Mohammed on March 2nd, 2024 at Al Awda Clinical and Social Center, Nuseirat. The following letter was written by her mother, Shahd J. Albadrasawi, speaking as the voice of baby Heba:

I watched the world unfold from a tiny corner of my heart, cradled in the warmth of my mother's love. My name is Heba, and I came into existence during a time overshadowed by chaos. Yet within me burned a quiet dream—a yearning for peace and a life filled with hope.

It all began with a moment of pure joy when my mother discovered she was pregnant with me. That news ignited a spark in her heart, and she began weaving a tapestry of dreams. She envisioned a home that was not just a shelter but a kingdom filled with laughter and warmth. I can picture her excitement as she planned my nursery, decorated in soft pastels with cozy blankets, each detail crafted with love. She dreamt of how she would welcome me, surrounded by family and friends who would celebrate my arrival with open arms.

But as life often teaches us, dreams do not always materialize as expected. The morning of October 7th shattered our peaceful aspirations. The world outside turned into a cacophony of terror, with the sounds of bombs echoing through the streets. I felt my mother's body tremble, her heart racing with fear. This would become my first memory—an imprint of chaos shadowed by the warmth of her love, holding me close as if to shield me from the world's horrors.

As the days turned into weeks, circumstances forced my family to move from one place to another. Every time they found a semblance of safety, the threat would loom again, sending us fleeing into the unknown. We lived in a tent, a fragile barrier against the elements, where the cold air seeped through every crack. Yet my parents worked tirelessly to make it feel like home. They gathered scraps of fabric to create a small corner for me, a sanctuary filled with hopes and dreams.

The day of my birth arrived amidst the turmoil. As we rushed to the hospital, the streets felt deserted, the sounds of conflict echoing all around. The hospital itself was dimly lit, filled with the cries of others seeking refuge from pain. My father spent that night on the hospital floor, anxiously waiting outside my mother's room, where helicopters circled above, and bombs shook the building. His presence was a testament to his love and devotion, even in the face of fear and uncertainty.

My father, a steadfast pillar of strength, had always been the one to shield us from despair. He worked tirelessly, often taking on multiple jobs just to ensure we had enough to eat. In those uncertain days, his determination shone brighter than ever. He would venture out into the chaos, risking his safety to find food and essentials, often returning with little more than scraps, but he always wore a smile, determined to protect our spirits.

When I entered this world, cradled in my mother's arms, I felt a surge of hope. In that moment, I was part of something greater—a symbol of resilience against the backdrop of despair. My father was right there, his eyes filled with tears of joy and pride, reflecting a love that could conquer any storm.

As I grew, I began to grasp the harsh realities of our existence. Explosions echoed in the distance, and I could see the fear in my mother's eyes every time the ground shook beneath us. Yet through it all, she never wavered. She often told me I was the reason for her strength, a beacon of light in their darkest days. She taught me that love could transcend any challenge and that hope could flourish even amidst chaos.

My father played a crucial role in shaping my understanding of courage. I remember the nights when fear would creep in, and my mother would hold me tightly, whispering words of reassurance. But it was my father who would sit with us, recounting stories of bravery and resilience, instilling in me a sense of strength. He would speak of our ancestors who faced adversities yet persevered, reminding us that we carried their legacy within us.

Now, at seven months old, I find myself in a cramped room we share with other families. It's a small space filled with the laughter and cries of children, yet it's also a reminder of our struggles. I see my father's efforts to secure food and basic necessities, his determination unwavering even in the face of scarcity. He searches for nourishment not just for me but for our dreams of a better future.

The small room we share is a testament to our resilience. Though it is cramped, it is filled with love. My father often plays with me, making silly faces to elicit my laughter, his smile a reminder that joy can exist even in the direst of circumstances. He would say, "Heba, as long as we have each other, we can withstand anything." His words resonated in the air, filling our tiny space with warmth.

But challenges persisted. I saw the toll that the ongoing conflict took on my father. His face, once bright and full of hope, began to show signs of weariness. The weight of responsibility rested heavily on his shoulders, yet he never let it dim his spirit. He would stay up late into the night, planning for our future, imagining a day when we could live freely, without fear.

I dream of a day when peace will blossom, when we can live as everyone deserves to live—free from fear, in a world where laughter reigns. I long for the moment when my parents' dreams will finally come to fruition, when they can watch me grow without the shadow of conflict looming overhead.

As I continue to grow, I will learn to tell my story. I will speak of the resilience that blossoms in the darkest of times, the love that nurtures us amidst chaos, and the unwavering hope that flickers like a candle in the night. One day, I will share my journey with others, not just to recount the hardships but to inspire strength and courage.

My father often speaks of hope as if it were a living thing, something we must nurture and protect. He tells me stories of gardens blooming after harsh winters, drawing parallels to our own lives. "We, too, will bloom," he reassures me, "as long as we hold onto hope."

For now, I remain a small child, cocooned in my parents' dreams, hopeful for a future where love conquers all, and where our story unfolds with the promise of brighter tomorrows. I envision a day when my father can stand tall without the burdens of fear, and my mother can smile without worry.

And as I grow, I will remember the sacrifices they made, the love they poured into every moment, and the strength they showed in the face of adversity. Together, we will write a new chapter in our story—a chapter filled with peace, joy, and the unwavering belief that love can overcome anything.

Acknowledgments

I find the task of writing these acknowledgments, hands-down, the most intimidating part of this book.

How can I adequately thank everyone who has stood up for Palestinians over the past year (and all the years prior)? How can I possibly recognize everyone who's educated me on these topics? How can I begin to express the depth of my admiration for all those who've fought for liberation, and particularly for the Palestinian people who have survived a year of genocide—and a hundred years of ethnic cleansing before that—how do I possibly thank you all?

It's a fool's errand, and I will fail miserably to credit everyone to whom credit is due, but here are a few key folks who made this book possible:

Obviously, to all the journalists, artists, scholars, researchers, and historians I've mentioned in this text and credited in the end notes, thank you for teaching me.

I have also learned from countless other journalists, podcasters, and content creators not credited in the endnotes. I've consumed a zillion tweets and memes and TikToks over the past year, many of which have shaped my opinions on Palestine or pointed me down a new avenue of research. I've credited a handful of those creators within this text, but there are so many more. You know who you are, and if one of my arguments sounds a lot like that shitpost you made a year ago, it's very possible I saw it while scrolling, and it seeped into my brain. Thank you for dodging censorship, hijacking shitty algorithms, dropping knowledge and keeping me sane through this long, dark year of horrors.

Thank you to Ganzeer, for creating yet another stunning, iconic, and perfectly suited cover for one of my books.

Thank you to my patreons, who pay for my groceries. And a special thank you to Jeff Spakowski and Laura Mandelberg who helped fund the cover art.

Thank you to my social media mishpocha, my followers, subscribers, and fans! Every heart, comment, share, and donation have made a difference. It's my honor to make content for such an empathetic, passionate, and radical community!

To my agent, Becca Podos, a fellow anti-Zionist Jew, thank you for fighting the good fight in publishing spaces. It would be so very lonely out here without your advocacy.

Thank you to David Klein for your attention to detail on the copy edits for this book, and for letting me keep so many "fucks" and exclamation marks and italics and parentheses and em dashes and stylistic lists and, yes, even many of those wretched scare quotes.

Thank you to the small but mighty team at Interlink: Michel, Maha, Pam, Harri, Leyla, Shell, Becca, and Greta.

Thank you to Dr. Rashid Khalidi who offered notes on an early draft of Chapters 3 and 6. And thank you Dr. Nadim Bawalsa, associate editor of the Journal of Palestine Studies, who provided fact-checking for historical content about Palestine.

Thank you to Nour, Waseem, and Shahd for the honor of getting to know you this year and for letting me share your words in these pages. Thank you for being amazing parents in the most horrifying circumstances.

Thank you to my spouse, without whom this book could not have been written, and who is my anchor and buddy and port in a storm. Thank you big kid for coming with me to protests and JVP meetings and for keeping me in touch with that Gen Z slang and hot goss. Thank you middle kid for being the funniest, fiercest person I know and for reminding me to get off my phone when I really need to hear it! And thank you littlest kid for making so many diapers, and needing so many naps, and continually interrupting me throughout the writing of this book with those little reminders to touch grass, breathe, and appreciate the way your smile lights up the world.

Thank you, Dad, for your love and humor and skepticism and open-mindedness and for being Jewish in all the best ways.

Acknowledgments

Finally, thank you to my dear editor, Hannah Moushabeck, for giving me a purpose and a direction in this year of darkness. This whole book was your idea. Your soul and your activism and your writing are all so completely beautiful and inspiring to me and many, many others.

Endnotes

Find a digital list of endnotes with working hyperlinks at simkern.com/ genocide-bad-endnotes

1   *UN Special Committee finds Israel's warfare methods in Gaza consistent with genocide, including use of starvation as weapon of war | ohchr.* United Nations Press Release. (2024, November 14). www.ohchr.org/en/press-releases/2024/11/un-special-committee-finds-israels-warfare-methods-gaza-consistent-genocide

2   *Amnesty International concludes Israel is committing genocide against Palestinians in Gaza.* Amnesty International. (2024, December 5). https://www.amnesty.org/en/latest/news/2024/12/amnesty-international-concludes-israel-is-committing-genocide-against-palestinians-in-gaza/

3   Maad, A., Audureau, W., & Forey, S. (2024, April 3). *"40 beheaded babies": Deconstructing the rumor at the heart of the information battle between Israel and Hamas.* Le Monde.fr. www.lemonde.fr/en/les-decodeurs/article/2024/04/03/40-beheaded-babies-the-itinerary-of-a-rumor-at-the-heart-of-the-information-battle-between-israel-and-hamas_6667274_8.html

4   Gupta, A. (2024, March 6). *Claims of mass rape by Hamas unravel upon investigation* . YES! Magazine. www.yesmagazine.org/social-justice/2024/03/05/israel-hamas-oct7-report-gaza

5   9572nd Meeting, S. C. (2024, March 11). *Reasonable grounds to believe conflict-related sexual violence occurred in Israel during 7 October attacks, senior UN official tells Security Council | Meetings coverage and press releases.* United Nations Security Council. https://press.un.org/en/2024/sc15621.doc.htm

6   Kubovich, Y. (2024, July 7). *IDF ordered Hannibal Directive on October 7 to prevent Hamas taking soldiers captive.* Haaretz.com. www.haaretz.com/israel-news/2024-07-07/ty-article-magazine/.premium/idf-ordered-hannibal-directive-on-october-7-to-prevent-hamas-taking-soldiers-captive/00000190-89a2-d776-a3b1-fdbe45520000

7   Bergman, R., & Goldman, A. (2023, December 1). *Israel knew Hamas's attack plan more than a year ago.* The New York Times. www.nytimes.com/2023/11/30/world/middleeast/israel-hamas-attack-intelligence.html

8   Egypt intelligence official says Israel ignored repeated warnings of 'something big' | The Times of Israel. (2023, October 9). https://www.timesofisrael.com/egypt-intelligence-official-says-israel-ignored-repeated-warnings-of-something-big/

9   Statistics on Palestinians in the custody of the Israeli security forces | B'Tselem. (2024, September 2). https://www.btselem.org/statistics/detainees_and_prisoners

10 Middle East Monitor. (2024, November 8). *Israel passes law allowing Palestinian children under 14 to be jailed.* https://www.middleeastmonitor.com/20241108-israel-passes-law-allowing-palestinian-children-under-14-to-be-jailed/

11 Oltermann, P. (2023, October 15). *Palestinian voices "shut down" at Frankfurt Book Fair, say authors.* The Guardian. www.theguardian.com/world/2023/oct/15/palestinian-voices-shut-down-at-frankfurt-book-fair-say-authors

12 Diamond, J. (2023, December 12). *This weird NYC couple doesn't want you to read Palestinian children's books.* Literary Hub. lithub.com/this-weird-nyc-couple-doesnt-want-you-to-read-palestinian-childrens-books/

13 Táíwò, O. O. (2022). *Elite capture: How the powerful took over identity politics (and everything else).* Haymarket Books. 12.

14 Ibid, 10.

15 Ibid, 7.

16 Schaefer, B. (2014, February 21). *Israeli military one of the world's most LGBT friendly, report says.* Haaretz.com. www.haaretz.com/2014-02-22/ty-article/.premium/idf-one-of-worlds-most-lgbt-friendly

17 *Vice president Harris to protesters: "I'm speaking."* C-Span. (n.d.). www.c-span.org/video/?c5127583%2Fvice-president-harris-protesters-im-speaking

18 Ibid, 112.

19 Ibid, 113.

20 Sato, M. (2024, June 5). *Israel reportedly used fake social media accounts to influence us lawmakers.* The Verge. www.theverge.com/2024/6/5/24172002/israel-gaza-war-covert-influence-camapaign-meta-openai

21 United Nations. (2024b, March 27). *Gaza war: "direct hits" on more than 200 schools since Israeli bombing began | UN news.* United Nations. news.un.org/en/story/2024/03/1148031

22 Krever, M., & Diamond, J. (2024, October 24). *The Israeli military has used Palestinians as human shields in Gaza, soldier and former detainees say.* CNN. www.cnn.com/2024/10/24/middleeast/palestinians-human-shields-israel-military-gaza-intl/index.html

23 *Israeli forces use Palestinian children as human shields during siege of hospital | defense for children Palestine.* Defense for Children International . (2024, September 23). www.dci-palestine.org/israeli_forces_use_palestinian_children_as_human_shields_during_siege_of_hospital

24 Al Jazeera. (2024, June 23). *"human shielding in action": Israeli forces strap Palestinian man to Jeep.* www.aljazeera.com/news/2024/6/23/human-shielding-in-action-israeli-forces-strap-palestinian-man-to-jeep

25 Esensten, A. (2023, December 19). *Black Israelis mobilized for their country, as soldiers, volunteers and Social Media Warriors.* The Jerusalem Post | JPost.com. www.jpost.com/israel-hamas-war/article-778604

26 Bohbot, A. (2024a, November 18). *Historic first: Female israeli combat soldiers conduct Lebanon operations.* The Jerusalem Post | JPost.com. www.jpost.com/israel-news/article-829602

27 Schaefer, B. (2014, February 21). *Israeli military one of the world's most LGBT friendly, report says.* Haaretz.com. www.haaretz.com/2014-02-22/ty-article/.premium/idf-one-of-worlds-most-lgbt-friendly/0000017f-f8b2-d2d5-a9ff-f8be12420000

28 BBC. (2022, October 7). *Gay Palestinian Ahmad Abu Marhia beheaded in West Bank.* BBC News. www.bbc.com/news/world-middle-east-63174835

29 Price, A. (2023, June 12). *Texas woman killed after shooter shouted anti-gay slur, per affidavit.* Axios Austin. www.axios.com/local/austin/2023/06/12/akira-ross-murder-shooting

30 Williams, R. (2015, August 2). *Shira Banki, Israeli teen attacked at Jerusalem Gay Pride Parade, dies from injuries.* NBCNews.com. www.nbcnews.com/news/world/shira-banki-israeli-teen-attacked-jerusalem-gay-pride-parade-dies-n402576

31 #OUTLAWED: *"The love that dare not speak its name."* Maps of anti-LGBT Laws Country by Country | Human Rights Watch. (n.d.). https://features.hrw.org/features/features/lgbt_laws/

32 *Gaza Strip Demographics Profile.* Index Mundi. (2021, September 18). www.indexmundi.com/gaza_strip/demographics_profile.html

33 Allen, M., & VandeHei, J. (2024, May 6). *Biden vs. Trump: 6% of Americans in these states will decide who wins.* Axios. www.axios.com/2024/05/06/biden-trump-election-swing-states

34 *200 days of military attack on Gaza: A horrific death toll amid intl. failure to stop Israel's genocide of Palestinians.* Euro-Med Human Rights Monitor. (2024, April 24). euromedmonitor.org/en/article/6282/200-days-of-military-attack-on-Gaza:-A-horrific-death-toll-amid-intl.-failure-to-stop-Israel%E2%80%99s-genocide-of-Palestinians

35 *Israel's Likud signs coalition deal with anti-LGBTQ Radical.* AP News. (2022, November 28). apnews.com/article/middle-east-religion-israel-gay-rights-d525655630fcf17082d0a6b8a8a998c8

36 Ben David, T., & Ben David, L. (2021, September 17). *"I'd rather die in the west bank": LGBTQ Palestinians find no safety in Israel.* +972 Magazine. www.972mag.com/lgbtq-palestinians-israel-asylum/

37 Ashly, J. (2019, August 27). *PA rescinds ban on LGBTQ Group after protests.* The Electronic Intifada. electronicintifada.net/content/pa-rescinds-ban-lgbtq-group-after-protests/28201

38 de Guzman, C. (2023, October 20). *In Gaza, "queering the map" shows heartbreaking LGBT notes.* Time. time.com/6326254/queering-the-map-gaza-lgbt-palestinians/

39 Al Jazeera English. *"Black faces in high places are not going to save us'"* – Quotable. YouTube. (April 17, 2024). www.youtube.com/watch?v=javaZtuESR4

40 Pew Research Center. (2021, May 11). *Jewish Americans in 2020, 9. race, ethnicity, heritage and immigration among U.S. Jews.* Pew Research Center. www.pewresearch.org/religion/2021/05/11/race-ethnicity-heritage-and-immigration-among-u-s-jews/

41 Pew Research Center. (2021, May 11). *Jewish Americans in 2020, 11. economics and well-being among U.S. jews.* Pew Research Center. www.pewresearch.org/religion/2021/05/11/economics-and-well-being-among-u-s-jews/

42 Jews from the Middle East - Jewish Voice for Peace Fact Sheet. (n.d.). https://www.jewishvoiceforpeace.org/wp-content/uploads/2015/07/ JVP-Jews-of-the-middle-east-fact-sheet.pdf

43 MEE Staff. (2021, June 11). *Education and income gaps widening between Israel's different Jewish groups, says report.* Middle East Eye. www.middleeasteye.net/news/israel-education-ashkenazi-mizrahi-report

44 Goldstein, T. (2019, July 8). *Ethiopian-israeli community has hit boiling point, leading activist says | The Times of Israel.* The Times of Israel. www.timesofisrael.com/ ethiopian-israeli-community-has-reached-boiling-point-leading-activist-says/

45 Greenwood, P. (2013, February 28). *Ethiopian women in Israel "given contraceptive without consent."* The Guardian. www.theguardian.com/ world/2013/feb/28/ethiopian-women-given-contraceptives-israel

46 *Israel's apartheid against Palestinians: A cruel system of domination and a crime against humanity.* Amnesty International. (2022, February 1). www.amnesty.org/ en/latest/news/2022/02/israels-apartheid-against-palestinians-a-cruel-system-of- domination-and-a-crime-against-humanity/

47 Johnson, A., & Ali, O. (2024, January 10). *Coverage of gaza war in the New York Times and other major newspapers heavily favored Israel, analysis shows.* The Intercept. theintercept.com/2024/01/09/newspapers-israel-palestine-bias-new-york-times/

48 Al Jazeera. (2023, November 7). *Is Israel's Gaza War the deadliest conflict for children in modern times?* https://www.aljazeera.com/news/2023/11/7/ is-israels-gaza-war-the-deadliest-conflict-for-children-in-modern-times

49 Ibid.

50 Al-Kassab, F. (2024, January 26). *A top U.N. Court says Gaza genocide is "plausible" but does not order cease-fire.* NPR. www.npr.org/2024/01/26/1227078791/ icj-israel-genocide-gaza-palestinians-south-africa

51 *Museum condemns recent antisemitism on college campuses.* Illinois Holocaust Museum. (2024, April 22). www.ilholocaustmuseum.org/ museum-condemns-recent-antisemitism-on-college-campuses/

52 Miszak, D. (2024, May 31). *A Holocaust Museum cut a survivor from its speaker's list - for protesting the war in Gaza.* The Forward. forward.com/news/618082/holocaust-survivor-cut-museum-protest-gaza/

53 *The jewish museum cancels two Jewish artists descended from holocaust survivors for supporting Palestinians*. World Art News. (2024, March 13). worldart.news/2024/03/13/the-jewish-museum-cancels-two-jewish-artists-descended-from-holocaust-survivors-for-supporting-palestinians/

54 *Holocaust books for Young Adults*. Jewish Book Council. (2023, September 20). www.jewishbookcouncil.org/books/reading-lists/holocaust-books-for-young-adults

55 *Holocaust books for Middle Grade Readers*. Jewish Book Council. (2023, September 20). www.jewishbookcouncil.org/books/reading-lists/holocaust-books-for-middle-grade-readers

56 Zion, I. B., & Scharf, I. (2022, January 27). *One-third of Israeli holocaust survivors live in poverty, advocates say*. PBS. www.pbs.org/newshour/world/one-third-of-israeli-holocaust-survivors-live-in-poverty-advocates-say

57 Dorman, J. L. (2023, October 14). *Descendants of holocaust survivors protesting Israel's "genocide" of Palestinians among those arrested in front of sen. Chuck Schumer's house in New York*. Business Insider. www.businessinsider.com/israel-pro-palestinian-arrests-descendants-holocaust-gaza-ceasefire-schumer-brooklyn-2023-10

58 Danailova, H. (2017, November). *PJ Library and its children of the (free monthly) book: Charleston jewish federation*. Charleston Jewish Federation. www.jewishcharleston.org/news/pj-library-and-its-children-of-the-free-monthly-book

59 Cox, M.-L. (1999, October 14). *Author Hochschild recounts lost history of Horror in the Belgian congo*. Wilson Center. www.wilsoncenter.org/article/author-hochschild-recounts-lost-history-horror-the-belgian-congo

60 David Michael, S. (2019, September). *Counting the Dead: Estimating the Loss of Life in the Indigenous Holocaust, 1492-Present*. Southeastern Oklahoma State University. www.se.edu/native-american/wp-content/uploads/sites/49/2019/09/A-NAS-2017-Proceedings-Smith.pdf

61 *Palestinian American Community Data: Center Arab narratives*. Palestinian American Community Data | Center Arab Narratives. (n.d.). https://www.arabnarratives.org/narrative/palestinian-american-community-in-numbers

62 Berger, M. (2023, September 29). *Sudan's diaspora sends home aid as world's attention drifts*. Washington Post. www.washingtonpost.com/world/2023/09/29/sudan-war-diaspora-aid/

63 Wikimedia Foundation. (2024, August 4). *Congolese Americans*. Wikipedia. en.wikipedia.org/wiki/Congolese_Americans

64 *Christian Zionism*. Jewish Virtual Library. (n.d.). www.jewishvirtuallibrary.org/christian-zionism

65 Irfan, A. (2023, August 23). *Why Palestinians are known as the world's "Best educated refugees"anne Irfan - Columbia University Press Blog*. Columbia University Press Blog . cupblog.org/2023/08/23/why-palestinians-are-known-as-the-worlds-best-educated-refugeesanne-irfan/

66 Konieczny, Piotr (2021-06-23). "From Xenophobia to Golden Age: "Jewish Paradise" Proverb as a Linguistic Reclamation". *Contemporary Jewry*. **41** (2): 517–537. doi:10.1007/s12397-021-09380-4. ISSN 1876-5165. S2CID 236146777.

67 Ben-Naeh, Y. Blond, tall, with honey-colored eyes: Jewish ownership of slaves in the Ottoman Empire. *Jew History* **20**, 315–332 (2006). doi.org/10.1007/s10835-006-9018-z

68 Sand, S. (2020). *The Invention of the Jewish People* (Y. Lotan, Trans.). Verso. 247.

69 Khalidi, R. (2021). *The Hundred Years' War on Palestine: A History of Settler Colonialism and Resistance, 1917-2017*. Picador. 97.

70 Ibid, 97.

71 Ibid, 98.

72 Ibid, 104.

73 Ibid, 104.

74 Schmidt, E. (2022, March 16). *Reading the numbers: 130 million American adults have low literacy skills*. APM Research Lab. www.apmresearchlab.org/10x-adult-literacy

75 Librarians and Archivists with Palestine. "Author Meets Booktok: Sim Kern and Rashid Khalidi on 'The Hundred Years' War on Palestine.'" YouTube. (2023, December 4). www.youtube.com/watch?v=Y9z6SdKDvi8

76 Maad, A., Audureau, W., & Forey, S. (2024, April 3). *"40 beheaded babies": Deconstructing the rumor at the heart of the information battle between Israel and Hamas*. Le Monde.fr. www.lemonde.fr/en/les-decodeurs/article/2024/04/03/40-beheaded-babies-the-itinerary-of-a-rumor-at-the-heart-of-the-information-battle-between-israel-and-hamas_6667274_8.html

77 AJ+. (2024, June 5.). *The child beheaded in the Rafah tent massacre was named Ahmed Al-Najjar. He was only 18 months old. Here's what his family had to say about Ahmed*. X (formerly Twitter). x.com/ajplus/status/1798535281081278893

78 *Hamas Covenant 1988.* The Avalon Project : Hamas Covenant 1988. (n.d.). https://avalon.law.yale.edu/21st_century/hamas.asp

79 *Hamas in 2017: The document in full.* Middle East Eye. (2017, May 2). www.middleeasteye.net/news/hamas-2017-document-full

80 *What is known about Israeli hostages taken by Hamas.* AJC. (2024, October 14). www.ajc.org/news/what-is-known-about-israeli-hostages-taken-by-hamas

81 *Number of Palestinian children in Israeli detention .* Defense for Children Palestine. (2024, June 30). www.dci-palestine.org/children_in_israeli_detention

82 *640 Palestinian children detained in West Bank since October 7.* The New Arab. (2024, June 18). www.newarab.com/news/640-palestinian-children-detained-west-bank-october-7

83 *Child casualties in the West Bank Skyrocket in the past nine months.* UNICEF. (2024,July22).www.unicef.org/press-releases/child-casualties-west-bank-skyrocket-past-nine-months

84 *Counting the dead in Gaza: difficult but essential.* Khatib, Rasha et al. (2024, July 10). The Lancet, Volume 404, Issue 10449, 237 – 238 https://www.thelancet.com/journals/lancet/article/PIIS0140-6736(24)01169-3/fulltext

85 Mohammad, L. (2023, October 19). *Children make up nearly half of Gaza's population. here's what it means for the war.* NPR. https://www.npr.org/2023/10/19/1206479861/israel-gaza-hamas-children-population-war-palestinians

86 BBC. (2024, October 18). *IDF drone footage "shows sinwar in final moments."* BBC News. https://www.bbc.com/news/videos/c8djz4rn144o

87 *How the Killing of Yahya Sinwar shattered Israel's narrative.*(2024, October 19). Al Jazeera English. YouTube www.youtube.com/watch?v=S0-8ZjygzpE&t=1232s

88 Hezbollah vows escalation after Sinwar's death, Iran says "resistance will endure" | The Times of Israel. (2024a, October 18). https://www.timesofisrael.com/hezbollah-vows-escalation-after-sinwars-death-iran-says-resistance-will-endure/

89 Reyes, R. (2024, October 10). *I interrogated Oct. 7 mastermind sinwar for 180 hours - there can be no peace as long as he lives.* New York Post. nypost.com/2024/10/06/world-news/israeli-who-interrogated-oct-7-mastermind-yahya-sinwar-on-why-he-must-be-killed/

90 Gardner, F. (2024, October 17). *Yahya Sinwar: Who was the Hamas leader?.* BBC News. www.bbc.com/news/world-middle-east-67473719

91   Ginbar, Y. (2019, March 21). *It's now (even more) official: Torture is legal in Israel.* OMCT. www.omct.org/en/resources/blog/its-now-even-more-official-torture-is-legal-in-israel

92   Ibid.

93   United States Holocaust Memorial Museum. (2023, April 17). *Warsaw Ghetto Uprising.* United States Holocaust Memorial Museum. encyclopedia.ushmm.org/content/en/article/warsaw-ghetto-uprising

94   Rabbani, M. (2002, May). *The only truth about Jenin is the Israeli cover-up.* Washington Report on Middle East Affairs. https://www.wrmea.org/2002-may/the-only-truth-about-jenin-is-the-israeli-cover-up.html

95   A. Polonsky, (2012), The Jews in Poland and Russia, Volume III, 1914 to 2008, p. 537

96   *How Hamas' Leader in Gaza Reacted to the Ceasefire.* (2021, June 21). Vice News. Youtube. www.youtube.com/watch?v=1Px6AyVjw2A

97   Enes Çalli, M. (2024, April 6). *Amount of Israeli bombs dropped on Gaza surpasses that of World War II.* Anadolu Ajansı. https://www.aa.com.tr/en/middle-east/amount-of-israeli-bombs-dropped-on-gaza-surpasses-that-of-world-war-ii/3239665

98   *2021 was the deadliest year since 2014, Israel killed 319 Palestinians in opt 5-year record in House demolitions: 895 Palestinians lost their homes | b'tselem.* B'tselem. (2022, January 4). www.btselem.org/press_releases/20220104_in_deadliest_year_since_2014_israel_killed_319_palestinians_in_opt

99   Middle East Monitor. (2024a, October 2). *902 Palestinian families wiped out in Gaza by Israel over past year: Media Office.* https://www.middleeastmonitor.com/20241002-902-palestinian-families-wiped-out-in-gaza-by-israel-over-past-year-media-office/

100 Khalidi, R. (2021). *The Hundred Years' War on Palestine: A History of Settler Colonialism and Resistance, 1917-2017.* Picador. 179.

101 Ibid, 179–180.

102 Ibid, 174.

103 Ibid, 169.

104 Ibid, 174.

105 Ibid, 198.

106 Ibid, 198.

107 Ibid, 203.

108 Ibid, 214.

109 Ibid, 215.

110 Ibid, 215.

111 Ibid.

112 Fayyad, H. (2019, March 30). *Gaza's Great March of return protests explained.* Al Jazeera. www.aljazeera.com/news/2019/3/30/gazas-great-march-of-return-protests-explained

113 Hamama, M. (2024, October 20). *Surprise Unto Death: The legend of sinwar.* Mada Masr. www.madamasr.com/en/2024/10/20/feature/politics/surprise-unto-death-the-legend-of-sinwar/

114 Middle East Eye. (2024, October 17). *"I prefer to die as a martyr" says Yahya Sinwar in old resurfaced footage.* YouTube. www.youtube.com/watch?v=I269qRt-75s

115 Guiza, I. (2024, October 18). *"in a keffiyeh, calm and fighting to the last": Social media reacts to killing of Yahya Sinwar.* Middle East Eye. www.middleeasteye.net/trending/yahya-sinwars-killing-mourning-celebration-online-reactions

116 MEE Staff. (2024, November 22). *One-third of Jewish-American teens say they "sympathise" with Hamas, Israeli government poll shows.* Middle East Eye. www.middleeasteye.net/news/one-third-american-jewish-teens-say-they-sympathise-hamas-israeli-government-poll-shows

117 Oz-Salzberger, F. (2024, November 25). *We have to choose: Do we back Bibi or support Israel?.* We have to choose: Do we back Bibi or support Israel? - The Jewish Chronicle. www.thejc.com/lets-talk/we-have-to-choose-do-we-back-bibi-or-support-israel-bzfu17q5

118 Chambers, S. (2024, July 1). *Shuttered Israeli port seeks financial shield.* Splash247. splash247.com/shuttered-israeli-port-seeks-financial-shield/

119 Young, E. (2024, October 27). *Israel may drop out of developed world if key professionals emigrate - expert.* The Jerusalem Post | JPost.com. www.jpost.com/israel-news/article-826287

120 Kubovich, Y. (2024, October 31). *Weapons rationing leading to more deaths of Israeli soldiers by explosive devices in Gaza.* Haaretz.com. www.haaretz.com/israel-news/2024-10-31/ty-article/.premium/low-arms-supply-leading-to-more-israeli-soldiers-being-killed-by-explosive-devices-in-gaza/00000192-e20d-d6c4-adfe-e6cfa4620000

121 Inlakesh, R. (2024, October 25). *"the platoons are empty": Israeli army battles low morale, soldier defections.* MintPress News. www.mintpressnews.com/the-platoons-are-empty-israeli-army-battles-low-morale-soldier-defections/288514/

122 Stockholm International Peace Research Institute. (2024, April 22). *Global military spending surges amid war, rising tensions and insecurity.* SIPRI. https://www.sipri.org/media/press-release/2024/ global-military-spending-surges-amid-war-rising-tensions-and-insecurity

123 Bicer, A. (2024, March 13). *Israel killed more children in Gaza in last 5 months than all conflicts worldwide for last 4 years: Un Rapporteur.* Anadolu Ajansı. www.aa.com.tr/en/middle-east/israel-killed-more-children-in-gaza-in-last-5-months-than-all-conflicts-worldwide-for-last-4-years-un-rapporteur/3163509

124 Williams, D. (2014). *I Freed Myself: African American self-emancipation in the Civil War era.* Cambridge University Press. erenow.org/modern/i-freed-myself-african-american-self-emancipation-civil-war-era/3.php

125 Encyclopædia Britannica, inc. (2024, September 27). *Slave rebellions.* Encyclopædia Britannica. www.britannica.com/topic/slave-rebellions

126 Williams, D. (2014). *I Freed Myself: African American self-emancipation in the Civil War era.* Cambridge University Press. erenow.org/modern/i-freed-myself-african-american-self-emancipation-civil-war-era/3.php

127 Ibid.

128 Ibid.

129 National Archives and Records Administration. (2022, January 28). *The Emancipation Proclamation.* www.archives.gov/exhibits/featured-documents/emancipation-proclamation

130 Williams, D. (2014). *I Freed Myself: African American self-emancipation in the Civil War era.* Cambridge University Press. erenow.org/modern/i-freed-myself-african-american-self-emancipation-civil-war-era/4.php

131 Ibid.

132 Ibid.

133 Plett-Usher, B. (2024, June 10). *South Africans still battling 'economic apartheid' 30 years on.* BBC News. www.bbc.com/news/articles/c4nn035zqqqo

134 Qumsiyeh, M. B., & Abusarhan, M. A. (2021, November 3). *An environmental nakba: The Palestinian environment under Israeli Colonization.* Science for the People Magazine. magazine.scienceforthepeople.org/vol23-1/an-environmental-nakba-the-palestinian-environment-under-israeli-colonization/

135 Middle East Eye. (September 22, 2024). *Israeli students chant 'may your village burn' at Palestinian girl.* Facebook. www.facebook.com/watch/?v=1170764674222593

136 Haaretz Editorial. (2024, September 24). *Israel is instilling mob values in its children: Editorial.* Haaretz.com. www.haaretz.com/opinion/editorial/2024-09-25/ty-article-opinion/israel-is-instilling-mob-values-in-its-children/00000192-259c-d815-a393-7ffe091e0000

137 Trachtenberg, J. (2013). *Jewish Magic and Superstition: A Study in Folk Religion.* Martino Publishing. p. 4.

138 Ibid, p. 5.

139 Chajes, J.H. (2003). *Between Worlds: Dybbuks, Exorcists, and Early Modern Judaism.* University of Pennsylvania Press. p. 61

140 Ibid, 65.

141 Ibid, 9.

142 Ibid, 42.

143 Ibid, 57.

144 Climenhaga, L. (2012, May 9). *Imagining the witch: A comparison between fifteenth-century witches within medieval Christian thought and the persecution of jews and heretics in the Middle Ages.* Constellations. https://journals.library.ualberta.ca/constellations/index.php/constellations/article/view/17200, p. 119-120.

145 Ibid, 121.

146 Trachtenberg, J. (2013). *Jewish Magic and Superstition: A Study in Folk Religion.* Martino Publishing. p. 2.

147 Climenhaga, L. (2012, May 9). *Imagining the witch: A comparison between fifteenth-century witches within medieval Christian thought and the persecution of jews and heretics in the Middle Ages.* Constellations. https://journals.library.ualberta.ca/constellations/index.php/constellations/article/view/17200, p. 124-125.

148 Lubrich, N. (2015). The Wandering Hat: Iterations of the Medieval Jewish Pointed Cap. *Jewish History, 29*(3/4), 203–244. http://www.jstor.org/stable/24709777, p. 222-223.

149 Council Fathers. (1215). *Fourth lateran council : 1215.* (Tanner, N. trans.) Papal Encyclicals. www.papalencyclicals.net/councils/ecum12-2.htm

150 LUBRICH, N. (2015). The Wandering Hat: Iterations of the Medieval Jewish Pointed Cap. *Jewish History, 29*(3/4), 203–244. http://www.jstor.org/stable/24709777, p. 227-228.

151 Ibid, 233.

152 *New exhibition at the wiener library features "jews out!" – a children's board game from Nazi Germany*. Tel Aviv University News. (2023, January 24). english.tau.ac.il/news/wiener_exhibition_2023

153 Cassen, Flora. (2019). *Jewish Travelers in Early Modern Italy: Visible and Invisible Resistance to the Jewish Badge*. in *Dress and Cultural Difference in Early Modern Europe*. www.researchgate.net/publication/336347490_Jewish_Travelers_in_Early_Modern_Italy_Visible_and_Invisible_Resistance_to_the_Jewish_Badge, (pp.73-89)

154 Horowitz, E. (n.d.). *Sumptuary Legislation*. The YIVO Encyclopedia of Jews in Eastern Europe. encyclopedia.yivo.org/article/305

155 Varyash, I. (2024, January 17). *The persecutions of the Jews and Muslims in the West*. Qalam. https://qalam.global/en/articles/the-persecutions-of-the-jews-and-muslims-in-the-west-en-1

156 Ibid.

157 Ford, R.T. (2022). *Dress Codes: How the laws of fashion made history*. Simon & Schuster Paperbacks. p. 53.

158 Shirbon, E., & Grzanka, P. (2024, March 28). *Israeli soldiers play with Gaza Women's underwear in online posts | reuters*. Reuters. https://www.reuters.com/world/middle-east/israeli-soldiers-play-with-gaza-womens-underwear-online-posts-2024-03-28/

159 Al-Mughrabi, N. (2023, December 8). *Israeli images showing Palestinian detainees in underwear spark outrage | Reuters*. Reuters. https://www.reuters.com/world/middle-east/hamas-condemns-israel-over-images-showing-semi-naked-palestinian-prisoners-2023-12-08/

160 Mączak, A. (1995). *Travel in Early Modern Europe*. Polity Press. p. 245.

161 Ibid, 248.

162 Evangelisti, S. (2007). *Nuns: A History of Convent Life*. Oxford University Press. p.33.

163 Mohsen, T. (2022, August 6). *How colonizers weaponize rape: Reflections from the Palestinian case*. Mondoweiss. https://mondoweiss.net/2022/08/how-colonizers-weaponize-rape-reflections-from-the-palestinian-case/

164 Inlakesh, R. (2024, March 12). *On Israel and rape*. thecradle.co. https://thecradle.co/articles/on-israel-and-rape

165 Goldberg, E. L. (2011). *Jews and Magic in Medici Florence: The secret world of Benedetto Blanis*. University of Toronto Press. p. 23.

166 Ibid, 103.

167 Ibid, 103.

168 Abu Sneineh, M. (2021, May 6). *Sheikh jarrah explained: The past and present of east jerusalem neighbourhood.* Middle East Eye. www.middleeasteye.net/news/ israel-palestine-sheikh-jarrah-jerusalem-neighbourhood-eviction-explained

169 Goldberg, E. L. (2011). *Jews and Magic in Medici Florence: The secret world of Benedetto Blanis.* University of Toronto Press. p. 91.

170 Ibid, 98.

171 Ibid, 105.

172 Ibid, 105.

173 Ibid, 108.

174 Stone, D. (1997). Knowledge of Foreign Languages among Eighteenth-Century Polish Jews. In G. D. Hundert (Ed.), *Polin: Studies in Polish Jewry Volume 10: Jews in Early Modern Poland* (pp. 200–218). Liverpool University Press. doi.org/10.2307/j.ctv39x6j8.16, p. 205.

175 Stampfer, S. (2003). What Actually Happened to the Jews of Ukraine in 1648? *Jewish History, 17*(2), 207–227. http://www.jstor.org/stable/20101498

176 Zimmermann, Moshe. *Wilhelm Marr: The Patriarch of Antisemitism.* New York and Oxford: Oxford University. p. 18.

177 Philologos. (2020, May 20). *How "anti-semitism" replaced "jew-hatred" and why it shouldn't have.* Mosaic. mosaicmagazine.com/observation/history-ideas/2020/05/how-anti-semitism-replaced-jew-hatred-and-why-it-shouldnt-have/

178 UNESCO. (1950). *The Race Question.* unesdoc.unesco.org/ark:/48223/pf0000128291 p.8

179 Gannon, M., & LiveScience. (2016, February 5). *Race is a social construct, scientists argue.* Scientific American. www.scientificamerican.com/article/ race-is-a-social-construct-scientists-argue/

180 Harpham, G. G. (Ed.). (2023). *François Bernier: 1620–1688.* Theories of Race: An annotated anthology of essays on race, 1684–1900. www.theoriesofrace.com/1/

181 Wikimedia Foundation. (2024, June 30). *Johann Christoph Gatterer.* Wikipedia. en.wikipedia.org/wiki/Johann_Christoph_Gatterer

182 *File:first depiction of historical ethnology by Semitic, Hamitic and Japhetic, 1771, Gatterer.jpg - Wikipedia republished // Wiki 2.* Wikipedia. (n.d.). wiki2.org/en/File:First_depiction_of_historical_ethnology_by_Semitic,_ Hamitic_and_Japhetic,_1771,_Gatterer_jpg

183 Charmantier, I. (2020, September 3). *Linnaeus and Race*. The Linnean Society of London. www.linnean.org/learning/who-was-linnaeus/linnaeus-and-race

184 Reid, Gordon McGregor (2009). "Carolus Linnaeus (1707–1778): His Life, Philosophy and Science and Its Relationship to Modern Biology and Medicine". *Taxon*. **58** (1): 1831. doi:10.1002/tax.581005. JSTOR 27756820.

185 Weisberg M, Paul DB. Morton, Gould, and Bias: A Comment on "The Mismeasure of Science". PLoS Biol. 2016 Apr 19;14(4):e1002444. doi: 10.1371/journal.pbio.1002444. PMID: 27092558; PMCID: PMC4836680. www.ncbi.nlm.nih.gov/pmc/articles/PMC4836680/

186 Darwin, C. (1871). *The descent of man, and selection in relation to sex*. John Murray. darwin-online.org.uk/content/frameset?viewtype=side&itemID=F937.1& pageseq=214 p. 201.

187 *World Court finds Israel responsible for apartheid*. Human Rights Watch. (2024, July 19). www.hrw.org/news/2024/07/19/world-court-finds-israel-responsible-apartheid

188 David Feldman, Toward a History of the Term "Anti-Semitism", *The American Historical Review*, Volume 123, Issue 4, October 2018, Pages 1139–1150, doi.org/10.1093/ahr/rhy029 p. 1141

189 Ibid, 1143.

190 Rosselson, L. (2018, October 25). *Theodor Herzl, founder of Zionism. not quite what you might imagine*. Jewish Voice for Labour. www.jewishvoiceforlabour.org.uk/article/theodor-herzl-founder-of-zionism-not-quite-what-you-might-imagine/

191 Hurwitz, S. (2024, March 6). *Why does Biden keep making the same dangerous comment about jews?*. The Nation. www.thenation.com/article/politics/biden-jews-israel-safety

192 Feldman, p. 1146.

193 Feldman, p. 1147.

194 Massad, J. (2012, December 24). *Zionism, anti-Semitism and colonialism*. Al Jazeera. www.aljazeera.com/opinions/2012/12/24/zionism-anti-semitism-and-colonialism

195 Ibid.

196 *Anti-Nazi Boycotts*. Jewish Virtual Library. (n.d.). www.jewishvirtuallibrary.org/anti-nazi-boycotts

197 *Haavara winds up Reich-Palestine transfer operations; handled $35,000,000 in 6 years*. Jewish Telegraphic Agency. (1939, September 10). www.jta.org/archive/haavara-winds-up-reich-palestine-transfer-operations-handled-35000000-in-6-years

198 Massad, J. (2012, December 24). *Zionism, anti-Semitism and colonialism*. Al Jazeera. www.aljazeera.com/opinions/2012/12/24/zionism-anti-semitism-and-colonialism

199 Abu-Diab, Fawzi: *Immigration to Israel: A Threat to Peace in the Middle East* (Information Paper #12; New York: Arab Information Center, 1960). archive.org/details/ImmigrationToIsraelAThreatToPeaceInTheMiddleEast, p.6

200 Margaliot, Abraham. (1989). *THE PROBLEM OF THE RESCUE OF GERMAN JEWRY DURING THE YEARS 1933-1939; THE REASONS FOR THE DELAY IN THEIR EMIGRATION FROM THE THIRD REICH. Volume 2*, edited by Michael Robert Marrus, Berlin, Boston: De Gruyter Saur. doi.org/10.1515/9783110968729.553, pp. 559-60.

201 Shohat, E. (1988). Sephardim in Israel: Zionism from the Standpoint of Its Jewish Victims. *Social Text, 19/20*, 1–35. palestinecollective.wordpress.com/wp-content/uploads/2013/10/sephardim-in-israel_-zionism-from-the-standpoint-of-its-jewish-victims.pdf, p. 9

202 Ibid, 9.

203 Ibid, 10.

204 Ibid, 11.

205 Ibid, 11.

206 Ibid, 12.

207 MEE Staff. (2023, June 17). *Avi Shlaim says he has "proof of Zionist involvement" in 1950s attack on Iraqi jews*. Middle East Eye. www.middleeasteye.net/news/avi-shlaim-proof-israel-zionist-involvement-iraq-jews-attacks

208 Shohat, E. (1988). Sephardim in Israel: Zionism from the Standpoint of Its Jewish Victims. *Social Text, 19/20*, 1–35. palestinecollective.wordpress.com/wp-content/uploads/2013/10/sephardim-in-israel_-zionism-from-the-standpoint-of-its-jewish-victims.pdf, p. 4

209 Ibid, 15.

210 Ibid, 16.

211 Pacchiani, G. (2024, June 22). West Bank Palestinian laborers in despair after eight months without jobs in Israel | The Times of Israel. https://www.timesofisrael.com/west-bank-palestinian-laborers-in-despair-after-eight-months-without-jobs-in-israel/

212 Yang, J. (2024, April 26). *Israel is desperate to replace Palestinian farmhands*. Foreign Policy. https://foreignpolicy.com/2024/04/25/israel-agriculture-india-palestinians-foreign-workers-rights/

213 Ibid, 15.

214 Ibid, 17.

215 Ibid, 17.

216 Ibid, 18.

217 Ibid, 17.

218 Times of Israel Staff. (2021, February 22). *Government expresses "regret," will compensate for disappeared yemenite children | The Times of Israel.* Times of Israel. www.timesofisrael.com/government-set-to-express-regret-compensate-for-disappeared-yemenite-children/

219 Ehrman, A. (1976). THE ORIGINS OF THE RITUAL MURDER ACCUSATION AND BLOOD LIBEL. *Tradition: A Journal of Orthodox Jewish Thought, 15*(4), 83–90. www.jstor.org/stable/23258406

220 Climenhaga, L. (2012, May 9). *Imagining the witch: A comparison between fifteenth-century witches within medieval Christian thought and the persecution of jews and heretics in the Middle Ages.* Constellations. journals.library.ualberta.ca/constellations/index.php/constellations/article/view/17200

221 Maad, A., Audureau, W., & Forey, S. (2024, April 3). *"40 beheaded babies": Deconstructing the rumor at the heart of the information battle between Israel and Hamas.* Le Monde.fr. www.lemonde.fr/en/les-decodeurs/article/2024/04/03/40-beheaded-babies-the-itinerary-of-a-rumor-at-the-heart-of-the-information-battle-between-israel-and-hamas_6667274_8.html

222 Syed, A. (2023, December 15). *What Palestinian children face in Israeli prisons.* Time. time.com/6548068/palestinian-children-israeli-prison-arrested/

223 Najjar, F. (2024, September 1). *To be a Palestinian child, trying to survive Israeli jail.* Al Jazeera. www.aljazeera.com/features/2024/8/31/to-be-a-palestinian-child-trying-to-survive-israeli-jail

224 Kinder, T. (2014, November 22). *Israel: 240 Palestinian children "sexually abused" in jerusalem detention centres, group claims.* International Business Times UK. www.ibtimes.co.uk/israel-240-palestinian-children-sexually-abused-jerusalem-detention-centres-group-claims-1476061

225 Forensic Architecture. (n.d., accessed 2024, December 8). https://forensic-architecture.org/investigation/the-killing-of-hind-rajab

226 Agency, A. (2024, July 11). *"Suffering Horrifically": 10 months of Israel's "War on Children" in Gaza.* Middle East Monitor. www.middleeastmonitor.com/20240711-suffering-horrifically-10-months-of-israels-war-on-children-in-gaza/

227 @Doamuslims. (2024, May 18). *Israeli soldier playing with killed Palestinian children's toys in Gaza.* Instagram. www.instagram.com/doamuslims/reel/C7H1ozMrmIy/

228 Shehadeh, R. (2023). *We Could Have Been Friends, My Father and I: A Palestinian Memoir.* Other Press.

229 Khalil, Z. (2024, February 11). *Israeli soldiers steal over $54 million from Gaza Bank: Report.* Anadolu Ajansı. www.aa.com.tr/en/middle-east/israeli-soldiers-steal-over-54-million-from-gaza-bank-report/3134166

230 Johnson, J. (2024, August 28). *"Very bad sign for democracy": AIPAC has spent over $100 million on 2024 elections.* Common Dreams. www.commondreams.org/news/aipac-100-million

231 McGreal, C. (2024, February 4). *CNN staff say network's pro-Israel slant amounts to "journalistic malpractice."* The Guardian. www.theguardian.com/media/2024/feb/04/cnn-staff-pro-israel-bias

232 Valdez, J. (2024, August 29). *Columbia cuts due process for student protesters after Congress demands harsher punishment.* The Intercept. theintercept.com/2024/08/29/columbia-campus-protests-gaza-subpoena/

233 Weinberg, D. A. (2021, August 6). Proven false 100 years ago, antisemitic 'protocols' document is still being exploited | arab news. www.arabnews.com/node/1906891/middle-east

234 Durgham, N. (2024, July 15). *Palestinians raped and tortured in Israeli detention, says prisoners group.* Middle East Eye. https://www.middleasteye.net/news/gaza-israel-detainees-abuse-torture-sde-teiman-ofer

235 Graham-Harrison, E., & Kierszenbaum, Q. (2024, July 30). *IDF charges reservist with aggravated abuse of Palestinian prisoners.* The Guardian. https://www.theguardian.com/world/article/2024/jul/30/idf-charges-reservist-with-aggravated-abuse-of-palestinian-prisoners

236 *Gaza: Israeli army systematically uses police dogs to brutally attack Palestinian civilians, with at least one reported rape.* Euro-Med Human Rights Monitor. (2024, June 27). euromedmonitor.org/en/article/6383/Gaza:-Israeli-army-systematically-uses-police-dogs-to-brutally-attack-Palestinian-civilians,-with-at-least-one-reported-rape

237 Ziv, O. (2024, August 1). *A riot for impunity shows Israel's proud embrace of its crimes.* +972 Magazine. https://www.972mag.com/sde-teiman-beit-lid-protests-detainees/

238 *Israeli lawmaker justifies rape of Palestinian prisoners.* Middle East Eye. (2024, July 30). https://www.middleeasteye.net/live-blog/live-blog-update/israeli-lawmaker-justifies-rape-palestinian-prisoners

239 Nilus, S. (Marsden, V. E. trans.) (2014). *Protocols of the Learned Elders of Zion.* Mercian Free Press. (Original work published 1905). ia803409.us.archive.org/6/items/books_202012/The%20Protocols%20of%20the%20Learned%20Elders%20of%20Zion%20(%20PDFDrive%20).pdf

240 Al Jazeera. (2003, June 5). *Israel's Latin American trail of terror.* Al Jazeera. www.aljazeera.com/news/2003/6/5/israels-latin-american-trail-of-terror

241 Al-Anani, K. (2023, May 11). *The sudan crisis: How regional actors' competing interests fuel the conflict.* Arab Center Washington DC. arabcenterdc.org/resource/the-sudan-crisis-how-regional-actors-competing-interests-fuel-the-conflict/

242 Nilus, p.39

243 Jabotinsky, V. (Jabotinsky Institute in Israel trans.) (1923). *The Iron Wall.* Razsviet. en.jabotinsky.org/media/9747/the-iron-wall.pdf

244 Kampeas, R. (2024, April 19). *Poll: Months into Gaza War, most US jews feel close to Israel -- not its government | The Times of Israel.* The Times of Israel. www.timesofisrael.com/poll-months-into-gaza-war-most-us-jews-feel-close-to-israel-not-its-government/

245 *Poll: 72% support humanitarian pause; 20% favor unconditional ceasefire.* The Jewish Federations of North America. (2023, November 22). www.jewishfederations.org/fedworld/poll-72-support-humanitarian-pause-only-20-favor-unconditional-ceasefire-452801

246 Rosenberg, D. (2022, June 27). *The ideals of the Jewish Labor Bund have outlived Nazi genocide.* Jacobin. jacobin.com/2022/06/jewish-labor-bund-nazi-genocide-wwii-labor-migration-anti-zionism

247 Kraus, K. (2017). *In These Great Times: Selected Writings* (P. Healy, Trans.). November Editions. p. 56

248 Sand, S. (2014). *The Invention of the Land of Israel: From Holy Land to Homeland* (G. Forman, Trans.). Verso. p. 70

249 (2013). *The Skeptic's Annotated Bible: The King James Version from a skeptic's point of view.* SAB Books. Genesis 12:1

250 Ibid., Genesis 12:10

251 Watanabe, T. (2001, April 13). *Doubting the Story of Exodus.* Los Angeles Times. www.latimes.com/archives/la-xpm-2001-apr-13-mn-50481-story.html

252 Sand, S. (2014). *The Invention of the Land of Israel: From Holy Land to Homeland* (G. Forman, Trans.). Verso. p. 70–71.

253 Ibid, 71.

254 (2013). *The Skeptic's Annotated Bible: The King James Version from a skeptic's point of view.* SAB Books. Deuteronomy 7:3

255 Ibid, Exodus 21:15-22:20.

256 Sand, S. (2014). *The Invention of the Land of Israel: From Holy Land to Homeland* (G. Forman, Trans.). Verso. p.76.

257 Ibid, 72.

258 (2013). *The Skeptic's Annotated Bible: The King James Version from a skeptic's point of view.* SAB Books. Exodus 23:27.

259 Ibid, Exodus 23:29.

260 Ibid., Joshua 6:21 and 11:14.

261 Ibid, Joshua 6:24.

262 Sand, S. (2014). *The Invention of the Land of Israel: From Holy Land to Homeland* (G. Forman, Trans.). Verso., p. 75.

263 Ibid, 74.

264 Ibid, 74.

265 Ibid, 85.

266 Shlomo, S. (2014, October 10). *Shlomo Sand: "I wish to resign and cease considering myself a Jew."* The Guardian. www.theguardian.com/world/2014/oct/10/shlomo-sand-i-wish-to-cease-considering-myself-a-jew

267 United Nations. (2023, September 27). *Settlement expansion in Occupied Palestinian territory violates international law, must cease, many delegates tell Security Council | Meetings Coverage and press releases.* United Nations. press.un.org/en/2023/sc15424.doc.htm

268 United Nations. (2004, July 9). *International Court of Justice Advisory Opinion finds Israel's construction of wall "contrary to international law" | meetings coverage and press releases.* United Nations. press.un.org/en/2004/icj616.doc.htm

269 United Nations. (2022, March 25). *Israel's occupation of Palestinian territory is "apartheid": UN rights expert .* United Nations. news.un.org/en/story/2022/03/1114702

270 United Nations. (2024, March 26). *Rights expert finds "reasonable grounds" genocide is being committed in Gaza | UN News.* United Nations. news.un.org/en/story/2024/03/1147976

271 United Nations. (2024b, May 20). *ICC seeking arrest warrants for Hamas leaders and Israel's Netanyahu* . United Nations. news.un.org/en/story/2024/05/1149966

272 Little, B. (2023, October 4). *How did humans evolve?*. History.com. www.history.com/news/humans-evolution-neanderthals-denisovans

273 Haddad, M. (2024, July 11). *Visualising how Israel keeps stealing Palestinian land*. Al Jazeera. https://www.aljazeera.com/news/2024/7/11/how-israel-keeps-stealing-palestinian-land

274 Sand, S. (2014). *The Invention of the Land of Israel: From Holy Land to Homeland* (G. Forman, Trans.). Verso. p. 12

275 Rubin, R. (2013, May 7). *"Jews a race" genetic theory comes under fierce attack by DNA expert*. The Forward. forward.com/israel/175912/jews-a-race-genetic-theory-comes-under-fierce-atta/

276 Elhaik E. (2017, July 28) *Editorial: Population Genetics of Worldwide Jewish People.* Frontiers in Genetics. 8:101. doi: 10.3389/fgene.2017.00101 PMID: 28804494; PMCID: PMC5532521. www.ncbi.nlm.nih.gov/pmc/articles/PMC5532521/

277 *Indigenous (adj.)*. Etymology. (n.d.). www.etymonline.com/word/Indigenous

278 Verhulst, S. (2023, March 9). *It's time to rethink the idea of "Indigenous"* . The Living Library. thelivinglib.org/its-time-to-rethink-the-idea-of-Indigenous/

279 Peters, M. A., & Mika, C. T. (2017). *Aborigine, Indian, Indigenous or first nations?* Educational Philosophy and Theory, 49(13), 1229–1234. doi.org/10.1080/00131857.2017.1279879

280 Evri Y, Kotef H. (2022). *When does a native become a settler? (With apologies to Zreik and Mamdani).* Constellations. doi.org/10.1111/1467-8675.12470

281 Ibid.

282 Ibid.

283 United Nations. (2022, June 6). *Fact sheet on environment in Palestine in Palestine.* United Nations. https://palestine.un.org/en/185047-fact-sheet-environment-palestine

284 Evri Y, Kotef H. (2022). *When does a native become a settler? (With apologies to Zreik and Mamdani).* Constellations. doi.org/10.1111/1467-8675.12470

285 *What is Ladino?*. Sephardic Brotherhood. (n.d.). www.sephardicbrotherhood.com/what-is-ladino

286 Mendel, Y. (2020). *On Palestinian Yiddish and Ashkenazi Arabic in 18-19 century Palestine: a language-oriented new look on Jewish-Arab relations.* British Journal of Middle Eastern Studies, 49(2), 204–222. doi.org/10.1080/13530194.2020.1778444

287 Wikimedia Foundation. (2024, October 11). *Modern Palestinian Judeo-Arabic.* Wikipedia. en.wikipedia.org/wiki/Modern_Palestinian_Judeo-Arabic

288 Shohat, E. (1999). The Invention of the Mizrahim. Journal of Palestine Studies, 29(1), 5–20. https://doi.org/10.2307/2676427

289 Rapoport, M. (2015, December 15). *Israel's forgotten Arabic language.* Middle East Eye. www.middleeasteye.net/opinion/israels-forgotten-arabic-language

290 Fellman, J. (n.d.). *Hebrew: Eliezer Ben-Yehuda & the Revival of Hebrew.* Jewish Virtual Library. https://www.jewishvirtuallibrary.org/eliezer-ben-yehuda-and-the-revival-of-hebrew

291 Socquet-Juglard, M. (2022). Persistence of Silenced Toponymic Landscapes in Disputed Territories : The Case of Arabic in West-Jerusalem. *Judaica. Neue Digitale Folge, 3.* https://doi.org/10.36950/jndf.2022.22

292 (2018, August 14). *Arabic Downgraded in Israel.* Language Magazine. www.languagemagazine.com/2018/08/14/arabic-downgraded-in-israel/

293 Arianti, F. (2024, September 16). *Forests thrive when Indigenous people have legal stewardship of their land.* Resilience. www.resilience.org/stories/2024-09-16/forests-thrive-when-Indigenous-people-have-legal-stewardship-of-their-land/

294 (2022, November 3). *Fact Sheet: Israel's Environmental Apartheid in Palestine.* IMEU. imeu.org/article/environmental-apartheid-in-palestine

295 Pearce, F. (2019, September 30). *In Israel, Questions are Raised about a Forest that Rises from the Desert.* Yale Environment 360. e360.yale.edu/features/in-israel-questions-are-raised-about-a-forest-that-rises-from-the-desert

296 Ibid.

297 Bentley, Elizabeth. *Between Extinction and Dispossession: A Rhetorical Historiography of the Last Palestinian Crocodile (1870–1935).* Jerusalem Quarterly 88 (2021): 9-29. /www.palestine-studies.org/sites/default/files/jq-articles/Between%20Extinction%20and%20Dispossession.pdf

298 Al Jazeera English. (2023, July 27). *Israeli army pours cement into Palestinian water source.* Facebook. www.facebook.com/watch/?v=315029630956152

299 *The Right to Water in Palestine: A Background.* Center for Economic and Social Rights. (n.d.). www.cesr.org/sites/default/files/Palestine.RighttoWater.Factsheet.pdf

300 Deprez, M. (2018, August 20). *Even animals are divided by Israel's wall and occupation threats to the local environment.* Middle East Monitor. www.middleeastmonitor.com/20180820-even-animals-are-divided-by-israels-wall-and-occupation-threats-to-the-local-environment/

Endnotes

301 Kawas, M. (2020, February 18). *Solidarity between Palestinians and Indigenous activists has deep roots.* Palestine Chronicle. www.palestinechronicle.com/solidarity-between-palestinians-and-Indigenous-activists-has-deep-roots/

302 Central Intelligence Agency. (2024, October 10). *The World Factbook: Israel.* Central Intelligence Agency. www.cia.gov/the-world-factbook/countries/israel/

303 Knell, Y., & Luckhurst, T. (2024, August 27). *Under cover of war, extremists are seizing Palestinian land – they hope permanently.* BBC News. https://www.bbc.com/news/articles/c624qr3mqrzo

304 Gopal, P. (2023, November 22). *Is decolonization "genocide"? let's see.* Medium. zen-catgirl.medium.com/is-decolonization-genocide-lets-see-de91184cb8af

305 Jaffer, H. (@hjaffer). (2024, October 10). *Free the Zionists.* Instagram. www.instagram.com/reel/DA62jyJIGkP/

306 von Aue, M. (2017, January 4). *How the CIA infiltrated the world's literature.* VICE. https://www.vice.com/en/article/how-the-cia-infiltrated-the-worlds-literature/